VICTORY

IN THE NO-GO ZONE

**WINNING THE FIGHT
AGAINST TWO-TIER POLICING**

GARY MCHALE

FOREWORD BY CHRISTIE BLATCHFORD

FRE3DOM PRESS
CANADA INC.

About the Book:

Our values of Freedom, Equality and the Rule of Law are quickly sacrificed on the altar of political correctness whenever the special interests of favoured groups are at stake. Caledonia is all about how the Ontario Provincial Police violated the fundamental trust that we, as citizens, place in our police forces: thousands of families lived in fear because "Public Safety" became a mere political buzz word while the full resources of the state were used to silence the victims' voices. This book exposes the corruption of race-based policing while demonstrating how average citizens can take back control when the system fails.

About the Author:

Gary McHale has a strong belief in Dr. Martin Luther King Jr.'s approach of direct action and peaceful protest, sharing his goal that someday all people will be judged by the strength of their character and not the colour of their skin. He has received death threats from Native protesters and has been assaulted numerous times in the presence of OPP officers. He was the victim of a vicious smear campaign by OPP leadership and sued for $7.1 million by officers. He has been arrested illegally nine times without a single case making it to trial. Yet, in the end, the court would order OPP Commissioner Julian Fantino and Deputy Commissioner Chris Lewis to face criminal charges for their actions against McHale.

Endorsements:

Canadians believe that racism, supported by the law, is a legacy of the South - the American South and South Africa. That's history. But the ugliness of institutional racism, supported by the police and the provincial government, is alive and thriving in Southern Ontario. How much longer will we accept ugly racism staining this nation? The story of Caledonia is one that has been ignored by most of the media, to their shame. This story will anger you and it should provoke you to action.

• *Jerry Agar*
talk host on Newstalk1010 Toronto.

"Caledonia" will forever remain an icon of shame in the annals of Canadian justice. This book takes us behind the scenes, providing step-by-step insight into OPP operations, as they and their political masters consciously chose political correctness over the rule of law and the security of Canadian citizens. Gary McHale is the only player in this long, sordid drama to emerge with honour. He is a Canadian hero.

• *Barbara Kay*
Columnist for National Post
and Postmedia Network.

VICTORY IN THE NO-GO ZONE:

Winning the Fight Against Two-Tier Policing

by Gary McHale

Dedicated to:

Merlyn Kinrade who loved his family, his community
and his country and passed away after battling cancer
in 2012 at the age of 77.

I wish to thank OPP Officer Jeff Bird who attended Merlyn's funeral
in full dress uniform and took part in a Canadian Flag folding ceremony
in Merlyn's honour.

I wish also to thank Stuart Laughton, Mark Vandermaas
and my wife Christine McHale for the hundreds of hours they committed
to ensure this book became a reality,
as well as Tristan Emmanuel of Freedom Press Canada Inc.
for his encouragement and his vision of a publishing house
for conservative ideals.

Finally, I thank God for sending Christine to be my wife, my friend
and my partner whose steadfast loyalty and support has aided
and comforted me, especially during the darkest days
of our struggle for justice.

Cover Photo:

The cover photo was taken by Christine McHale at a Canadian flag-raising rally in Caledonia on January 20, 2007. OPP Commissioner Julian Fantino was in town to personally supervise the OPP's plan to ensure non-Native people could not walk down the town's main road and raise a Canadian flag across from the Douglas Creek Estates occupation site. Meanwhile, dozens of Six Nations and Mohawk Warrior flags were allowed to be placed throughout the town.

Fantino was so determined to stop the Canadian flag from offending those who terrorized Caledonia that he called in hundreds of OPP officers as well as the London Police Service riot squad to demonstrate his willingness to use extreme force against non-Native people. The photo of the squad was taken at the edge of private property where about a dozen non-Natives stood by a small fire to keep warm while drinking hot coffee. They left within minutes after the media started taking photos of them lining up against law abiding citizens and never returned.

Contents

Foreword: By Christie Blatchford.. 1

Introduction: Setting the Context 3

1   Average Citizens Standing up for Equality 11

2   The OPP Lies to the Court and the Public about Criminal Behaviour.............. 23

3   The Canadian Flag is Illegal but Native Flags are Legal 41

4   Julian Fantino: The Gift That Keeps on Giving 65

5   The Fleming Rally: A Pivotal Event 87

6   Desperate Measures: A Long, Drawn Out Prosecution 101

7   Cop Assaulter Clyde Powless Gets a Sweetheart Deal 121

8   "Cashedonia": A Town Where Officers Get Rich.................................... 131

9   McGuinty's Ipperwash Cover-Up: The Caledonia Legacy 155

10   Standing Up Against Institutionalized Racism 167

11   Five Myths of the Caledonia Occupation that Threaten Our Rule of Law 177

12   How We Won Caledonia in the 2008 Federal Election 193

13   Hope For The Future 199

FOREWORD

The first few times I met Gary McHale, I was cautious and kept a nervous distance. His reputation – or should I say the vile rumours of his reputation – had preceded him. He was a racist, a boor and worse, the old epithet favoured by the former Ontario Provincial Police commissioner Julian Fantino, "an interloper," an outsider.

Christine was something else.

McHale's wife is gentle, pretty, quiet and the perfect antidote to her husband. She is, and seems to be, refined and utterly lovely. She's easier to like at first sight, as it were.

It's only later on, when you get to know her a bit, that you realize she is also possessed of a bitter, cutting humour and sardonic wit.

Of course, it's also only later that I figured out that McHale was not as advertised – nothing like it – and that the reason he seems so foreign, even odd, is because he's that rarest of modern Canadian creatures – a man who acts on principle, lives and breathes it in fact.

In our collective defence, there are so few of these folks around it's little wonder we're suspicious of them.

The McHales gave up so much in what might be called, though it's a bit of a stretch, the fight for a free Caledonia – financial security, the trappings of an ordinarily comfortable, if not affluent, life – in exchange for permanent poverty, vilification by the state and a generally sleepy press, and arrest and harassment by the OPP.

In the years I've known them, they rarely complained – though once or twice, Christine would say in her quiet voice that she yearned for some stability – and more important, they didn't give up, which is useful for the rest of us, because if Caledonia was once like a patient in acute crisis, the town and the province, and to a degree the whole country, is now firmly in the grip of a chronic illness.

The problems that culminated in the occupation in Caledonia – native and non-native Canadians badly served by all levels of government; cowardly or dishonest leaders as far as the eye can see; a politicized police force; a lazy or timorous press, and all of this playing into the great Canadian longing for peace at all costs – remain. McHale in this book sees reason to hope; I am not nearly so optimistic.

In his early days as a rabble-rouser (another Fantino favourite), McHale was occasionally prone to exaggerating the facts on his website. But he's become a much more careful witness-cum-reporter, as this assiduously footnoted book demonstrates, just as he has turned himself into an excellent self-taught lawyer. He's a quick study.

It's funny. McHale ran unsuccessfully for office in the federal election of 2008; I was enraged that he was defeated, though he did far better than he had a right to do.

Two years later, his old nemesis, Julian Fantino, ran in a federal by-election, won, and is now a federal MP. He lives in Ottawa.

For a glorious few months after his election, before he went on to greater responsibilities, Fantino got a junior cabinet post, and I was able to refer to him at every opportunity as "the junior Minister for Seniors".

As for Gary, he still lives with Christine in a rented joint near Caledonia, if not hand-to-mouth, then close enough that it counts. As this book shows, he's still fighting.

Well, at least one of them made something of himself.

August, 2013

Christie Blatchford
Columnist for *National Post* and Postmedia Network
Recipient of Governor General's Literary Award
and National Newspaper Award

Introduction

Setting the Context

As I write this book in the spring of 2013, I have been arrested illegally nine times and have been charged during three of those arrests, yet not a single case has made it to trial. I was once prosecuted for 30 months before the Crown stayed the charge. I have been sued by the Ontario Provincial Police (OPP) to the tune of $7.1 million for making public statements which accused them of disobeying their oath of office. I have been beaten in the presence of OPP officers, and have been taken to the hospital. I have received death threats. I have been cursed and assaulted numerous times. I have been branded a "racist" and "white supremacist" by Natives, the media and the OPP.

This book is about the battle to expose corruption in the Ontario police force and political establishment. It is about what some ordinary citizens have done – and are doing – to force some degree of law and order to be restored. It is about fighting the unlimited resources of the state which are being used to protect institutional racism and which have led to the injustice in Caledonia. There is no *Fighting for Your Rights for Dummies* handbook to tell you how to restore equality and freedom for all. Looking back after seven years, there are things I would have done differently, but, sadly, I don't have a time machine, and thus cannot change the past. Events have been described as they occurred, not as how I wish they might have happened. No doubt my critics will have a field day with what I have written, but I have recorded events honestly and as I experienced them, and I hope that even my critics will be willing to focus on the serious issues that have been uncovered.

This book will not sugarcoat the reality of just how far our leaders have allowed our system of justice to be corrupted. I will name the police officers and Crown lawyers who have played a role in this corruption, and provide the hard evidence so that readers can understand the depth to which racism has become institutionalized in Canada. We should be outraged by the complete abandonment of the principle that we all have equal benefit and equal protection under the law. It is ordinary Canadians who pay the price when our leaders allow – and even encourage – the corruption of justice.

While some may see this book as negative, it contains a very positive message. When the full force of the state is used to suppress the fundamental rights of a whole community, it is the individual who must stand against that injustice. Our freedoms are not "free" – those who came before us paid a price on our behalf. When governments fail us, when our institutions fail us, when the police fail us, and when the political parties are nowhere to be found, it is the individual Canadian who is the last line of defence for democracy. People like you and I must take up the cause and pay the price to ensure that we remain free. Freedom is not automatic, nor is it inherently Canadian – it is always under attack.

Those in power always want more power. Of course, they claim they will only use their power in the citizens' best interests. The residents of Caledonia came to realize the hard way that this is simply not true. As Caledonia has repeatedly shown, we do not even have the checks and balances in place to deal with institutional racism – provided it has the support of political parties and the media. Our Charter of Rights and Freedoms is merely words on a piece of paper, and can be destroyed at will by the very people sworn to uphold the law. Our system assumes that our leaders will act in a way that is beneficial to society, but in Caledonia police officers became pawns of the politicians. Caledonia is all about the absolute failure of the system to protect average people – a failure that is rooted in a race-based approach to policing and public policy.

* * *

In December 2005 the sleepy town of Caledonia was preparing for Christmas, a time when family, friends and neighbours celebrate "peace on earth; good will to all men." Like many communities in Ontario, Caledonia has families who trace their residency back 200 years, as well as newer arrivals. And, as in every community, there are people of every political stripe – Conservatives, Liberals, NDPers, independents, and many others who don't really care about politics. You will also find the things that make a community a community – the service clubs, sports teams and family businesses.

Caledonia is located 15 minutes south of Hamilton along Hwy #6. With a population of approximately 10,000, it is one of the larger towns in Haldimand County. Within a five minute drive of Caledonia is the Six Nations reserve, which has approximately the same population, but which has a land mass approximately the size of the city of Hamilton (pop. 500,000). The people of Six Nations and Caledonia have lived in peace for the past 250 years. Their children go to the same schools, play on the same sports teams and compete for the same jobs; inter-marriages are a common occurrence. Unbeknownst to these families, the seeds of destruction that would undermine everything we in a free and democratic society hold dear had already been planted and well-watered over the course of the previous four decades. A perfect storm had been brewing as racism within Canada's political parties, government departments, the mainstream media and many aboriginal communities had become endemic and systemic.

On February 28, 2006, a small group of Native protesters led by 2 women from Six Nations decided to illegally occupy a Caledonia sub-division development called Douglas Creek Estates (DCE). Ten model homes had been completed, with 70 more to come. Two additional building phases were in the planning stage. The developer of the sub-division, Henco Industries Limited, was owned by John and Don Henning, two brothers who lived locally. All the construction was being done by local tradesmen, which would ensure years of employment for many people. Henco's homes were priced from $320,000 to $370,000. In a small community like Caledonia this represented a major economic stimulus.

By April, several court orders had been issued stating that the protesters were on this property illegally, and that they must be removed. The OPP and Ontario government lawyers, however, were doing everything they could to stall the enforcement of these orders. This despite the fact that, in mid-March, Mohawk Warriors had joined the occupation, and the OPP believed (correctly, as it turned out) that these "protesters" were nothing more than an organized crime gang that was smuggling drugs, cigarettes, guns and people across the USA border. It is no wonder that by June, agents from the U.S. Bureau of Alcohol, Tobacco, Firearms and Explosives (BATF) arrived to videotape the so-called grassroots movement to reclaim "Native" land – and were attacked by Native protesters on June 9.

The courts made it clear that they were becoming increasingly frustrated by the OPP's refusal to enforce its directive. On April 20, 2006, the OPP finally enforced the court order and raided the occupied sub-division at 4:30 a.m. (Native protesters would later express public anger over the raid, claiming the OPP had promised them that no such action would be taken. The OPP probably did make such a promise, but had to break it because the court insisted it uphold the law rather than appease the radical law-breakers.)

The police raid on the DCE sub-division was poorly planned and any reasonable person could see that it was destined to fail. It doesn't take a mastermind to realize that when you raid a hostile protest site, the first thing you do is contain the protest, and ensure that reinforcements don't arrive. But during the two months it had taken the OPP to launch the raid, many other Native protesters had come from Ontario, Quebec, New York, Manitoba and even as far away as British Columbia. And police were well aware of the ominous presence of the Mohawk Warriors, a group that had been established as an armed response to so-called government interference with their illegal smuggling activities. Over the years Warriors had killed law enforcement officers,[1] had offered money to anyone who would shoot down police helicopters, and had been involved in gun battles with law enforcement officers on both sides of the Canada-US border.

The OPP could have simply removed the Native protesters at the beginning of the occupation, but political correctness wouldn't allow for it. Instead, they waited, thereby escalating the crisis. By the time they finally acted, the occupying forces were prepared, armed and far more numerous. Here's how the April 20, 2006 OPP press release described the action:

> Today, members of the Ontario Provincial Police arrested and removed 16 protesters occupying a housing development in Caledonia, Ontario in contravention of a court order issued by the Ontario Superior Court of Justice on March 3, 2006... The site was secured, however a short time later the site was re-occupied. During this time three OPP officers were injured and required medical attention. Our officers showed tremendous restraint while confronted by the protesters with weapons which included axes, crowbars, rocks and a various assortment of make-shift batons.[2]

The protesters also set several large tire fires on the road at key points in Caledonia, with the result that the only highway through and around town was now on fire. Gangs of thugs wearing masks and carrying bats and other weapons roamed the streets. The days that followed brought chaos. The highway was dug up; truckloads of gravel were poured on the roads; and projectiles of all sorts were hurled from highway overpasses (including a van that was pushed off the bridge to the highway below). Hydro towers were cut down; fires were set in barns and on other property; a wooden overpass bridge was burnt down; guns were drawn on firemen as they responded to the numerous fires; residents were harassed day and night for weeks; non-Natives had to show Native-issued passports in order to travel through parts of the town; numerous officers and residents were hospitalized; and two OPP officers were kidnapped, their guns taken from them and their vehicle destroyed.

Even though there were daily threats to kill area residents and destroy their property, Six Nations spokespersons such as Hazel Hill would repeatedly tell the media that the protesters were peaceful (well, if you're going to lie, you may as well lie big!) and, in a May 16 press release, even Haldimand County put a positive spin on "ongoing negotiations." Ironically, less than a week later the county was forced to declare a state of emergency because protesters fire-bombed the power station. They took a truck and smashed through the security gates. After ramming the truck into the station they set the gas tank of the truck on fire. The fire caused $1.5 million in damages and knocked out the town's hydro for days.

Even after this terrorist action – which, clearly, was intended to terrorize and threaten the government, police and residents so that they would submit to the political will of the Native protesters – the OPP refused to provide any security for the power station. Ontario Hydro did place a security car with a driver at the station, but two weeks later, on June 4, 2006, Native protesters swarmed the vehicle, smashing out the windows and threatening the 20-year-old security guard with death. After the guard ran away they poured gasoline on the car and set it on fire.

Throughout May and June, 2006, Native protesters would swarm various media reporters, threatening them, stealing their camera equipment and harassing them about negative coverage. These types of crimes were committed against CBC, CHCH TV, *Kitchener Record* newspaper and the *Regional News*, the local newspaper. By June 9, a pattern had been established: protesters did whatever they pleased, and the OPP did nothing to stop them. An OPP press release issued on that day demonstrates just how far Native thugs were prepared to go, and the unwillingness of police to do anything to curtail the ongoing crime spree. It states:

> *On Friday June 9, 2006, the O.P.P. investigated three violent altercations that took place within one hour in the south end of Caledonia. The first incident took place before noon and involved an elderly couple from Simcoe who were visiting the Caledonia area when an altercation occurred between themselves and the 'occupiers'. An elderly male victim was taken to West Haldimand General Hospital in Hagersville as a precaution.*

> *The second incident involved two news cameramen that were filming the incident. One was swarmed, assaulted and had his camera stolen. He was transported to West Haldimand General Hospital with non-life threatening injuries.*

> *The third incident involved the theft of a motor vehicle. This vehicle was swarmed, the occupants forcibly removed, and then the vehicle was stolen.* [NOTE: this is a reference to the assault on the US BATF agent and a US border guard] *During the theft an O.P.P. officer was injured and deliberately driven at by the stolen vehicle. Other officers at the*

scene pulled him to safety. The O.P.P. officer was transported to hospital with serious injuries.

Overnight, there were several clashes between Police and Caledonians. Five persons were arrested for Breach of the Peace. Two were released shortly after their arrest and three were held overnight. All parties were released unconditionally.[3]

The last paragraph of the press release is quite telling. Instead of detailing how police took steps to prevent these crimes or to arrest the Natives who committed them, the release talks about arresting Caledonia residents. Readers of this book should be aware that when the OPP arrests you for what is technically called "To Prevent A Breach of the Peace," it isn't a criminal charge. In fact, the OPP cannot legally file any actual charge for this type of arrest. I should know because I have been arrested for "Breach of the Peace" six times.

The OPP's statement made it appear to the general public that non-Native residents from Caledonia were doing something illegal, but that's untrue. Each of my arrests took place because police believed Native protesters were about to assault me, or to prevent Native protesters from continuing to assault me, or to prevent Native protestors from continuing to assault OPP officers. In the one-sided world of racial policing in Caledonia, the OPP are prepared to stand by while fellow officers and non-Native residents are assaulted, and will arrest non-Natives in order to "prevent further assaults." However, they refuse to arrest the Natives committing the assaults. I kid you not.

While all this crime (and too many other examples to relate here) was occurring, OPP officers merely stood and watched. They watched, and they watched, and then watched some more, as the people of Caledonia, who expected these public servants to protect them, lived in fear. Hours of violence turned into days, then weeks, then months, while police and Ontario Premier Dalton McGuinty repeatedly urged Caledonians to be patient. Up until September 2006, McGuinty publicly bragged that he was going to solve the Caledonia situation, and even former Liberal Premier David Peterson, who he sent to Caledonia to try to improve the situation, told the media at the time that the problem would be resolved in a matter of weeks, not months. McGuinty declared that the Native protesters would not be allowed to remain on DCE through the winter of 2006.

Seven years after these bold statements were issued, Peterson has disappeared, along with all the others McGuinty sent to Caledonia. Also gone is Gwen Boniface, OPP Commissioner since 1996, who fled the country suddenly in August, 2006 for a job in Ireland, thereby reneging on her promise to retain her OPP position until 2009. Gone, too, are the various OPP detachment commanders, inspectors and officers who all publicly promised to address the local issues.

McGuinty himself has fled the scene, resigning as premier in an effort to evade financial scandals and proroguing his party's rule, and there is no evidence that his replacement, Kathleen Wynne, is plugged into the issue. Meanwhile, Conservative leader Tim Hudak barely knows where Caledonia is, even though his riding is right next to Haldimand County.

At the same time, the media, for the most part, failed to keep the public informed, and seem intent on remaining ignorant about the problems. Over the years I have heard many reporters refer to Caledonia as "the longest occupation in Canadian history." That is demonstrably false: the Oka occupation in Quebec, which began in 1990, and the Ipperwash occupation in Ontario, which began in 1993, remain unresolved to this day. The Federal government made an offer to settle Ipperwash in 1998, but as of this writing Natives have yet to vote on it. (The Ontario government gave Ipperwash Provincial Park to the Natives in 2009 even though the park was never part of the land claim.) I realized in 2006 that the political game of appeasement would mean that Caledonia would follow in the footsteps of Oka and Ipperwash and be quickly forgotten once the media attention had turned elsewhere. Given that history, I could never understand how anyone in Canada could actually believe that politicians would follow any course but appeasement. Tragically, for Caledonians and all freedom-loving Canadians, my prediction has turned out to be correct.

Believe it or not, despite Caledonia representing one of the greatest rule of law failures in modern Ontario history, with the exception of a French CBC television documentary that never made it to air (built around Native-OPP radio transmissions that prove native occupation leaders authorized their compatriots to shoot civilians and police officers, and interfered with an ambulance trying to reach an injured OPP officer), only one investigative reporter has ever contacted us to review our mountain of evidence in depth: the award-winning journalist Christie Blatchford, who would go on to write the shocking story of Caledonia's betrayal at the hands of our government in which she credits my wife Christine and me for our extensive assistance. Her 2010 book, *Helpless: Caledonia's Nightmare of Fear And Anarchy, And How The Law Failed All Of Us*[4] recounts Caledonia's agony from the residents' perspective. It also introduced readers to the ordinary people who fought back to restore the rule of law, and equality. This book tells more of that story.

---

1   P. Whitney Lackenbauer, *Ph.D., Journal of Military & Strategic Studies*, Winter 2008: Carrying the Burden of Peace: The Mohawks, the Canadian Forces and the Oka Crisis, p.71, footnote 36. "The Mohawk Warriors claimed publicly that the police fired first, and that Lemay had been a victim of fratricide (killed by a police bullet). Five years after the standoff, a coroner's report concluded that the shot was fired by a Mohawk warrior, but the report did not identify the killer and no one was charged with Lemay's murder." http://www.jmss.org/jmss/index.php/jmss/article/download/89/99.

2   OPP news release, April 20, 2006, Protesters removed from Caledonia housing development. *

3   OPP news release, June 11, 2006, *O.P.P. Investigate Three Violent Altercations Within One Hour* *

4   Christie Blatchford, *Helpless: Caledonia's Nightmare of Fear And Anarchy, And How The Law Failed All Of Us*, Doubleday Canada, 2010. See also: www.HelplessByBlatchford.ca

* See http://www.GaryMcHale.ca/book for additional information, links to documents, videos and photos

Chapter 1

Average Citizens Standing up for Equality

In 2006 I was living in Richmond Hill, just north of Toronto, with my wife Christine. Over the years many have asked why I was the one who got involved in Caledonia. I have never really answered this question fully because in my mind the question should really be, "Why didn't everyone else get involved?" However, a more complete answer should be provided so that my actions can be judged based on some understanding of my motives. We are all products of our past – our experiences shape our view of life and what is important to us. I am no different.

I am the youngest of six boys. My oldest brother, Greg, is eight years older than me. I was born in 1962 in Kingston, Ontario, where both my parents worked, but where my father never had a stable job until after my mother died in 1972. Early on, my brothers and I headed down a path of crime. My brother, Mike, (two years older than me) was brought home by the police for accidentally burning down a barn (he'd been smoking cigarettes) and for stealing – all before his tenth birthday. At the age of seven, I set the family record for most chocolate bars stolen in a single trip to the store – 27. In that year we moved to an area just outside of Odessa, Ontario, and then to Violet, Ontario, a very small town of fewer than 50 homes – no stores or gas stations. We were very poor, but somehow, as a child, I didn't really notice. Violet was good for our family because with no stores to steal from and with a small town awareness of which child belonged to which parent, there was a limit to how much trouble we could get into.

I can still remember almost word for word everything that happened the morning I woke up and was told we weren't going to school. When I asked why, one of my brothers said, "Mom died last night in a car accident." I remember thinking that it was a very odd thing for him to say, so I repeated my question. It wasn't until my father returned a few minutes later and asked, "Has he been told?" that I realized my brothers were not playing a joke on me.

My mother's funeral was the first occasion I can remember ever walking into a church. While I had relatives who were religious, religion was never discussed in our home. Although my parents may not have been the greatest role models, I have many fond memories of my mother.

After her death, our home life changed quite a bit. We were always a bit rebellious – hey, six boys with no girls is guaranteed to challenge anybody's parenting skills. However, after my mother's death, I rarely saw my father, even though he came home regularly. When I turned 12, we moved back to Kingston, which created problems almost immediately.

By the time I was 13, one of my brothers was stealing cars and motorcycles and two other brothers were selling drugs. I recall being very angry and resentful. I saw my future as being a life of crime, with little hope that that could change. But I was wrong. In the summer of 1975, I returned to Violet to visit cousins still living there (we had lived across the road from them). I went there every weekend for six months. Finally, my aunt, Mary Shook (my mother's sister who had eight children of her own), asked if I wanted to live with them. So on Christmas morning 1975, I woke up, unwrapped my presents, packed my bags and went to my aunt's home, never letting on to anyone that I was leaving. I never returned.

Aunt Mary would save me and change the course of my life, but I was still a very angry and bitter person. I found it almost impossible to live in a house where, suddenly, I had to follow rules, where parents were there every day and corrected you, and where people said prayers before every meal. Within a year the Shook family moved to Sydenham, Ontario. My anger and bitterness had completely destroyed any sense of self-worth. In 1977 I tried drugs for the first time. Within days, I was lost in an imaginary world of my own creation. The drugs allowed me to forget the bitterness and mask my pain. I can remember spending several nights sleeping at the local park, without a care in the world because I was so high.

Aunt Mary recognized how much I had changed and asked my oldest brother, Greg, if I could come live with him; she thought he would be a good influence on me. By this time, Greg was living in St. Catharines, Ontario. He had a successful career repairing main-frame computers for IBM, and was married to Donna. They had no children. So once again, in Grade 12, I moved, the fourth year in a row I had moved somewhere else – from Kingston to Odessa to Sydenham to St. Catharines – and gone to a different school. Clearly, the concept of lasting relationships and close friends wasn't part of my experience.

That all changed in Grade 12, however. A crazy girl in my math class kept bugging me. She was cute, so I married her. I put it that way because I realized in Grade 12 that I needed to be married, needed a stable home life, needed to be with someone who would never, ever leave me. I have now been married to Christine for 32 years, and as time has passed she has only grown more beautiful in my eyes. Christine came from a terrible, abusive home. So in Grade 13, I found a full time job (I still went to school full time), Christine found a few part time jobs, and we moved in together – quite the scandal for two students to be living together back then.

Right after Grade 13, we moved to Kingston and got married, but old habits and deep bitterness soon took hold again. I started stealing professionally as a way to pay the bills. I was caught but, luckily, I was given a second chance. I remember going to court to face shoplifting charges and doing some serious thinking about what I wanted out of life. I got another break when I landed a great computer technician job in Toronto even though I had no education beyond grade 13. (I had my first paying computer job when I was 15 and was a whiz kid with computers.) The job actually paid more than computer science university graduates were earning at the time, so Christine and I moved to Toronto and started life over.

Soon after this move, and as a result of much hard work by my brother Greg and Christine, I became a Christian. I was 21, and this intellectual and spiritual experience formed the basis of everything I now do. Self-worth was no longer measured by what others thought of me or even by what I could or couldn't do, but by the fact that God, the creator of heaven and earth, cared for me, a rebellious sinner. He intervened in my life and saved me through the death of His Son.

At this time, I could barely read and write – that is a fact. This was due in part to my lack of interest in school, but mainly because of a serious reading and writing disability that I had to work constantly to overcome, but especially so once I began using the media and the courts to fight for justice in Caledonia much later in life. My first serious prayer asked God for the ability to read so that I could understand what He had written in the Bible. It took years to be able to read the Bible stories about how evil men like me had come face to face with God and had to deal with their own demons, their own sinful characters, and walk away as changed people. It took well over ten years to deal with the bitterness, anger and hatred toward others, but I know myself now, and regardless of my failings, God remains faithful.

By the spring of 2006, I had been a Christian for 25 years. I attended a Baptist Seminary and received two awards: best marks in Theology and best leadership skills. I had come to see that we could never control others because it takes all our efforts simply to control ourselves. I had come to see that God works through the weak, the poor and the foolish in order to put to shame those who are strong, wealthy, and see themselves as wise.

In early June of 2006 I heard on Michael Coren's Crossroads Television System (CTS) television show that two OPP officers had been kidnapped by Native protesters in Caledonia, that the officers' guns had been taken and their car destroyed, and that they had been held hostage for several hours. I couldn't believe this was happening in Canada. The worst of it was that the Toronto media reported – or rather, misreported – it as being a simple matter of two officers who got lost, and who had been escorted back to their fellow officers by "helpful" Native protesters. There was nothing about the kidnapping and other criminal actions.

On June 9, I heard that Native protesters had swarmed an elderly couple at the Canadian Tire store in Caledonia, attacked the CHCH TV camera crew covering the story and, half an hour later, surrounded and attacked an unmarked OPP van containing an OPP officer, U.S. border guard and an American BATF agent.[1] All the while, the OPP stood by and watched the crimes take place, and did nothing to protect the innocent or arrest the criminals. The next day I made the decision to become involved in Caledonia.

All my life I had seen how the criminal mind operates and how hatred controls people, and I knew it would not stop until people stepped forward. For me, there were always certain crimes you just didn't commit – call it honour among thieves. That's why prisons have to separate criminals who violate this code from the general prison population, because otherwise they would likely be killed. To my mind, the three crimes I mentioned above violated this code and represented an attack on the very foundations of Canadian society. To swarm elderly people was unimaginable to me, even with my criminal background. To openly attack police officers – and put a knife to a BATF agent's throat– demonstrated that there was no limit to the violence of these Native protesters. To swarm members of the media was, as I saw it, an attack on free speech with the intent of suppressing the truth.

But what was worse was that the provincial police allowed each of these crimes to occur. Every town has its criminals and those willing to commit violence against others. What was unique in Caledonia wasn't the violence but the way the OPP stood by and abandoned people to be victimized day after day, for weeks and then months – a flagrant dereliction of duty, I thought. This posed a dilemma and a challenge.

How could I, someone claiming to be a Christian, claiming to believe in God's sacrifice for me, be unwilling to sacrifice myself for others? How could I look myself in the mirror knowing that my neighbour needed me, but be unwilling to come to his aid? What is astonishing isn't that I stepped forward, but that the churches in Caledonia failed to do so. As we will see in a later chapter, the local pastors were paralyzed by fears that their church or their families could be the next target. To me that was a lame excuse for those who claimed to believe in a sovereign God, One who has called Christians to be Good Samaritans.

Prior to my involvement in Caledonia local residents had been seeking to expose the lawlessness and the OPP's refusal to enforce the law. It would be difficult to name all the people who paid a price to ensure fundamental freedoms and equality for all, but Kevin Clark; Bo Chausse; John Roza; Mark Watson; Dave Hartless; Doug and Randy Fleming; Lisa and Mike Parent; AnneMarie VanSickle; Ken and Lorna Watson; Steve Tong; and Tom Peddle are among them. Many of these people became targets of both radical Native protesters and the OPP, and many were forced to give in to the pressure. This isn't a negative statement about these people, but simply the reality of what can happen when we find ourselves face to face with the massive combined force of government and armed police supporting the violent radicals.

On June 17, 2006, I started my website www.CaledoniaWakeUpCall.com. I went to Caledonia a few weeks later, for the first time in my life. From that point forward I became a target of Native protesters, the OPP and the media who have a bias towards Native protesters.

* * *

By mid-2007, it had become clear that in order to have law and order restored, a long-term plan was needed to expose the OPP. As part of the plan, a group called Canadian Advocates for Charter Equality (www.CanACE.ca) was formed. Although the group was and remains very small, to this day it has had the greatest impact of any individual or organization on events in Caledonia. The group was comprised of a core of four individuals, with two to three other key people who helped plan events with larger groups also committed to participating in the various rallies that were organized. CanACE's founding members were me, Merlyn Kinrade, Jeff Parkinson and Mark Vandermaas, plus "honorary founder" Mary-Lou LaPratte, who led a group numbering six hundred to address the related injustices occurring in Ipperwash, Ontario. Later, Bonnie and Larry Stephens would play key roles, as would Randy and Doug Fleming.

A rational observer would immediately conclude that our motley crew of wildly differing characters (with no training relevant to the task at hand) was completely unequal to the challenge of opposing a provincial government and a monolithic police force. However, God doesn't choose people because of their university degrees, their wealth, or their connections to government. He selects them because their hearts are willing. As such, this book is meant to inspire the average Canadian so that he and she can and will change the course of history if they simply resolve to do so. Many of us sit around and do nothing because we think someone else, someone wiser or richer or stronger or more influential, will step up to the plate. But Caledonia is all about average people standing up against injustice – and winning.

I first met Mark Vandermaas two weeks before my first rally, scheduled to take place on October 15, 2006. He had sent an e-mail expressing his interest in participating, and I think he was intrigued by my website, where my colourful and unorthodox spelling and grammar were revealed for the entire world to see. So began a great partnership.

Mark traveled from London, Ontario to Brantford to hear me speak at the local Lion's Hall. I had rented the hall so that I could explain to the public why rallies in Caledonia were so crucial to restoring law and order there. Things became interesting when Brantford Mayor Mike Hancock summarily cancelled my booking. Not only that, he paid for large commercial signs informing the public about the cancellation. (Rest assured that the mayor has never cancelled any meetings convened by Natives.) It is one of my core beliefs that every obstacle in life is actually an opportunity. I would be the first to admit that I dislike confrontations and obstacles; I'm like everyone else who prefers life to be enjoyable and easy. However, as a Christian who believes that Christ's crucifixion wasn't negative at all, but was the opportunity that allowed for the salvation of humanity I see life's obstacles in a different light.

Mayor Hancock's actions forced me – enabled me – to deliver my speech in the parking lot of the Lion's Hall as Brantford police stood nearby. When Mark saw this public spectacle – 90 minutes of harassment and intimidation by Native protesters as I spoke about the equality of all people – he decided then and there he had to join the fight against racism in Caledonia. Mark has flaws just like me and everybody else, but I have no doubt that he is the single hardest worker for justice in Ontario. He has spent thousands of hours documenting details of events to ensure there is a body of evidence to support our public statements. He also created the websites VoiceofCanada.ca, CaledoniaVictimsProject.ca, HelplessbyBlatchford.ca, and IpperwashPapers.ca, all of which keep the public informed about events which most of the media have ignored. In 2012, after some Jewish students were intimidated at the University of Western Ontario (now Western University) while campus police refused to intervene (the Caledonia Disease at work), he founded Israel Truth Week (IsraelTruthWeek.org) in order to not only counter the lies of Israel Apartheid Week, but to help unite Jewish and non-Jewish groups in defence of shared liberal values of freedom, equality and the rule of law which are under attack around the world. For these reasons, I actually owe Mayor Hancock my deepest thanks. Had it not been for his undemocratic tactics, I might never have met Mark.

Jeff Parkinson was also a founding member of CanACE. He emailed me right before my first rally to say he'd be there, and from the tone of his email it sounded like he was coming to confront Native protesters. I told him he could come, but only if he could control himself and if his purpose was to confront injustice and not Native people. He showed up at the rally, but I don't think I met him until January, 2007. My first impression was that he was young and wanted to knock heads. I must admit that it occurred to me that he might be an OPP plant, sent to create trouble and turn my rallies into violent confrontations.

Jeff has proven to be worth his weight in gold. He has been a key person at every rally because, despite whatever madness happens to be going on around him, he retains his cool, remains unobtrusive and videotapes it all. That's an extremely difficult feat. I am convinced that, had it not been for Jeff, the OPP would have been able to lay many false criminal charges against us. As it is, we rarely give our video footage to the police, so they never know exactly what evidence Jeff has collected. Jeff has spent countless hours creating videos and documenting the OPP's ongoing violations of the law. You can find his work at www.JeffParkinson.ca, and more than 140 of his videos are posted at www.CanACEHD.com. Jeff's high quality videos have been used many times by various TV news stations.

When I met Merlyn Kinrade, he was 72-years-old and, in my view, simply a force of nature. This was on January 20, 2007, but God's timing couldn't have been better. Under Commissioner Julian Fantino's leadership, the OPP had started a campaign to publicly smear me and anyone associated with me: There is strong evidence on file to indicate that the OPP worked with a Native person to create a neo-Nazi website, supposedly created by me, in an attempt to persuade the public that I was a white supremacist.

Merlyn was a Caledonia businessman, who in the 1950's-60's ran the local dairy shop, managed a kid's hockey team and later became a plumber. Over the years he fought for local issues such as preserving a local park and ensuring that a "public" swimming pool not be built at the school because he feared the school board would then control the use of the facility. Merlyn was an extremely honourable person who demonstrated great loyalty. Rough around the edges (and with a colourful vocabulary acquired during his days in the navy), he was exactly what was needed. Divisive gossip was spreading throughout Caledonia, and rumours were replacing facts. After nine months of violence, many residents had started to believe that the "poor" Native protesters had no option but to use violence because that "nasty" Gary McHale was coming

to town. The fact that most of the serious crimes committed at Caledonia occurred before I ever entered the picture didn't change many people's thinking.
The OPP propaganda machine proved to be very effective, persuading people
– for a while – that Gary McHale was responsible for Caledonia's ongoing
problems.

Merlyn was relentless at confronting the gossips. If you visited the local Tim
Horton's outlet (as Merlyn did most every day), you had better not bad-mouth
any member of CanACE because he would walk right up to your table and demand that you either prove your statements or apologize. At town hall meetings, in restaurants or at any other business location, and even at the local fair
or Santa Claus parade, if anyone called those standing up for freedom "racist,"
that person had to answer to Merlyn Kinrade.

Once, while I was running in the 2008 federal election, a local businessman
walked behind me down a hallway while repeatedly whispering "racist." Merlyn heard him, and a week-long battle ensued. Merlyn confronted the businessman again and again, and asked if he had ever spoken to me or heard any
of my speeches. He demanded that the man either prove his point or apologize
to me. The businessman had a booth at the Caledonia Fair, as did I, because I
was running in the election. Merlyn got the businessman to come over to my
booth and apologize for his comment.

Over the years Merlyn channeled his anger at injustice into a newfound sense
of God's peace and love for others. He left his colourful navy language behind,
at least in my presence, and in a true working of the heart, learned not to be
angry with people, but rather with injustice. Single-handedly, he put an end to
the gossip that had almost destroyed our efforts to hold the police force and
Premier Dalton McGuinty publicly accountable. Sadly, though, Merlyn was
battling an even more formidable foe – cancer. It was a battle he could fight
bravely and stoically, but couldn't win; he succumbed to his illness on Saturday, October 6, 2012 at the age of 77. It was only the year before that the OPP
had arrested him for trespassing because he had dared to walk down a public
road carrying a Canadian Flag.

Merlyn never understood those who claimed they supported the cause but
could not get involved because of their need to protect their family. His daughter was four years old when the illegal occupation began, but he maintained
that "It is because of my daughter that I must get involved and ensure that her
future is free from racist policies."

Bonnie and Larry Stephens became involved during our "Protect Our Families
Rally" in August, 2008 at the Cayuga police station.[2] A retired couple, they
lived in the nearby town of Cayuga. Throughout 2007-2009, Merlyn wrote

many letters to the local paper reminding people of the crucial local issue and bluntly calling people cowards. The Stephens were among the few to heed his call for help, and soon become vital to the cause. Bonnie and Larry attended every rally, opened their home for our meetings, spent tens of thousands of dollars earmarked for their retirement money supporting the cause, and risked their own personal safety and their property by simply being involved. On December 3, 2011, Bonnie was arrested along with Merlyn, Jeff, Mark, me and 3 others (Doug & Randy Fleming, Jack Van Halteren) on the false charge of trespassing when we walked down a public road with a Canadian Flag. All charges were eventually dropped against the 'Caledonia 8'.[3] Larry and Bonnie were also illegally arrested on September 2, 2012 on yet another false charge of trespassing.

Everyone involved in the struggle brings his/her own particular style to the cause, and it is amazing to watch videos of Bonnie politely but firmly confronting OPP officers as they stand by and watch crimes being committed. The Stephens have demonstrated that they are willing to go the distance, and won't be deterred by false arrests, economic hardship, threats and intimidation or lies and defamation

Finally, I must mention the high price paid by the spouses of those involved. Debbie Vandermaas and Patricia Kinrade have had to put up with a lot, including a changed lifestyle; financial hardship; endless discussions about justice; the fear of being targeted; the fear that their husbands will be harmed or jailed; and having to live 24/7 with the cause. The economic hardship they have endured has been huge: no one hands you a paycheck for fighting to restore justice. Over the years, some people have stepped up and donated money to our cause, but seven years of battle has drained everyone's RRSPs, bank accounts and more. My wife Christine has had to endure intense anxiety knowing that I am the focal point of the radicals' hatred and anger at our rallies. Her greatest fear has been that the OPP would do little to stop an assault on me. In these past six years, not a day has gone by without something to do with Caledonia interrupting our home life, be it a phone call or posting news stories on the website or something else.

Over the course of our struggle, dozens of individuals have attempted to stand up to the government. Some have been involved for a few weeks, some for a few months and some for a few years. All have paid a price and all have faced the pressure. I will not bad mouth anyone who has bent under it. When faced with the task of changing the views of a government and political parties, and the very way the public thinks, it can often appear to be so hopeless and, therefore, so discouraging. It is usually very hard to see a light at the end of the tunnel. The greatest hardship is staying the course and remaining steadfast when facing down a government that has all the time and money in the world. But while enduring all the abuse, CanACE, a small group of misfits, not only confronted the full force of the McGuinty government but also compelled the provincial police to make some real changes to ensure the rights of all citizens.

The battle isn't over. There is no guarantee that the OPP's racist policies – racist because they consistently and unlawfully favour one group of people over another – have truly ended, but there is light and hope. There is a way to force the government to ensure equality for all.

* * *

Throughout 2006-2007, the OPP and the McGuinty government argued that police were engaged in a "peacekeeping mission" in Caledonia. At one press conference, McGuinty even stated that he should be issuing blue helmets to OPP officers in Caledonia, as if to suggest that their work was the equivalent of the noble work of Canadian peacekeepers throughout the world. OPP Commissioner Julian Fantino would regularly refer to the OPP officers as "peacekeepers."

That sounds nice and reasonable until you understand that a primary purpose of the United Nations is to establish the rule of law so that all people are subject to the law and all people are protected by the law. As the UN website explains:

> *Promoting the rule of law at the national and international levels is at the heart of the United Nations' mission. Establishing respect for the rule of law is fundamental to achieving a durable peace in the aftermath of conflict, to the effective protection of human rights, and to sustained economic progress and development. The principle that everyone – from the individual right up to the State itself – is accountable to laws that are publicly promulgated, equally enforced and independently adjudicated, is a fundamental concept which drives much of the United Nations work.*[4]

Both Mark Vandermaas and Merlyn Kinrade were actual peacekeepers, serving Canada under the UN Flag in the Middle East; Merlyn served in 1955 and Mark served in 1978. In response to McGuinty describing the OPP in Caledonia as "peacekeepers," they wrote him a letter which included the following:

> *'Law Enforcement' is a role performed by police officers in a functioning, vibrant, healthy First World democracy in order to preserve the Rule of Law and protect law-abiding citizens from criminals irrespective of their race, religion, national origin or grievance. It requires that citizens respect both the law and the willingness of police officers to enforce it justly.*

'Peacekeeping' is a role performed mainly by soldiers trained to kill, and is used as a deterrent during civil war in failed states where the Rule of Law has broken down, or in the aftermath of international warfare to prevent further hostilities.

It disturbs us greatly that people in positions of power talk of 'peace-keeping' as if it were some kind of innocuous, refined and noble form of policing when, in fact, their use of this word is the surest confirmation that the foundation of our society – the rule of law – is collapsing.[5]

The Ontario Police Services Act does say police officers are peace officers that keep the peace. However, the same Act demands all officers "prevent crimes," "encourage other persons to prevent crimes," "assist victims of crime," "apprehend criminals," "lay charges," and "participate in prosecutions," etc.

In effect, what Fantino and McGuinty were saying is that it is okay for officers to *not* assist victims of crime, to *not* prevent crimes, to *not* apprehend criminals and to *not* lay charges. Can you imagine if an OPP officer refused to "participate in prosecution" of a case by refusing to testify? Would it be okay as long as the officer was keeping the peace? If the OPP and Ontario's premier will not uphold the rule of law in Caledonia, thugs will rule the town. Citizens will be forced to take the law into their own hands, and fights will break out in the streets. Fundamental to all democratic societies is the understanding that the primary role of the government is to ensure that law and order is established and upheld.

Canadians, through their British heritage, have entered into a contract with the government whereby we, the citizens, charge the government with upholding community peace and order. In return we have agreed not to bear arms for self-protection. We, as Canadians, have rejected the Hatfield/McCoy view of law enforcement whereby citizens take the law into their own hands. Prior to 1880 in Canada, we did not have Crown prosecutors, but our nation has evolved and we have turned over all aspects of justice to government agents. In return citizens pay an increased tax to ensure that the government has the resources to hire police, Crown prosecutors and court staff so that all people can resolve their conflicts in court, rather than in the streets.

McGuinty and the OPP have violated this long established contract between the citizens and their government. They have failed to uphold the law; failed to assist the victims; failed to prosecute the criminals; failed to prevent further crimes; and, due to these failures, have emboldened those who use violence instead of the courts. They have a great deal to answer for.

1   OPP news release, June 11, 2006, O.P.P. Investigate Three Violent Altercations Within
    One Hour. *
2   'Protect Our Families' Rally, Aug. 23, 2008. *
3   *Hamilton Spectator*, Feb. 4, 2012: McHale plans new protest after charges dismissed. *
4   *United Nations, United Nations and the Rule of Law*, accessed June 8, 2013. http://www.
    un.org/en/ruleoflaw/.
5   Mark Vandermaas & Merlyn Kinrade letter to former Ontario Premier Dalton McGuinty,
    May 8, 2007. *

    * See http://www.GaryMcHale.ca/book for additional information, links to documents,
    videos and photos

Chapter 2

The OPP Lies to the Court and the Public about Criminal Behaviour

By July 2006, serious crimes had been repeatedly committed in Caledonia, and the OPP had done little to prevent them. After Native protesters attacked the CHCH TV camera crew and other media outlets, though, the tone of media coverage began to change. It went from characterizing Native protesters as "poor" and "innocent" to showing the violence and lawlessness that was taking place.

The McGuinty government's response was, in a word, outrageous. In July of that year, it bought Douglas Creek Estates for $23 million, and then immediately authorized the Native protesters (the same ones whose violence has put dozens of officers and residents in the hospital) to live there for free in existing houses. Living expenses for heat, gas, water, etc., were passed on to Ontario's taxpayers. In other words, instead of upholding the law and defending the innocent victims, McGuinty rewarded Natives for their bad – unlawful – behaviour.

Of course, instead of solving the problems, McGuinty's "remedy" succeeded only in creating new ones. Early in August, Native groups began to quarrel over who would get to occupy the newly built homes on Douglas Creek Estates. One group set a house on fire because another group wanted to take it over.

The fire department and police were sent to DCE but refused to enter, heeding the Natives' order to keep out. As per usual in Caledonia, the OPP obeyed these orders. The firefighters parked their truck down the road at the Canadian Tire and watched the house burn. A Native group put out the fire. (Of the 10 homes on DCE that were completed or near completion, only one now remains. McGuinty allowed – and, I have reason to believe, paid – the very same Native protesters that had been living in the others to gut them, removing all the stoves, refrigerators, furnaces, wood, carpet, etc. Someone made thousands of dollars from these items, proof that, in McGuinty's Ontario, some crimes certainly *did* pay.)

On August 8, 2006, Superior Court Judge David Marshall ordered the OPP to arrest all protesters who remained on DCE.[1] The OPP and McGuinty appealed this decision to the Court of Appeal for Ontario, arguing that since McGuinty was now the "owner" of this property, he was allowed to let whomever he wanted to live there (which apparently included people committing crimes).

Throughout July and August of 2006 the OPP had refused to launch criminal investigations against Native protesters. The County further whitewashed the issue by refusing to issue by-law violations against the protesters or the McGuinty government for which, as owner of the property, it was liable. Consequently, when the Court of Appeals heard the appeal against Judge Marshall's ruling, it was led to believe that the crime rate in Caledonia was actually declining and that by-law violations were not occurring. The court stated in its ruling:

> *Ontario is content to permit the peaceful occupation of its property. It has the right to do so. As a property owner it has the right to use its own land as it sees fit, as long as it complies with municipal by-laws and the laws concerning nuisance and public safety. Ontario has complied with its legal obligations. The record does not show that by permitting the protestors to remain, the government has breached any municipal requirements, created a nuisance or adversely affected public safety. Nor even does the record show that after July 5 the public's right to use the highways has been impeded.[2]*

It is quite incredible that, while the Criminal Code and local by-laws had been violated dozens of times every day in July, August and September of 2006, the appeals court stated that there was no record to show that the government had "breached any municipal requirements" by permitting protesters to remain. It is hard to know whether the OPP simply lied to its lawyers about what was happening, or whether the lawyers knew about the daily criminal acts and lied to the court. Either way, the Court of Appeals was lied to, as subsequent court cases would reveal by exposing just how many crimes were actually taking place on, and from, McGuinty's Caledonia property. The McGuinty government would end up paying $20-million to Caledonia residents, compensation awarded to over 400 families victimized by Native crimes who had filed a class action lawsuit[3] against his government. The settlement also included damage

24

done to 440 businesses which had lost money as a direct result of the ongoing violence.

From May to September 2006, residents living near Douglas Creek Estates were harassed and threatened daily, and even throughout the night, as Native protesters lined up cars and shone their lights into people's homes, made loud noises, and generally made it difficult, if not impossible, for residents to sleep. The government would admit in its $20 million settlement that residents experienced ongoing harassment by Native protesters in the form of "frequent gunfire, loud noises, smoke, verbal assaults, personal property damage, ATV traffic in backyards, bright lights, etc."[4] On August 31, various media outlets reported that "The federal and Ontario governments are telling Six Nations leaders to stop aboriginal protesters from harassing residents in Caledonia... They call for an end to 'loud noises, firecrackers, bright lights from ATVs and other vehicles, and other activities that disturb the peace in neighbouring areas.'"[5] Of course, later the government would admit that there were no "firecrackers," and that those sounds were actually part of the 'frequent gunfire.'

In early August 2006, Haldimand Mayor Marie Trainer and I were interviewed on CHCH TV about Native protesters who were throwing objects from the overpass bridge onto the highway below in Caledonia. Several cars and trucks had been damaged and Mayor Trainer reported that a number of trucks had had their windshields smashed. Throughout 2006, an OPP police car was stationed within a few feet of the bridge, but officers in the vehicle had been ordered not to intervene when Native protesters committed such crimes.

On Sept. 6, 2006, the local newspaper, *Regional News*, reported that two Six Nations teenagers were seen throwing debris off the bridge at a truck driver below:

> All of a sudden the pickup truck he was driving was showered with rocks, some of them the size of a baseball, his wife explained. Because the teens were situated on the train bridge, her husband turned down Ross Street and chased the teens down on Sutherland Street as they were coming off the tracks... However police just sat in the park adjacent to the train bridge while the incident was taking place, noted the woman. And another local homeowner backs up her story. An officer sitting in the park nearby said he wasn't responsible for anything 'on that side', which they both interpreted to mean 'on that side of the river'. But the victims' main reason for contacting the paper was to spread awareness about the incident and to let people know that debris is still flying from the sky onto Highway 54. They're scared someone will get maimed, or worse. No warning or notice has been issued by the OPP in the form of a press release.[6]

Throughout 2006 the OPP would do nothing but watch as Native protesters threw objects from the bridge onto drivers below them. Officers would tell residents there was nothing they could do because, "We'd have to cross native land to get to those bridges and we can't drive there." Native protesters in Caledonia had created a "no-go zone" for OPP, a list of roads the police were not allowed to use. Yes, you read that correctly – the OPP meekly obeyed as Native protesters laid down the law *to them*, refusing to intervene as they watched crimes being committed before their eyes.

In public, at least, the OPP refused to acknowledge that these crimes were even occurring. Finally, a year later, on June 16, 2007 the OPP issued a press release which revealed that "A 44-year-old Caledonia woman escaped injury after her windshield was shattered by a rock that was thrown from the Stirling Road overpass... A malicious and senseless act such as this could have had devastating consequences. Those responsible will face a charge of Mischief Endangering Life."[7] You have to give the OPP credit: it took only a year for it to admit that these acts could actually kill someone! However, that's as far as it went: Native people were caught hurling objects from the bridge for years, and not a single person was ever charged. In 2010, the OPP would be forced – in connection with the death of a motorist – to produce the record of all incidents near the overpass bridge. The court record shows that police recorded 1,500 incidents that they knew of over a 5-year period.

Of course, Caledonia also has a fire department – an extremely busy one that seemed to be getting busier all the time. In 2005, for example, it responded to a total of 135 incidents; in the first six months of 2006, it responded to 111 calls. From March to June, 2005, it responded to 41 calls; in the same period in 2006, it responded to 81 incidents, an increase of almost 100 percent. The first time I went to Caledonia, in mid-July 2006, I photographed fires Native protesters had set in two different locations on that day alone. Neither of the fires was reported to the fire department, so neither made it into department statistics. Who knows how many other fires have also gone unreported?

On August 8, 2006, the Natives were incensed by Superior Court Judge Marshall's court order which called for them to be removed from DCE and arrested. In his ruling he stated:

> *Ladies and gentlemen we speak of the Rule of Law. This case deals with an issue that is arguably the pre-eminent condition of freedom and peace in a democratic society. It is upheld wherever in the world there is liberty... It is the rule that every citizen from the prime minister to the poorest of our people is equally subject to and must obey the law... Whenever it is broken – even in a small way, we say there is injustice. We see the unfairness. It is a rule that is woven into every part of our*

social contract to live peacefully together. Even a small tear in the cloth of our justice system spoils the whole fabric of society. Who is responsible for upholding the Rule of Law? The answer, of course, is, each of us. I and each of my neighbours are equally responsible.

But the courts have a central role. It is the courts who are the arbiters. The crown and the police play a role – but the courts have the difficult role of applying equally to everyone the laws passed by our elected representatives. Should the court defer to the government its role as arbiter of the Rule of Law? No indeed, but that has been submitted in this court in this case. The counsel for the crown said here, and I quote: "Almost everyone you've heard from has asked that you (the court) leave the matter with those that are responsible for dealing with the rule of law"; meaning leaving that to the crown and the police. With respect, that submission could hardly be further from the mark. The Superior Courts, of which this court is a part, are the custodians of the Rule of Law.

*Consider this statement by the Chief Justice of Canada's Supreme Court: "In the constitutional arrangements passed on to us by the British and recognized by the preamble of the Constitution Act 1867, the provincial superior courts are the **foundation of the rule of law itself.**"[8] [emphasis in the original]*

Native protesters were outraged by the idea that they, too, were subject to the law and were expected to live peacefully with their neighbours. In response to the ruling, they set fires at the base of hydro towers, thereby threatening the major hydro grid that was near DCE.[9] They then blocked the road that led onto DCE and attached a fire hose to a fire hydrant, using it as a water cannon to assault OPP officers and residents. The police response was typical: no Native protesters were arrested. However, police did arrest a non-Native resident who attempted to remove a Native Flag from the side of the road. Let's face it – Native protesters used the residents of Caledonia as pawns to force the government to comply with their wishes. Instead of protesting in a peaceful manner, using the court to decide any legal issues, they were emboldened by the OPP's and McGuinty's weakness to use extreme force and violence.

Two days before Judge Marshall's August 8 ruling, Native protesters harassed an 86-year-old World War II veteran who lived beside DCE. From 10 p.m. to 3 a.m., protesters threw rocks at the man's home, making holes in the aluminum siding. At one point Mayor Trainer tried to speak to the Natives to persuade them to stop this harassment, but the OPP refused to allow her to cross the police line. The OPP stood there watching these crimes being committed, essentially functioning as security guards for the Natives to ensure that no one could or would interfere with them.

Observing that the Rule of Law had been replaced by the rule of thugs, some Caledonia residents began throwing objects at the Native protesters. According to the OPP press release, "... just after 12:00 midnight, police attended and observed approximately 40 citizens in opposition with numerous occupiers. At one point the numbers grew to approximately 100 citizens. The situation escalated to the point where projectiles such as rocks and golf balls were thrown from both sides."[10] I must have ESP because the OPP claimed they didn't arrive at the scene until midnight, and yet I had posted my first story about the incident by 10:15, almost two hours earlier. At the time, the OPP had many checkpoints in Caledonia that operated 24 hours a day, including one within a few hundred feet of where this incident took place. How could it take the OPP two hours to travel a few hundred feet?

The OPP press release makes it appear that the two sides were equally culpable in the altercation instead of reporting that the Native protesters were to blame because they had attacked the homes along the edge of DCE. In addition, Native protesters had built large bonfires near homes on DCE and then prevented the fire department from extinguishing them. Natives had pulled out hydro towers, destroyed Canadian flags and raised the Native flag throughout the same day in Caledonia. All this took place *before* the residents took any action; when they did, it was only in response to this flagrant provocation. Obviously, the OPP didn't want to report these facts.

Local reporter Karen Best (who is now doing media relations for the Six Nations band council) witnessed the whole event and reported, "Over 20 rocks were hurled at the home of a Second World War veteran. No longer counting on police for protection, neighbours stood watch over his backyard all night and refused to leave when OPP asked them."[11] The next day I phoned and asked her what she thought of the OPP press release. After laughing, she said, "Caledonians didn't start this, because they suffer the consequences whenever anything happens... [Native-owned] ATVs were just roaring around by people's homes at 3 a.m."[12]

There were far too many events throughout July to October to report, but it's safe to say that Native protesters committed crimes against Caledonia residents on a daily basis. It is thus almost impossible to understand how the Ontario Court of Appeals could conclude, in the words of its ruling: "Ontario has complied with its legal obligations. The record does not show that by permitting the protestors to remain, the government has breached any municipal requirements, created a nuisance or adversely affected public safety."[13]

* * *

OPP brass was beginning to get push-back from some police officers, disgusted because Native crimes were being allowed to continue with impunity. Officers were beginning to step forward and tell the media that there was a two-tier justice system in Caledonia – one for Natives and one for non-Native residents, with the Natives getting preferential treatment because police were under orders to not arrest them. The Ontario Provincial Police Association (OPPA) was under pressure to address issues relating to the failed policing in Caledonia. They sent a list of questions to OPP brass that revealed exactly what the average OPP officer was thinking. Among the questions:

- Why is it that when Federal and Provincial Statutes are being contravened in the presence of OPP officers in Caledonia they are not taking the appropriate and immediate action that they would if they were anywhere else in the Province?

- Prior to, or following any arrest or contact with individuals in Caledonia, why is the Command Post asking our members if the person in question is white or non-white? When the person is non-white or First Nations, they are being told to "stand down" or "release".

- Our members are highly trained professional police officers. Why are our members not being told and then supported by Command to enforce all the laws of this Municipality, Province and Country?

- Why were the OPP placed in the role of peacekeepers and not law enforcement officers?

- Why are the First Nations people treated differently than any other citizen?

- Why has the government perpetuated a two tier judicial system?

- "Why were officers deployed with direction that would violate policy or SOP? [Standard Operating Procedures]"

- Given that weapons have been seen and intelligence would indicate they are present, why is Caledonia not a level II incident? [14]

Of course, the public was never told that that the OPPA, which represents Ontario's 6,200 OPP officers, was demanding answers to these questions. The OPP would repeatedly tell the public there was no two-tier system of justice, that Natives were not being treated differently and that there were no weapons on DCE.

The way senior OPP brass responded to these questions was also very telling. For example, its response to the question "Why has the government perpetuated a two tier judicial system?" was not "There is no government policy to create a two tier justice system." It was "The OPP does not comment on government policies." That's perhaps no surprise, given that a two tier system is both government policy *and* OPP policy. However, it wouldn't be until December

2007 that anyone in the OPP would publicly admit that the policy it was following in Caledonia had actually been enacted back in 2002. The policy was called *A Framework for Police Preparedness for Aboriginal Critical Incidents* or *The Framework*, for short.[15]

While Native protesters had known about *The Framework* since November 2005, non-Native people and local government officials were never told that such a policy existed. OPP officers had received training about *The Framework*, so they knew exactly what it required of them. In December 2007, OPP Superintendent John Cain swore out an affidavit stating, in part: "To assist the police in responding to land disputes involving Aboriginal persons, the OPP developed a policy entitled *The Framework*. *The Framework* is the OPP's strategic and operational policy for dealing with such disputes... The OPP endeavours not to take sides in blockades, occupations or land disputes..."[16]

Supt. Cain may believe that the OPP doesn't take sides, but the truth is that they do. Once any Native protester walks onto private property and starts an occupation, it is the OPP, not the Natives, who ensure the property owner is rendered powerless. It was the OPP that stopped construction trucks, cars and property owners from entering the construction site. In every case, police would line up dozens of officers and prevent non-Natives from entering their own property.

The Framework is quite clear on what it is trying to accomplish. While it quotes Section 25 and Section 35 of the Canadian Constitution about the rights of Aboriginals, it omits all sections about the rights of non-Aboriginals. The entire document is focused on Native rights and excludes the rights of non-Natives. At every step, the OPP officer is directed to negotiate with the Natives committing crimes instead of arresting them.

The Framework states that its purpose is to ensure a "flexible approach to resolving conflict," create a "mutual respect of difference, positions and interests of the involved Aboriginal community and the OPP" and promote and develop "strategies that minimize the use of force to the fullest extent possible." Nowhere does it state that its purpose is to prevent crimes, aid the victims of crime and see to it that officers and non-Native residents do not end up in the hospital. *The Framework*'s entire *raison d'etre* is to prevent arrests of Native protesters; to make officers "flexible" so that all they will do is "talk" to Natives, even when there is an attempt on the life of one of their fellow officers. On June 9, 2006, for instance, OPP officers were so "flexible" that they watched as Natives assaulted a fellow officer; so "flexible" that they did not lift a finger to assist him or to prevent his assailants from fleeing the scene of the crime.

OPP brass will say that it is better to make an arrest weeks later than to have a confrontation at the scene. Do the police in Toronto, Montreal or anywhere else view law enforcement this way? Can I rob a bank, point a gun at an officer or hospitalize someone in Toronto while the police simply watch me drive away? The question is ridiculous. There is only one reason for the OPP's stance: the people committing the crimes are Native. There is no way a police officer would ever say it was okay to stand by and watch white people beat up a black person. There is no way the police would ever create a policy that allowed heterosexuals to attack a gay person. No commissioner of the OPP, no superintendent or inspector, would ever instruct officers to allow Christians to harm Jewish people and put them in the hospital.

There is no doubt that current policies which favour Natives are racist; there is also no doubt that such policies arose because of Canada's past history of racism against Natives, and because of the guilt many Canadians feel because of it. However, it makes no sense whatsoever to try to redress historical wrongs by pursuing new racist policies against another group. Surely it doesn't take an Einstein to figure out that the real solution is to treat all people with respect and equality under the law. Is it so hard for the OPP and the Ontario government to clue in to the reality that racist policies will always create victims, hatred and conflict? No matter what government lawyers or even courts say, they can never turn racism into something positive. The attempt to do so serves only to institutionalize it, which makes it even more evil.

At some level, McGuinty and the OPP must recognize that their two-tier justice system is unacceptable, for if they really believed that they were doing the right thing they'd be on TV trumpeting the benefits of their two-tiered system. They would be proud because they would be confident that it was the right thing to do. Instead, they have repeatedly hidden the truth from the public and have claimed that there is no official policy which would prompt police officers in Caledonia to apply the law differently according to race.

As previously mentioned, individual OPP officers had begun to spill the beans about *The Framework*, and the impact it was having in Caledonia. I had several OPP officers in court testifying as witnesses in 2008-9. Officer Jeff Bird, for one, wasn't about to lie on the stand about what was really happening. Over strenuous objections by the Crown, he admitted that he had heard officers being told over OPP radio to identify the race of the person involved in a crime.[17] If the individual happened to be Native, police were to let that person go. Officer Bird further testified that he had received training regarding *The Framework* and that, as he understood it, he was not supposed to arrest a Native person who was committing an assault, but that he was supposed to arrest a non-Native person committing one.

Under intense cross-examination by Crown prosecutor Mitch Hoffman, Haldimand Mayor Marie Trainer testified that she had come to firmly believe that the OPP were forcing race-based policing policies on the community. When Hofmann challenged her on this, she told the court she had witnessed it with her own two eyes, that numerous residents were reporting it, that retired OPP officers had privately apologized to her for the policy, and that serving OPP officers were complaining to her about their orders.[18] Having failed to discredit Haldimand's top municipal official, Hoffman was finally told by the judge that he was badgering the witness and instructed to move on.

* * *

In July and August of 2006, the OPP did everything in its power to ensure that crime reports would show a decline in incidents. That way they could proudly announce to the court and the public that their racist policies (which they would never admit were racist) were working. This propaganda was staggeringly effective.

In August 2006, I announced my first rally in Caledonia. I scheduled it for October 15 and called it "March for Freedom". The title came from Judge Marshall's ruling in which he wrote that the Rule of Law is a "pre-eminent condition of freedom and peace in a democratic society". All truly democratic societies must uphold the Rule of Law because, wrote Judge Marshall, "the fathers and mothers of my generation gave their lives to uphold this principle of the equality of each of us before the law." [19] Elsewhere in the ruling Marshall said this:

> It was, and is common knowledge that the law has not been enforced... The citizens of Caledonia may well ask why should I pay a fine, that a judge has ordered when, on DCE, the protesters do not have to obey the court's order? To that person, this court has no teeth. To that person, this is not a court at all... The court has been and will be patient but the court cannot turn a blind eye to the blatant contempt of the court's lawful order.... Whatever is being done should be done peacefully but also lawfully, within the Rule of Law...[20]

Judge David Marshall was an amazing man whose years of service to the Native community as a medical doctor had earned him the honorary title of Chief. A doctor since 1962 and a lawyer since 1972, Marshall had practised both professions, and for a time was a provincial coroner. In 1982, he was appointed Justice of the Supreme Court of the Northwest Territories and Yukon, and Judge of the Court of Appeal to the Northwest Territories and Yukon. In 2008, he was named Colonel Commandant of the Canadian Forces Medical and Dental Branch after being a reservist for over four decades. Justice Marshall was the founding director of the National Judicial Institute. And yet, his years of medical service to Native people throughout the Northwest Territories and Yukon did not prevent radicals from denouncing him as "racist" and "corrupt."

For example, on three occasions in a play created by University of Waterloo Professor Andy Houston and his students, Judge Marshall was called "corrupt." Of course, nothing in the play mentioned Marshall's years of devoted service to Native people: that would have conflicted with their politically correct narrative. No, he was called "corrupt" for only one reason: because he was the judge who had ordered law-breaking Natives to be removed and arrested in Caledonia.

On November 1, 2007 Mark Vandermaas and I spoke to Houston's class, which we were very pleased to do because we believed (wrongly as it turned out) that the university was taking an interest in understanding the impact of native lawlessness on innocent residents and would, hopefully, play a role in preventing similar crises in the future. We gave each student a CD containing supporting evidence along with our presentation notes. Our effort was in vain: What Professor Houston and his students neglected to tell the public is that the student actors themselves were pro-Native activists who had helped build the illegal structure at the entrance to DCE that Natives cheekily called their "embassy." We and our spouses attended the play only to sadly discover that it was blatantly biased toward the occupiers, downplaying their violence and lawlessness completely while portraying us as anti-Native troublemakers. Waterloo students have been bused into Caledonia to provide support for Native protesters. Whether Professor Houston has supported this I cannot say. I should also note that it was UofW radicals who disrupted – and forced the cancellation of – Christie Blatchford's originally-scheduled 2010 presentation in relation to the release of *Helpless*. (The university rescheduled her talk which she gave to a full house, without incident, all thanks to the publicity.)[21]

The point of our March for Freedom rally was to give Caledonia residents a platform so they could voice their views to the media, and an outlet through which they could vent their frustration over the thugs' actions and OPP inaction. I wanted there to be a single, simple message for the media and I wanted to unite the community, giving people a lawful way of expressing their outrage.

Almost immediately, the OPP and McGuinty went into panic mode, as if Ontario would wake up the next day to the news that Caledonia had been wiped off the map. The government's Caledonia negotiator, former premier David Peterson, actually referred to me and my supporters as "whackos", which only fueled more support.[22] For seven years Native protesters had held rallies in Caledonia and not once did the OPP or McGuinty discourage the public from attending them, or make any negative comments regarding them; on the contrary, at each rally the OPP provided the Natives with a police escort to ensure their rallies went off without a hitch. This was most emphatically not the case for us, non-Natives who the OPP saw as troublemakers. According to the OPP we were the real problem in Caledonia. It seemed as though they were saying things would be much better if only the community would go to sleep and wake up in 15 years, so the government could do as it pleased and appease those committing the crimes. My key message at the March for Freedom rally was this: we citizens must never surrender our rights and freedoms to the police or to the government, and must demand that the government uphold the equality of all people.

To this day, the Native protesters in Caledonia refuse to accept that non-Native people have the right to public protest. Not once have we held a counter-rally, or even been present in Caledonia when Native protesters have held their BBQs, rallies, marches, or other such events. At the same time, though, never once in seven years have Natives and their leftist union supporters failed to show up to confront and harass us at our rallies. As these radicals see it, Natives have the right to exercise their free speech in public. We, on the other hand, do not. Their implication is all too clear: How dare anyone stand up for the equality of all people? Anyone who would do so *must* be a "racist." And, indeed, there is racism. As Native protesters screamed out at one of my public speeches calling for equality before the law, "It's called special policing, Gary."

While the OPP was negotiating almost daily with Native protesters, the same OPP refused to meet with non-Native protesters. Local Detachment Commander, Insp. Dave McLean, was invited to several of our planning meetings to ensure the OPP knew every detail about our March for Freedom rally. Each time he failed to show up or send officers on his behalf. It wasn't until two days before the rally that McLean finally met with me.

In the days leading up to the rally the OPP was desperate to show the public that it was enforcing the law. On September 23, 2006, the OPP issued a press release stating that in seven months they had arrested 27 people, charging them with a total of 57 offences. Of course, over that same period hundreds, if not thousands, of crimes had been committed. And how many of these arrests were of innocent residents for "breach of the peace"? By contrast, to this day, the OPP has yet to arrest a single Native person for the bridge-burning episode; the firebombing of the power station; the kidnapping of two OPP officers; the kidnapping of Dave Brown; the six-week long barricading of Argyle St.; the numerous tire fires on the roads; the dumping of gravel on the highway; the nightly harassment of residents; the endless trespassing onto residents' properties; and the numerous instances of property damage. Recently, OPP Commissioner Chris Lewis, who replaced Julian Fantino in 2010, discussed the number of OPP arrests related to Caledonia, but he never mentioned the hundreds of events that the OPP simply failed to investigate. As for the OPP's numbers game: I have been arrested on nine different occasions, never mind the multiple arrests of my associates (as many as eleven of us at one time) who volunteered to be arrested while trying to raise a Canadian flag or simply walk down the public road through DCE. Do OPP numbers include these arrests?

After seven months of residents being harassed by Native protesters, the OPP suddenly wanted to create a no-go zone between residents' homes and DCE property. At first it appeared as though the OPP was trying to help the residents, but that wasn't the case. Not once did police enforce the no-go zone against Native protesters even though several times they had been videotaped crossing through the no-go zone and confronting OPP officers at one of their 24/7 check points. The no-go zone was created solely as a public relations counter-measure regarding my March for Freedom rally. It was to give the OPP an excuse to arrest non-Natives for trespassing (because the McGuinty government had put up "no trespassing" signs along this zone). The zone was activated just a few days before the rally and never again 'enforced' once the rally was over.

Following my call for a rally, the OPP created random no-go zones that applied only to non-Natives. In seven years, to the best of my knowledge, the OPP never once told Native protesters where they could or could not walk, and never arrested a single Native for "to prevent a breach of peace." By contrast, police have made dozens of arrests of non-Natives as a means of preventing Natives from assaulting them. In some cases, OPP officers simply jumped out of a police van and declared the area to be a no-go zone and then proceeded to arrest the non-Natives. At the same time, Native protesters were free to walk through police lines and to walk right up to non-natives to threaten them, harass them and attempt to intimidate them.

In August 2006, three non-Native Caledonia women took lawn chairs and sat themselves down 20 feet inside DCE, the previously private land that was now owned by Ontario taxpayers. This was before the police used the no-go zones tactic, so the OPP sent in 53 officers, at your expense, to cart away the one woman who refused to leave public property. As she sat in her lawn chair on the public's land, she was arrested by the OPP to prevent – you guessed it – a "breach of the peace."[24] The officers picked up the lawn chair with her in it, carried it ten feet outside DCE limits, and then released her. Since she had committed no crime she was never charged. Is this arrest included as one of the ones the OPP claims to have made in Caledonia?

Why would the OPP behave in this way? The answer is simple: because they were terrified of Native protesters. The mindset of the OPP was that protesters were violent, were more than willing to injure officers and could not be trusted not to attack residents. While the Natives claimed their protests were peaceful, the whole point of their exercise was to instill fear into people's minds, to convince the OPP, the government and the residents that they were prepared to use extreme violence. It was, quite simply, a form of terrorism: Attack bridges and power stations; hospitalize police; kidnap people; dig up roads and force Native-issued passports upon non-Natives – all in order to force their political will upon others.

When I first got involved in Caledonia in June 2006, I tried dozens of times to reach then-OPP Commissioner Gwen Boniface by phone, with no success. Finally, a senior officer agreed to speak to me. Of course, I taped the conversation, during which it was made clear that the OPP was convinced that Native protesters were willing to kill OPP officers and area residents.

Beginning in December 2006, and continuing for almost three years, a Caledonia resident taped all OPP radio transmissions, as well as Native protesters' security force radio transmissions. Based on these tapes, I reported to the CBC in March 2007 that I had evidence that Native protesters had authorized the killing of OPP officers, residents of Caledonia and County workers. In return for an exclusive story, the CBC promised to do a prime time documentary on the issue.

The CBC sent a camera crew and a reporter to my home. Their lawyers asked for three examples of Native radio transmissions which had authorized killing. We provided the examples, and the story got the go-ahead from lawyers. The CBC then sent a camera crew to interview Mayor Trainer and Native protesters. Following that, I received two separate phone calls from the reporter, informing me of the show time and confirming that the lawyers had approved the final story. However, the CBC got cold feet, and half an hour before airtime the show was pulled. My information and the documentary team's work were solid, but for reasons of political correctness, the CBC could not bring itself to tell the Canadian public that Natives in Caledonia had authorized the killing of non-Natives. At a press conference held at Queen's Park on April 17, 2007, we told Canadian media what had happened.[25]

Can anyone imagine CBC pulling the story if white people had authorized the killing of Natives? Can you imagine the media firestorm that would ensue in Canada if it was discovered that *any* group had been targeting Native people? Of course you can't. Apparently, though, Canadian media do not feel the same need to inform the public when Natives say they plan to kill non-Natives.

To the public, the OPP continued to insist that the Caledonia protests were peaceful, except, of course, for that troublemaker McHale and his group (even though none of us had ever assaulted or even threatened a single person). The October 15, 2006 March for Freedom was my way of getting the truth to the public and of exposing the OPP cover-up. It was the best way I could think of to get the media to pay attention to Caledonia, and to allow people who lived there to voice their concerns. The speakers at that event were: local MPP Toby

Barrett, Caledonia resident AnneMarie VanSickle[26], Ipperwash resident Mary-Lou LaPratte[27] and my wife Christine, who read a speech written by Native private investigator Jon Sabin[28] from New York State. I spoke, too, but it was Anne-Marie VanSickle who captured the hearts of the crowd with her bold statements. She said:

> We have been subjected to ATVs racing around our homes all hours of the night, some with their mufflers removed, as their drivers yell and scream. The sounds of hammering, banging and gunshots can frequently be heard. Our family and neighbours have had to endure sleep deprivation, verbal and physical assaults while law enforcement has turned their back. This directly violates our autonomy as well as violates the rule of law. My phone line has been cut in 3 places. Occupiers with bandanas covering their faces, continue to ignore the 'no go zone.' They enter at their leisure and then proceed to stand and stare at the residents and their children, take our pictures and shout obscenities. Occupiers have come onto my property and my neighbour's. The OPP continue to refuse to patrol 6th line, or the areas behind Braemar Ave, MacCrae St and Argyle St. Our children have had to witness fires, burned bridges, threats, blocked highways, anarchy and lawlessness.

> Premier McGuinty: you, sir, are a medical anomaly. The fact you can stand when you don't have a spine will surely be discussed for generations to come. Your signature phrase "be patient" has outlived its usefulness; we expect the leader of our great province to have greater words of wisdom. Premier McGuinty, where have you been? Our patience has run out.

> Some of our elected provincial government diatribe has stated that this illegal occupation has been incident free and is merely symbolic. Your lack of knowledge concerns me: how can educated decisions regarding the safety and well-being of the people you serve be made with such a blatant lack of insight?

The rally was a huge success, covered by many media outlets across Canada. The OPP would tell the media that only 400 people showed up, but local reporters put the number at 2,000. One thing is for sure: the photos of the event show that there were far more than 400 people there. [29]

After the speeches we marched to the local Catholic School so that the media could see that, because of ongoing Native violence, the government had thought it necessary to build a high fence, install cameras and station OPP officers there. Nowhere else in Canada has the government felt compelled to fence-in a school in this way. Nowhere else in Canada have parents been told that, because the government refuses to enforce the law, their children have to attend school with such security. This Caledonia school had gone into lock-down mode several times due to violent protesters. During the first year of the protest, many families with children at this school lived in constant fear– not a way of life most Canadians would ever imagine possible in peaceful Canada.

For the OPP and McGuinty, our rally was the worst possible thing that could have happened. No longer could they keep people in the dark. No longer could they control the public message. We had demonstrated that we could invite a large crowd into Caledonia and keep it peaceful, and we had shown that we were able to work well with the media. The rally empowered average people to step forward and speak out. For political reasons, McGuinty wanted Caledonia to fade away, but our rally sent a powerful message to the Premier that they and the OPP could no longer get away with keeping us in the dark. What was the Premier's response? Well, McGuinty had banned pit bulls in the province, but he unleashed his own pit bull – Julian Fantino, his new OPP Commissioner – to sink his teeth into any "mouthy" non-Native in Caledonia. And soon enough, Fantino did just that.

* * *

I'll close this chapter with a favourite story. Our great friend and supporter, Doug Fleming, was concerned because a growing number of illegal smoke shops were popping up in the Caledonia area. (Natives can lawfully sell un-taxed cigarettes only on their reserves, but police do not enforce this). Some people say that Doug has a twisted sense of humour. I'll let you be the judge.

The first thing Doug did was set up an illegal smoke shop in his truck on the edge of town to see whether the OPP would arrest him while ignoring the il-legal Native smoke shops nearby. The handmade sign on his truck advertised "Information, Coffee, Pumpkins, Smokes." He sold untaxed cigarettes at cost. His opening day special was a free pumpkin if you bought two baggies of ciga-rettes; and a free pumpkin and a *Toronto Sun* if you bought three baggies.[30] Merlyn Kinrade got in on the act, phoning the OPP repeatedly in an attempt to get Doug arrested. But the police were a no-show. Several hours later, spotting an OPP car on random patrol near Doug's truck, I stood in the middle of the road and forced the officer to stop. He got out, talked to Doug and interviewed a few people, but left without laying any charges.

Bizarrely, the OPP issued a press release the next day asking the public for any information that could identify the person who had set up Doug's illegal smoke shop. Merlyn phoned the OPP right away, but no officer ever spoke to him about it.

Of course, the police knew full well that Doug Fleming had opened the smoke shop. After all, he had a big sign at his truck saying "Doug's Smokes", and his truck had a license plate. What exactly was the point of the OPP press release? Was it merely to try to tell the public that somehow the OPP was investigating this? If so it was pure propaganda, designed to mislead the public. They couldn't arrest Fleming while allowing Native illegal smoke shops to operate.

The next week Doug opened his "smoke shop" directly in front of the OPP sub-station in Caledonia. Police officers watched as, mere feet away, he illegally sold his cigarettes. Although they promised to send a senior officer to talk to him about why the government and police were allowing Natives to sell illegal cigarettes to the town's children, the brass never showed up.

Even more brazenly, he also set up shop in front of the home of Haldimand County Mayor Ken Hewitt (who was elected 2010). Later he set up "Doug's Stop Smoking Clinic" at an illegal Native-run smoke shop (one of many in the area). On December 4, 2007 Doug spoke to the media about illegal tobacco and its effects on his town at our 'Doug's Smokes' news conference in the Queen's Park Media Studio[31] after we were viciously assaulted by Six Nations supporters of an illegal smoke shop, a milestone in the fight for justice that I will cover in later chapters.

Doug's inventive approach to getting media attention was very successful, and he had several letters published in the local newspaper. You would have had to be living on the moon not to be aware of Doug Fleming's smoke shop protests. It was hilarious.

---

1   *Henco Industries Ltd. v. Haudenosaunee Six Nations Confederacy Council*, 2006 CanLII 63728 (ON SC), http://canlii.ca/t/23418.

2   *Henco Industries Limited v. Haudenosaunee Six Nations Confederacy Council*, 2006 Can-LII 41649 (ON CA), see paras. 72-73, http://canlii.ca/t/1q58j.

3   Caledonia Class Action Lawsuit official website: www.CaledoniaClassAction.com.

4   Superior Court Judge Crane court order dated Sept. 28, 2011 regarding Caledonia Class Action settlement for $20 million. See page 35 which lists out 6 zones in Caledonia where residents experienced hardship due to the illegal occupation. *

5   Canadian Press, Aug. 31, 2006, Feds and Ont. tell Six Nations Chief to stop protesters from harassing locals. *

6   *Regional News This Week*, Sept. 6, 2006, Six Nations teens caught throwing rocks off bridge. *

7   OPP news release, June 16, 2007, OPP: Driver Escapes Injury – Rock Thrown From Bridge. *

8   *Henco Industries Ltd. v. Haudenosaunee Six Nations Confederacy Council*, Aug. 8, 2006, Judge Marshall's ruling. *

9   See various newspaper stories on Aug 8th and 9th, 2006. *

10 OPP news release, Aug. 7, 2006, DISTURBANCE IN CALEDONIA. *

11 *Dunnville Chronicle*, Aug. 8, 2006, Rocks fly in Caledonia dispute. *

12 Taped phone call with Karen Best – reporter for *Dunnville Chronicle*.

13 *Henco Industries Limited v. Haudenosaunee Six Nations Confederacy Council*, 2006 Can-LII 41649 (ON CA), para. 73. http://canlii.ca/t/1q58j.

14 Ontario Provincial Police Association questions, August 2006, Questions confirmed by OPPA President Karl Walsh in Christie Blatchford's book Helpless. *

15 OPP Policies Statement, passed as policy in 2002, *A Framework for Police Preparedness for Aboriginal Critical Incidents*. Copy of policy marked as exhibit #7 at Gary McHale's preliminary hearing. *

16 Affidavit by OPP Superintendent John Cain, Dec. 14, 2007, copy filed as exhibit #22 at Gary McHale's preliminary hearing. *

17 Court testimony on April 24 and 27, 2009 by OPP Officer Jeff Bird at Gary McHale's preliminary hearing. *

18 Court testimony on Nov. 25, 2008 by ex-Haldimand Mayor Marie Trainer at Gary McHale's preliminary hearing. *

19 *Henco Industries Ltd. v. Haudenosaunee Six Nations Confederacy Council*, Aug. 8, 2006, Judge Marshall's ruling, see pg 8. *

20 Ibid, pg 6. *

21 VoiceofCanada.ca, November 13, 2007: VoC, CWUC speak at University of Waterloo. *

22 Canadian Press, Sept. 24, 2006, Peterson comments critical of march in Caledonia 'offensive': organizer. *

23 OPP news release, Sept. 23, 2006, Key To Successful Negotiations and Community Safety Understanding, Mutual Respect and Meaningful Dialogue. *

24 Residents videotaped the arrest and videotaped each officer giving their names/badge #. *

25 Gary McHale presentation, OPP & Native Radio Transmissions, FantinoGate news conference, Queen's Park, April 17, 2007. *

26 Caledonia resident AnneMarie VanSickle, Oct. 15, 2006 speech at McHale's Freedom rally in Caledonia. *

27 Ipperwash resident Mary-Lou LaPratte, Oct. 15, 2006 speech at McHale's Freedom rally in Caledonia. *

28 Native private investigator Jon Sabin, Oct. 15, 2006 speech at McHale's Freedom rally in Caledonia. *

29 Posted news stories along with photos and videos of rally. *

30 Dozens of posted news stories along with photos and videos of Doug's Smokes operating out of his truck. *

31 Queen's Park media room presentation, Dec. 4, 2007, Illegal Smoke shops and Land claim Lawlessness. Presentation done by Caledonia residents Merlyn Kinrade, Brian Hagan and Doug Fleming. Gary McHale also presented his message of lawlessness in Caledonia. *

* See http://www.GaryMcHale.ca/book for additional information, links to documents, videos and photos

Chapter 3

The Canadian Flag is Illegal but Native Flags are Legal

By October 30, 2006, Julian Fantino had become the new OPP Commissioner. Many, including me, believed that Fantino would take steps to restore law and order. We learned all too soon that his primary mission appeared to be to silence and control non-Native people. Fantino would emerge as a key figure because he engaged in direct confrontation with Caledonia citizens. While Commissioners Gwen Boniface and Chris Lewis (who would replace Fantino as commissioner in 2010) worked behind the scenes to ensure the OPP's racist policies were upheld, Fantino would make it a public battle, appearing on TV and radio and giving interviews to the media throughout 2007. Fantino sought to control the media message and, in that way, control the public debate.

As I will show over the next few chapters, Fantino was and is nothing but a bully and a street fighter who rose through the ranks of the police force by taking on public issues. Eventually, we concluded that, as with most bullies, Fantino would go too far, and that our best strategy was to give him enough rope so that he could hang himself. At every opportunity we ensured that Fantino knew exactly what we were doing, knowing that he would overreact and abuse his authority.

One of Fantino's first provocations was to turn some areas in Caledonia into non-Canadian flag zones. For several months leading up to December 2006, Native protesters had raised their flags all over Caledonia. They placed them on treetops, atop hydro towers, on non-Native private property, along Caledonia's main street and elsewhere throughout DCE. In fact, starting in March 2006, Native protesters would in time raise over 100 flags. The point was to declare to everyone that they were no longer in Canada and, therefore, no longer protected by Canadian laws. As well, it underscored that all Caledonia residents were now subject to Native rule. But they didn't just raise Six Nations flags. They also flew Mohawk Warrior[1] flags, along with flags of Palestine, Venezuela and various unions.[2] And whenever they came across a flag of Canada, they destroyed it.[3]

At no time did the OPP interfere with the raising of Native flags or with the theft and destruction of Canadian flags. In one case, Chris Syrie, who owned land next to DCE, placed two Canadian flags on his property along with two 'No Trespassing' signs. On January 10, 2007, Native protester Brian Skye entered his private property, threw one of the flags on the ground, then pushed Syrie around and threatened him while OPP officers stood by and watched, refusing to arrest Skye despite Syrie's repeated requests.[4] Later, the OPP would tell Syrie that the reason they did nothing was because they couldn't identify Brian Skye even though he had been head of Native security on DCE for almost a year and was well known to the OPP.

Police also claimed they didn't know who had stolen Syrie's Canadian flag later that same day. We knew that wasn't true, though, because residents were taping OPP radio transmissions and heard officers radio in when they saw Native protesters enter the private property and steal the flag. The officers were ordered to do nothing.

In January 2007, Fantino held a semi-public meeting – it would turn out to be his only one – at the Caledonia Rotary Club. It was a members-only meeting which was attended by our lawyer John Findlay who would go on to win a $20M settlement for Caledonia's victims from the Ontario government in 2011. At the event, Fantino was asked directly about the Native flags that had been raised throughout Caledonia. He stated that the OPP had no authority to remove them or to prevent Natives from raising them. He said this knowing full well that in the 1993 Supreme Court case of *Ramsden v. Peterborough*[5] the court had ruled that citizens have the right to place objects on hydro poles as part of their freedom of expression, a freedom he would not allow non-Natives to exercise. Under his watch, that right was granted only to Natives, and Fantino's forces targeted and arrested non-Natives who dared to raise the Canadian flag on public land near DCE.

The first Canadian flag-raising event had taken place a month earlier, on December 2, 2006. This event had been organized by Caledonia residents on their own, without any input from our CanACE group. (Actually, we didn't know about the event until the night before it happened. Even so, the OPP blamed me for it.) As part of the event, the residents placed Canadian flags and yellow ribbons on hydro poles throughout Caledonia to honour our soldiers in Afghanistan. Learning of the flag-raising, I came to Caledonia, but only to take photographs. I saw that the OPP had created no-fly zones for Canadian flags while dozens of Mohawk Warrior flags flapped in the breeze.

The OPP stopped Randy and Doug Fleming, two Caledonians, as they walked down the road. The Flemings were headed for a hydro pole, where they wanted to hoist a Canadian flag. For 40 minutes police patrolled the road, preventing any non-Native from going beyond a certain point. One officer grabbed Randy Fleming's flagpole. After some time, the OPP suddenly arrested local resident Bo Chausse, who wasn't even one of the flag-raisers, and who had been watching the standoff from across the road.[6]

After the event, I drove to the Cayuga police station to pick up Chausse and to ensure that CHCH TV went there to interview him. He was released about two hours after his arrest. He was furious because police had claimed that the local Baptist church had accused him of trespassing, and that was why he had been arrested. A few days later two OPP officers visited Chausse and apologized for the arrest, leaving their business cards. Chausse later sued and the government settled out of court – more costs to taxpayers.

Chausse's arrest shocked me because it showed that Canada's Charter of Rights and Freedoms provided no real protection to those who were targeted by the OPP, that it was merely something written on a piece of paper that could be ignored at will. The OPP didn't care about the equal rights of all people. They were only interested in enforcing the political will of the McGuinty government. The OPP had become the Ontario Political Police.

Oh, sure, the OPP will claim again and again that an individual officer has complete discretion to enforce the law as he/she sees fit. How, then, is it possible for a hundred individual officers to make the same decisions at 15 different events – and for every decision to abridge the rights of non-Natives?

That first flag-raising, and Bo Chausse's arrest, shone a spotlight on Caledonia. For the first time, Canadians outside the community could see in simple terms how the OPP conducted themselves. They saw how police let Natives fly their flags, but refused to allow non-Natives to fly the Canadian flag – dramatic proof of favoritism and appeasement that the average Canadian could understand.

That flag-raising also provided the impetus for future CanACE flag-raising rallies.

CanACE asked a simple question: "Why can't a citizen walk down the side of a Caledonia road carrying a Canadian flag?" It was a question that the OPP could not answer in any reasonable way, thereby exposing police propaganda for what it was. To shine a light on this corruption, I called a flag-raising rally for December 16, 2006. All we wanted to do was walk down the road and place a Canadian flag on the same hydro pole the Flemings had wanted to use but had been barred from doing so by police.

Fantino went NUTS! Emboldened by his new power as OPP Commissioner, he ordered officers and government lawyers to target me for arrest. How dare I walk down a road with a Canadian flag! Meanwhile, remember, Fantino was insisting the OPP could do nothing about the many Native flags that had been hoisted in the area.

An October 18, 2007 OPP report prepared in response to my complaint for false arrest during the upcoming protest shows that on December 3, 2006, Fantino emailed the Director of the Legal Services Branch of the Attorney General's office requesting that it find some way to "deal with Mr. McHale".[7] Chris Diana, lawyer for the OPP, was tasked with finding a way to arrest me so they could restrict my travel. After all, if you can bar a man entry to a town, you don't have to worry that he might decide to exercise his Charter rights by walking down a road in that town.

Over the course of two weeks, about a dozen meetings were held to try to come up with a way – a novel, twisted way– to try to keep non-Natives out of Caledonia. Every person involved in these meetings knew two things: first, that their scheme targeted only non-Natives and, second, that these non-Natives had broken no laws. (I call it a "scheme" because a few OPP officers had the common sense to question how OPP had the authority to do this. They were told that government lawyers had worked it all out, so they should just go along with the plan.)

Not surprisingly, the OPP report cleared all officers of any wrongdoing for being part of this conspiracy to arrest people they knew had committed no crime. The report does admit that the tactics used were "unconventional" and not "commonly known" or even used at all "by the police community". In fact, I would say none of the officers involved had ever heard of any police force using such tactics against a law-abiding citizen. The report went on to say that the OPP couldn't determine whether this tactic would ever be used again. The writer of the report, Det. Staff Sgt. Robert Knipf, stated – the report was approved by Supt. M. MacLachlan – that, "the propriety of the continued use of this unconventional approach cannot be decided at the writer's level, or even in the police or judicial communities, with any certainty. It will likely have to be adjudicated by a court of competent jurisdiction."[8]

So let's get this straight: the OPP were about to use a tactic against a law-abiding citizen that officers have never heard of and, even after government lawyers and Crown attorneys got involved, could not determine was even legal. The OPP admitted that a court would have to decide whether or not the plan (cooked up on Fantino's behalf) was even lawful.

So who exactly was involved in this conspiracy to limit my freedoms, a plot that even OPP admitted was legally in doubt? The roster includes the following: OPP lawyer Chris Diana; Crown Attorney Alex Paparella; Assistant Crown Larry Brock; Chief Supt. Sue Dunn; A/Supt. Doug Babbitt; Insp. Dave McLean; D/Insp Bill Renton; Insp. Ross Nichols; Sgt. Bernie Cowan; D/Sgt. Heidi Stewart; Sgt. Mike McDonnell; Det. Staff Sgt. Greg Walton; and several officers of lower rank. And let's not forget Commissioner Julian Fantino, who got the whole thing rolling!

That's quite the list of senior OPP officers willing to engage in "experimental" justice in order to limit the Charter Rights of a law-abiding citizens they knew had not committed – and was not about to commit – a crime. Their little conspiracy might have worked, had it not been for Assistant Crown Attorney Andrew Goodman. He refused in no uncertain terms to go along with the plot. Moreover, he told the OPP repeatedly that it wasn't lawful.[9] At first, Crown lawyer Larry Brock, too, believed it was unlawful, but he ended up acceding to the OPP argument. However, once Goodman refused to back the plan in court, he suddenly found Paparella and Brock on his side.

The OPP then pressured Goodman to file false charges against me so Fantino and his senior brass could impose travel restrictions that would keep me out of Caledonia.[10] Goodman refused, and in the end the OPP officers were left to fend for themselves. It was Det. S/Sgt. Walton, lead officer in Cayuga, who made the decision to hold me in jail overnight on December 16, 2006. Once Walton realized the Crown wasn't going to back up the OPP's scheme he sent an email to officers telling them to prepare a document that would cover his own backside. He was concerned that he was going "to look like the bad guy in this matter and he was just following instructions."

A few officers questioned the OPP's authority to arrest me and hold me in jail. Sgt. Ben Gutenberg and Sgt. McDonnell both admitted they had never heard of anyone ever being held in jail and forced to appear in court to face travel restrictions when no crime had been committed. They were told that the OPP Crime Unit had investigated the issue and was being guided by the Crown's Office: that would be Paparella and Brock, since Goodman was refusing to go along.

I would later subpoena Andrew Goodman to testify against the OPP during the spectacularly unsuccessful attempt to prosecute me for 'counselling mischief not committed' in connection with a December 1, 2007 riot at an illegal smoke shack, an event covered in detail in later chapters. This is unheard of because you cannot force a lawyer to testify against his client, and in this instance the Crown's client was the police. However, the OPP was so desperate to prove that its officers had done nothing wrong that it made the mistake of quoting both Goodman and OPP lawyer Chris Diana throughout its report. Apparently, they hoped this would make it appear as though officers were merely following the lawyers' advice. The problem for the OPP was that, by quoting Goodman and Diana, they breached lawyer/client privilege, thereby enabling me to question their lawyers in court. Oops!

Goodman testified via written answers that he believed both Det. S/Sgt. Walton and Det. Alexander had tried to get him to charge me with a criminal offence of mischief. Goodman had refused to do so, explaining that the OPP's role is to lay charges and the Crown's role is to prosecute them. Goodman pointed out to these officers that the OPP had already decided not to lay a charge and said he doubted there was any possibility of conviction.

What is interesting is that the OPP had already determined that no crime had been committed, but still wanted to arrest me and force me into court. For two weeks, the OPP held meetings where these plans were discussed, and in which Walton was a key participant. When I was arrested on December 16, the OPP created a computer report. The report stated that, as of 2:18 p.m., the status of my arrest was "complete – solved (non-criminal)." Despite that designation, I was held in jail overnight and, the very next morning, Walton and Alexander tried to get the Crown to lay a criminal charge against me.[11]

It should be noted that those involved in the conspiracy were well aware of the many criminal acts, some quite serious, that had been committed by Native protesters, but there was nothing in the report that showed there was any plan to target them. Nor was there a plan to subject them to travel restrictions. No, Fantino and his forces wanted to reserve those restrictions for non-Natives who had exposed their failure to protect the town's residents.

In order to give the OPP plan a shot at succeeding, remote as it was, police decided to create a "No Whites Allowed" zone in Caledonia (while Natives, of course, faced no such restrictions). Police called it a "buffer zone" and tried to give the impression that they were attempting to keep the peace. They believed this would also help them persuade the courts that it was the non-Natives who were responsible for all the violence – an outright fiction.

The police strategy uses the same logic – if you can call it that – that police in the southern United States used for generations to suppress black people. Any time a black person attempted to address the injustice and/or expose the racism, police and the state twisted the evidence to convey the impression that it was the black person who was disturbing the community's peace. The historical record reveals the dreadful way Dr. Martin Luther King was treated by police, state authorities, and even some church leaders, when all he wanted was to march for his people's freedom.

Not to compare myself in any way to Dr. King, I was accused of creating all the problems in Caledonia – "everything would be peaceful in Caledonia but for McHale," said Julian Fantino, just as King had been accused of creating problems in the American south. Fantino and others were saying, in effect, if we non-Native troublemakers would just learn to shut up and allow ourselves to be victimized, then Native protesters wouldn't feel the need to attack people. If non-Natives would simply accept that some roads and neighbourhoods in Haldimand County were off-limits to us, then everything would be peaceful.

Please understand that I do not wish to compare the abuse suffered by generations of American Blacks to the suffering of non-Natives in Caledonia: there is, quite simply, no comparison. My point here is that the "logic" behind the authorities' response to our protest is the same. I am hardly the first person to observe that when we do not learn from history, we are doomed to repeat it. As Dr. King Jr. sat in a jail cell in Birmingham – arrested for not having a parade permit – he received a letter signed by pastors of eight leading churches. It was truly a sad day in the history of Christianity when these Christian leaders refused to stand in solidarity with Dr. King.[12] Even worse, they did their best to try to silence those who stood with him against the injustice. Decades later, silence from Christian leaders was also the reality for Caledonia. Where were the church leaders willing to stand up and speak out against the violence and injustice occurring right under their noses? The answer: they were nowhere to be seen. (Another oft-repeated quotation may be relevant here: "The only thing necessary for the triumph of evil is for good men to do nothing.")

Dr. King Jr., a Baptist pastor, responded to the church leaders' criticism with his magnificent "*Letter from Birmingham Jail*" dated April 16, 1963. The full text can be found on the Internet[13], and I'd urge you to take the time to read it. Dr. King's letter is remarkable for the way he addresses the faulty logic of police, government officials and many in the church. In Caledonia, those of us who wanted to restore law and order have always been told that "the government needs to negotiate." We still hear that to this day. But negotiate with whom? And what kind of negotiations would they be? Would such discussions equate law-abiding residents with violent, crime-committing thugs? Where is the justice in that? There isn't any. Hasn't history shown where this sort of appeasement can lead? To appeasement like Neville Chamberlain's "peace in our time" with Hitler. To say the least, that didn't turn out so well.

In their letter to Dr. King, church leaders wrote that: "... we are now confronted by a series of demonstrations by some of our Negro citizens, directed and led in part by outsiders. We recognize the natural impatience of people who feel that their hopes are slow in being realized. But we are convinced that these demonstrations are unwise and untimely. We agree rather with certain local

47

Negro leadership which has called for honest and open negotiation of racial issues in our area... we also point out that such actions as incite to hatred and violence, however technically peaceful those actions may be, have not contributed to the resolution of our local problems."

Let's consider the basic "logic" in this statement. First, Dr. King is an "outsider," which apparently means he shouldn't be involved. Second, demonstrations are "unwise and untimely" because of the tension they would cause. Third, negotiation is the proper path to take (apparently, to these leaders, public exposure of injustice is not a Christian concept). Fourth, demonstrations, regardless of whether or not they are peaceful, incite hatred and violence.

While few in today's churches, police or government would publicly denounce Dr. King for his tactics, there were plenty who did in the 1950's and 60's. Dr. King's response to these points is solidly Christian, and his letter provides dozens of Biblical examples of true Christianity and its commitment to justice.

At the heart of Christianity is the fact that we are our brother's keepers, as the story of the Good Samaritan shows us. There are no "outsiders" when it comes to Christians standing up against injustice. Throughout the ages Christians have travelled around the world addressing injustice and, truth be told, all missionaries are "outsiders" called to work in areas away from their homes on behalf of God and others.

As Dr. King states, "I think I should indicate why I am here in Birmingham, since you have been influenced by the view which argues against 'outsiders coming in.' ... I am in Birmingham because injustice is here. Just as the prophets of the eighth century B.C. left their villages and carried their 'thus saith the Lord' far beyond the boundaries of their home towns, and just as the Apostle Paul left his village of Tarsus and carried the gospel of Jesus Christ to the far corners of the Greco Roman world, so am I compelled to carry the gospel of freedom beyond my own home town. Like Paul, I must constantly respond to the Macedonian call for aid."

Dr. King continues: "I cannot sit idly by in Atlanta and not be concerned about what happens in Birmingham. Injustice anywhere is a threat to justice everywhere. We are caught in an inescapable network of mutuality, tied in a single garment of destiny. Whatever affects one directly, affects all indirectly. Never again can we afford to live with the narrow, provincial 'outside agitator' idea. Anyone who lives inside the United States can never be considered an outsider anywhere within its bounds."

People have asked why we believe in holding demonstrations rather than "negotiating." First of all, it is because the examples of Ipperwash and Oka and now Caledonia have shown that negotiations rarely succeed in resolving problems arising from racial issues. Second, political leaders and the media have short attention spans: They aren't able to keep the focus on these problems long enough ensure that they are truly resolved. Demonstrations by ordinary people force the media to pay attention to the problems, thereby forcing them onto the political landscape. Problems continue to exist at Oka and Ipperwash, but with no demonstrations to capture media attention, the public, for the most part, is unaware of them.

Here's how Dr. King puts it in his letter: "You may well ask: 'Why direct action? Why sit-ins, marches and so forth? Isn't negotiation a better path?' You are quite right in calling for negotiation. Indeed, this is the very purpose of direct action. Nonviolent direct action seeks to create such a crisis and foster such a tension that a community which has constantly refused to negotiate is forced to confront the issue... It seeks so to dramatize the issue that it can no longer be ignored. My citing the creation of tension as part of the work of the nonviolent resister may sound rather shocking. But I must confess that I am not afraid of the word 'tension.' I have earnestly opposed violent tension, but there is a type of constructive, nonviolent tension which is necessary for growth... The purpose of our direct action program is to create a situation so crisis packed that it will inevitably open the door to negotiation. I therefore concur with you in your call for negotiation. Too long has our beloved Southland been bogged down in a tragic effort to live in monologue rather than dialogue."

Premier Dalton McGuinty's Ipperwash Inquiry refused to address violence against non-Natives during these so-called peaceful land claims. In a later chapter I will talk about our Ipperwash Papers project that documents how non-Natives were first victimized by police and Native radicals, and then later by an Inquiry that deliberately excluded them and their testimony. A public dialogue regarding the victimization of non-Natives never took place. It was silenced both by politicians, who didn't want to discuss it, and by the media, which refused to report on it. We refused to let the same thing happen in Caledonia. That's the reason for our Canadian flag-raising events, for our marches down the road. We were determined to compel public debate in order to force political parties to muster the political will to deal with the issues in a just and timely fashion. We knew that if we didn't, attention would drift elsewhere, and the problems would never get solved.

It is easy for the OPP to say "be patient," or for our leaders to claim they are negotiating. After all, it isn't *their* families who are being traumatized or sent to the hospital. Does anyone doubt for a second that, were McGuinty's wife or child living in fear and being assaulted, he would say, "Give us more time"? Seven years have passed and who within the government even talks about Caledonia anymore? No negotiations have been held in the past two years – proof that, if you sit back, the issues will never be addressed.

Why should the residents of Caledonia have to wait for the OPP to understand that the Charter of Rights and Freedoms applies to all Canadians, Natives and non-Natives alike? How many families have to live in fear before an officer who took an Oath to serve and protect does his duty and prevents crimes? How many years should the government be allowed to turn a blind eye to the Caledonia resident who has permanent brain damage because of government policies? Do we say to Jewish people that, because you were victimized in Germany, we will allow you to track down and beat up Germans? Do we say to black people that, because you were slaves, you're allowed to wear a mask, carry a bat and beat up white people? How many people have to be harmed before an injustice is seen as being serious enough for the police and government to act?

Wherever racism becomes institutionalized, it is practiced by those within a government (politicians, lawyers, police, etc.) for a theoretical greater good. But racism is evil and always will be. Racism can never be a legitimate means to a greater good.

As Dr. King reminds us: "We should never forget that everything Adolf Hitler did in Germany was 'legal' and everything the Hungarian freedom fighters did in Hungary was 'illegal.' It was 'illegal' to aid and comfort a Jew in Hitler's Germany. Even so, I am sure that, had I lived in Germany at the time, I would have aided and comforted my Jewish brothers. If today I lived in a Communist country where certain principles dear to the Christian faith are suppressed, I would openly advocate disobeying that country's anti-religious laws."

Whenever racism is institutionalized, all citizens, especially those claiming to be Christians, must decide whether they are prepared to ignore the suffering of others, or whether they are willing to expose it. Sadly, as Dr. King observed many times, the very people who should stand up against injustice, but don't, become the greatest hindrance to confronting the injustice.

Dr. King states: "I must make two honest confessions to you, my Christian and Jewish brothers. First, I must confess that over the past few years I have been gravely disappointed with the white moderate. I have almost reached the regrettable conclusion that the Negro's great stumbling block in his stride toward freedom is not the White Citizen's Councilor or the Ku Klux Klanner, but the white moderate, who is more devoted to 'order' than to justice; who prefers a negative peace which is the absence of tension to a positive peace which is the presence of justice; who constantly says: 'I agree with you in the goal you seek, but I cannot agree with your methods of direct action'; who paternalistically believes he can set the timetable for another man's freedom; who lives by a mythical concept of time and who constantly advises the Negro to wait for a 'more convenient season.' Shallow understanding from people of good will is more frustrating than absolute misunderstanding from people of ill will. Lukewarm acceptance is much more bewildering than outright rejection."

These words apply to the Caledonia situation, too. I don't know a single leader in any church in Haldimand County who has publicly stood up for the equality of all people. I and members of my group have met with several church leaders in Caledonia and, although every single one agrees that the actions of police and government are unjust, not one leader has agreed to criticize it in public or help us work towards a reconciliation solution that includes asking those responsible – Six Nations included – to apologize for their role in terrorizing their neighbours. In short, what these leaders are really saying is: "I don't want to get involved because it is too confrontational and because I don't want to risk being called a racist."

Dr. King addressed the issue of 'provoking violence' via confrontation when he wrote: "In your statement you assert that our actions, even though peaceful, must be condemned because they precipitate violence. But is this a logical assertion? Isn't this like condemning a robbed man because his possession of money precipitated the evil act of robbery? Isn't this like condemning Socrates because his unswerving commitment to truth and his philosophical inquiries precipitated the act by the misguided populace in which they made him drink hemlock? Isn't this like condemning Jesus because his unique God consciousness and never ceasing devotion to God's will precipitated the evil act of crucifixion?"

If the rule of law is not restored, then people will be subject to the rule of thugs. If the police, government and Crown lawyers will not uphold the rights of all people, then people will turn to violence in an attempt to find justice.

Dr. King states: "And I am further convinced that if our white brothers dismiss as 'rabble rousers' and 'outside agitators' those of us who employ nonviolent direct action, and if they refuse to support our nonviolent efforts, millions of Negroes will, out of frustration and despair, seek solace and security in black nationalist ideologies – a development that would inevitably lead to a frightening racial nightmare... If one recognizes this vital urge that has engulfed the Negro community, one should readily understand why public demonstrations are taking place. The Negro has many pent up resentments and latent frustrations, and he must release them. So let him march; let him make prayer pilgrimages to the city hall; let him go on freedom rides – and try to understand why he must do so. If his repressed emotions are not released in nonviolent ways, they will seek expression through violence; this is not a threat but a fact of history."

The primary purpose of public demonstrations is to expose the issue, to expose the tension to ensure leadership responds, and to provide victims of the injustice a way to express themselves without resorting to violence. If you attempt to suppress public protests, to silence those who want to speak, jail those who walk peacefully down a road, and target those who commit no crimes, you pretty much assure that, at some point, an otherwise peaceful people will turn to violence. It must be said that Native protesters were put in a position such that many believed that only violence would be effective. While I do not believe this is the case in Caledonia because our courts, police and governments today are very pro-Native, it has been true in the past.

On October 8, 2007, two days before the provincial election, I held a rally in Caledonia, and many media outlets showed up to cover the event. However, they failed to report my main message which was that politicians, the media and churches had failed Native people by not speaking out against the problems in Residential Schools. I pointed out that to this day the CBC has a 1962 documentary on its website that showed "happy" Native children at these schools.[15] Where were the church leaders willing to stand up and denounce the schools? As I commented to several Caledonia church leaders, "Wouldn't it be nice to address the injustice of today instead of allowing the next generation to apologize for our failure?"

It is also worth noting that the speech Mark Vandermaas delivered at that rally (which the media also failed to cover) dealt with how race-based policing in Caledonia had created Native victims, too.[16] Once the OPP had sent their clear message to Native protesters that they would not be arrested for much of their lawlessness, they ensured that the various Native factions could commit violence against each other with impunity. The Native media reported some of these incidents on DCE that involved drugs, guns, fires, fights and two rapes.[17] Because of the OPP's hands off approach, though, none of these crimes were investigated.

Over the course of three years, we held about a dozen Canadian flag-raising events in Caledonia. The OPP burned through millions of your taxpayer dollars to prevent law-abiding citizens from strolling down a road with your nation's flag. The OPP arrested some of us, claiming to want to prevent a breach of the peace – code for "the OPP thinks Native protesters may be about to attack non-Natives." That's like police arresting a black person because they feared the Ku Klux Klan was about to beat him up.

At the first flag-raising we organized on December 16, 2006, the task, quite simply, was to walk to where Randy Fleming had been stopped by the OPP, and place a Canadian flag on the hydro pole there. The act was meant to symbolize that non-Natives have rights, too. Before I even got to Caledonia that day, I was pulled over on the highway by two OPP officers. They had been told to deliver a message (which, apparently, could not be delivered by phone, email or fax).

Det. Sgt. Bernie Cowan pulled me over and said, "We've been sitting there pretty much most of the morning looking for ya just because we wanted to have a couple of words with ya." [18] (That's a good use of taxpayers' money, don't you think…to have a Detective Sergeant and a second officer sitting in a car waiting hours for someone to drive by? I guess this detective had no crimes anywhere else in Ontario to investigate, and no constables were available to do this crucial job.)

D/Sgt. Cowan continued: "Anybody that attempts to raise those flags and ribbons in that restricted area will be arrested for Breach of the Peace." I replied, "So have Natives been arrested for putting up their flags?" Cowan replied, "They have not." I asked why. After talking in circles for a while, Cowan said, "I'm not here to comment on that. I'm just telling you what our plan is today and that's what my purpose is. What is your plan?"

I was getting really frustrated that once again the OPP were creating two sets of laws – one for Natives, who were free to go anywhere and one for non-Natives, who had to comply with restricted access provisions. It should be noted that the restricted zone was Caledonia's main road. I told Cowan, "My plan is to make you guys [the OPP] look like a bunch of assholes and you've done a great job. The media will be here and it will be quite clear to all Canadians across this country 'cause they will see the Native flags. The cameras will show the Native flags and you'll be there and your officers will be there saying, 'If you put up a Canadian flag we will arrest you'. Then everybody in Canada will see and ask how come the Native flags are up there. So, you may not want to answer me but this is building and building and building and you guys are looking more ridiculous as time goes by. You did nothing when the power station was burnt down and now we're talking about a simple flag. So when you say there's going to be a Breach of the Peace, then you are admitting, or the OPP is admitting, that there is one group that is going to Breach the Peace and it is none of the residents."

We then got into the subject of the restricted zone and I asked him whether it applied to Native people. He said it applied to "anybody that is in that restricted area."

"You mean non-Native," I said.

"No," he said. "I'm talking about you or anybody."

Believing that his phrase "you or anybody" meant my CanACE group, I asked him directly, "Are Natives allowed to be in that area?"

"I'm not here to get into an argument with you... I'm not here to talk about that...," he replied.

The OPP had brought in hundreds of officers to stop us from raising a Canadian flag and, sure enough, the camera showed that Natives were free to roam around in the so-called restricted zone. Mark Vandermaas and I, on the other hand, were arrested and placed in jail. Mark was released a few hours later but, as discussed earlier, the OPP had already planned to keep me in jail overnight because it wanted to get me into court in hopes it could impose travel restrictions against me. The OPP apparently wanted the court to uphold a 'no-whites' zone in Caledonia.

Following my arrest, the OPP issued a press release which admitted to bringing in additional officers from the Toronto Police Service. Commissioner Fantino stated, "I am proud and thankful to all of our officers..." The release added, "The organizer of the rally had been stopped by police prior to attending the rally and questioned as to his intentions. He said to police that his intent was **'just to make you guys look like a bunch of assholes like you already do'**." (Emphasis in the original.)

Fantino would later be forced to provide a written reason to the Ontario Human Rights Commission why Mark and I were arrested. His statement said, "Mr. Vandermaas' actions in relation to the situation at Caledonia have made him a potential target of the more extreme element who do not share his views. It is the Respondents' [Fantino and OPP officers] position that any actions it has taken in relation to Mr. Vandermaas have been to preserve the peace and to protect Mr. Vandermaas and his supporters from harm."[20]

So the reason Mark and I were stopped from raising Canadian flags, arrested and placed in jail was to stop the "extreme element" from attacking us. Isn't this the same logic of arresting black people because the KKK was about to attack them? Exactly when do the police actually arrest those threatening to do harm? Why didn't Fantino and the OPP create a plan to deal with these "extreme elements" and impose travel restrictions on *them*? Why not remove those who the OPP believed would commit the violence instead of putting innocent citizens in jail? Maybe it is time in Ontario to start putting Jews in jail if the police believe a Muslim is about to attack them!

I realized when the OPP arrested me that they were simply trying to intimidate me, not to protect me. Over the years I have been arrested several times on the pretext of "protecting me," so I have repeatedly asked officers, "Do you have any evidence that I am about to be attacked?" Each time I have asked, the answer is, "No". The truth is that the OPP arrests non-Natives in order to appease Native protesters and control free speech of non-Natives.

Anticipating jail, I thought it important to send OPP brass the message that jail time wasn't going to intimidate me, so I refused to give my name, or reply when asked if I wanted to speak to a lawyer. Over the course of about an hour I was asked repeatedly, "What is your name?" to which I replied, "I was the guy standing on the side of the road holding a Canadian flag." Of course the OPP knew my name because they had just spent two weeks planning this scheme. Once I was in a cell, I removed all my clothes except my underwear. I was held in jail for 20 hours – overnight – but when served dinner I left it on the bed uneaten until an officer removed it hours later. I didn't sleep and would not have dressed the next morning for a court appearance if I had known I was only going to appear by videophone.

It was in the dead of winter, and cells at any time are not the warmest of places – a steel bed with no blanket and cement walls. I had a cold and the OPP denied me the only thing in my pocket – cough drops. I guess they were worried I could use them to commit suicide – maybe swallow a bunch and choke myself to death. Let me tell you…the cell was freezing, but each time I coughed the OPP turned up the heat (there is a camera with sound in each cell). Within 30 minutes I was sitting very toasty in my cell. Meanwhile, Mark, over in in the next cell, was getting hotter and hotter.

The next morning, before appearing in court by videophone, I spoke with the duty counsel. He told me the OPP had not filed an "information" – the term used for the paperwork stating what a person has been charged with – for my case. He also told my wife Christine, Mark (he was released after only a few hours), and the other supporters at the Hamilton courthouse that the case "smells political, not criminal." I was told that the OPP wanted me to agree to travel restrictions. "Are they joking?" I thought. They arrested me even though I had committed no crime, held me in jail overnight knowing I had done nothing wrong, and now they want my consent for court-imposed travel restrictions? Needless to say, I didn't consent and my entire court case wrapped up in less than 40 seconds. The judge ordered my release because the court had no jurisdiction over me. Two officers tried to comply with instructions by giving me my clothes and having me sign a form verifying their return. I refused to do so unless the officers identified the name of the official who had made the decision to keep me in jail. After a few moments, they wrote down the name of Sgt. Greg Walton.

For most people, being arrested and placed in jail, or being targeted by the police, is so intimidating and unpleasant that people give up fighting, often unable to see anything positive emerging from such negative experiences. However, by the time I was arrested in 2006, I was 44 years old, and had been a Christian for more than 20 years. Over those years I had learned a very valuable lesson – that what man perceives as a negative situation is often the precise moment when God is accomplishing His purpose. In fact, I see every so-called negative event as evidence that God is trying to do something positive. That doesn't mean it is enjoyable, but it *is* necessary. The experience I've just related is a perfect example of that. The OPP, with all its high-priced lawyers, schemed to publicly expose me as a troublemaker, put me in jail, and tried to have a court restrict my travel. They had no idea that their actions would have a very positive result: I met John Findlay.

John and his wife, Margaret McCarthy, were the lawyers who represented Caledonia residents and businesses in their class action lawsuit.[21] While I knew of Findlay and had seen him at public meetings, I had never spoken to him. When I was arrested, my wife went to the couple's home in Caledonia and told them what had happened. Neither could believe what the OPP had done, that it had held me in jail overnight without a charge. The next day when the OPP was forced to release me, Findlay visited me to express his outrage. Both Margaret and John are very committed Catholics, and it was because of that commitment that Findlay became the lawyer who represented me in a number of very important civil cases. In March 2007, for example, 22 OPP officers sued me for $7.1 million because I said they had failed to uphold their oath of office. Findlay immediately stepped in and fought that case for 3 years without asking for a dime; in the end, the case was settled with conditions I am very happy with. Furthermore, when the government's high-priced lawyers won a motion to keep the lawsuit in Toronto the court ordered me to pay $18,000 – money I did not have. It was John's sister, unknown to me, who stepped in and paid the bill.

The names of the officers who sued me are: Steven Lorch; William Bittner; Stefan Chambers; Craig Cole; Douglas Dinner; Graham Ebert; Peter Fischer; Adoree Fleming; Jamie Gillespie; Guy Higgott; Preven Jepsen; Scott MacPhail; Kyle Miller; Kirkland Richardson; John Rosa; David Smith; Mark Smith; Scott Taylor; Robert Uridil; Michael Whitelaw; Kevin York; and Michael Zwarun.

In my view the lawsuit was launched because the OPP hoped to intimidate me into shutting down my website. The officers contended that I had accused them of being racist (because of the nature of their policing), but I had done no such thing. I accused them of not upholding their Oath of Office. The oath states: "I solemnly affirm that I will be loyal to Her Majesty the Queen and to Canada, and that I will uphold the Constitution of Canada and that I will, to the best of my ability, preserve the peace, prevent offences and discharge my other duties as a Commissioned Officer, faithfully, impartially and according to law." Notice that the oath includes preventing offences and upholding of the Canadian Constitution, which includes the Charter of Rights and Freedoms.

Many of these officers had seen Natives committing offences in Caledonia and had done nothing to prevent them. While these officers are not racist, they do enforce a policy, "*The Framework*," that virtually everyone outside the OPP has called racist.

In a media interview, my lawyer John Findlay, identified the OPP tactic as a SLAPP – Strategic Lawsuit Against Public Participation – lawsuit. Some provinces have laws against such tactics, but Ontario does not. I don't know who paid these police officers' legal fees, but I highly doubt it was the officers themselves. Was it perhaps the Ontario Provincial Police Association (OPPA) or was it the McGuinty government? Whoever it was, they ponied up over $150,000 for the tab. And, a funny thing: when it came time for each of the officers to be questioned under oath, 18 of them felt a sudden urge to drop the case, and filed to have their names removed from the suit. The court allowed this hasty change, but told the 18 who had, shall we call them second thoughts, that they were on the hook to cover their portion of my legal expenses. Clearly, some of these officers knew the case was bogus from the outset. I am sure many of them were also well aware that standing by as Natives committed crimes, even if officers were acting – or rather, failing to act – on orders, was not only a violation of their sworn oath, it was evidence of their participation in a racist policy. Many of these officers have been out to many events since 2006, and nothing has changed. They still stand around watching crimes being committed, and still do little or nothing to stop them.

CanACE's next flag-raising event was called for January 20, 2007. First, however, we held a town hall meeting to explain to the public why these rallies were necessary. Mark Vandermaas and I each presented a PowerPoint presentation to the public as OPP officers, Six Nations police and Native protesters sat and listened to our arguments. At the end I called for 50 volunteers who were willing to allow the OPP to arrest them for the non-crime of walking down a public road while carrying a Canadian flag.

Once again, Julian Fantino went nuts! He could not allow non-Natives to think that *they* had a right to expose OPP activity and hold him, the OPP boss, accountable for his failure to enforce the law. After all, he was the Commissioner, a very important man, and there was no way he was going to tolerate regular Canadians protesting against an injustice when he believed that the best, the *only*, way to keep the peace between Natives and non-Natives invariably favoured one side over the other, even if everyone with an ounce of common sense could see that this was a profoundly racist policy that conflicted with the officers' Oath. Fantino had two options: he could either continue the one-sided approach, and focus his policing on the law-abiding or, he could opt to go the other route, and make it clear to the Native "radical element" that they would be held accountable and could expect to face arrest should they continue to break the law. Of course he opted for the former: In his twisted worldview, it appeared logical to arrest those who weren't committing crimes, and to do so with a show of force that would terrify the public. There was no way he was going to risk his $256,000 a year job by upholding the rights of all citizens. Fantino decided to take personal charge of Caledonia and be present at the January 20 event.

On January 20, 2007, Fantino met with Native protesters. He assured them that he would deal with the non-Natives who dared to walk down the road. It seems that he felt quite safe meeting alone with the "radical elements," more than a few of whom had been known to engage in repeated violence. And yet, a year later, when he walked into a Hamilton courtroom filled with non-violent Caledonia residents, he felt the need to be "protected" by six OPP bodyguards. Later on, he whined about all the taxpayer money being spent on these events (including his posse of bodyguards in Hamilton?; including that OPP team ordered to waste hours waiting to waylay me on the highway to deliver a "message" to me?), but as OPP chief, the questionable decisions and the megabucks that paid for them stopped at his desk.

For the January 20 rally, Fantino would bring in the London Riot Squad and an OPP helicopter. Hundreds of OPP officers and senior brass were told to make the trip to Caledonia. Fantino, who was earning nearly $1,000 a day, would spend his day in Caledonia. Officers sat comfortably inside their Greyhound buses and the OPP rented many hotel rooms to ensure that their officers were up and ready for their 8 a.m. morning briefing. Fantino himself would hide out at the Union Road OPP Command Post and peek out the window when we asked to meet with him.

It was a cold day and at one point there were about 15-20 of us huddled around an open fire on private property. As we stood there sipping our coffee, we noticed the London Riot Squad forming a line at the property's edge. They were decked out in full riot gear.[23] Realizing how ridiculous it looked for police dressed up in their impressive Teenage Mutant Ninja Turtle-style riot garb lining up against a dozen or so ordinary folks drinking coffee, we walked to the edge of the property and pointed out the absurdity to the media, so they would capture it by taking some photos, including one of Mark Vandermaas wearing his blue United Nations peacekeeping beret and holding a Canadian flag while speaking to the officers about our reasons for being there. Not more than five minutes later, the officers boarded their buses and left the area. Not only had the OPP intimidation failed to work, it gave the media more evidence of just how far the OPP would go to target innocent non-Natives.

That day the OPP enforced a "no-go" zone that, incredibly, prevented non-Natives, and only non-Natives, from being on Caledonia's main street. Mark gave a speech[24] on the side of the road, on a hill near Canadian Tire while waiting (in vain, as it turned out), for a senior officer to come and explain why we couldn't put up Canadian flags. That was when we first met Merlyn Kinrade who volunteered to hold Mark's flag while he spoke to the crowd. At one point the OPP helicopter passed overhead forcing him to stop for a few minutes during which he and Merlyn doubled over in laughter at the silliness of the OPP helicopter and the hundreds of officers being used to make sure Canadians couldn't put up the flag both of them had served under in the military.

Faced with the barrier of police stopping us from walking down the road, and the ranks upon ranks of police enforcing it, we chose instead to walk on property belonging to Dave Brown and Dana Chatwell adjacent to the main street which bordered DCE. The police couldn't touch us, of course, because we were now on private property. We walked up and down, our wonderful Canadian flags held proudly, in full view of the public and glare of the media.

A group of about 100 occupiers – Native and union supporters – on DCE came to the edge of the Brown-Chatwell property and screamed obscenities at us as we stood in complete silence. A picture of them can be found in *Helpless*. After screaming insults and making obscene gestures at us for about 30 minutes they realized we were not going to return hate for hate and they slowly drifted away until none were left. It was a powerful lesson about the strength of Dr. King's non-violent approach; we had faced down those who had terrorized Caledonia with nothing more than silence and Canadian flags.

There was no doubt about it: our rally had been a resounding success. The same could not be said of Fantino's high-priced operation. As we saw the OPP helicopter we wondered if Fantino was sitting high overhead fuming that he couldn't stop us.

Native protesters had often terrorized Dave and Dana because of the location of their home, which bordered DCE. The OPP had stationed officers in a car in their driveway for many days. Of course, the officers never got out of their car to prevent any crimes. For almost a year, the OPP had refused to arrest any Native protesters who trespassed on a resident's private property. However, they called Dana again and again, pressuring her to agree to have us arrested for trespassing on her property.[25] Months later, the OPP went around to property owners, asking them to sign a form consenting to the arrest of trespassers. Thinking the OPP would use these consents to arrest trespassing Natives, a number of residents signed the form. When they found out that the consent would be used only against fellow residents, many asked for their forms back.

In the timeline of Caledonia flag protests, the January 20, 2007 flag rally was the third event (my inaugural October 15, 2006 'March For Freedom' rally was not a 'flag' protest), and the second one that I had called. On each occasion, the OPP employed a new tactic to arrest non-Natives. Residents had organized the first event, held on December 2, 2006. That day, the police used trespassing laws to arbitrarily and illegally arrest Bo Chausse. On December 16, 2006, they came up with the scheme to arrest and illegally hold me in jail overnight in an attempt to impose travel restrictions on me. On January 20, 2007, police threatened to charge non-Natives with obstructing the duties of a police officer if they crossed or went around a police line (a scheme cooked up because non-Natives were not intimidated by the false arrests).

To discourage attendance at our peaceful rallies the OPP issued a series of press releases[26] on January 4, 16, 18 and 19, 2007 stating that "O.P.P. are proactively warning anyone planning on protesting in Caledonia tomorrow that attempting to go around or through the Police Line could face criminal charges of obstructing police. Persons attempting to cross or crossing that police line could be arrested, charged, fingerprinted and photographed." Fantino would add in his two cents by saying in the press release that "The OPP and other legitimate stakeholders do not want 'mischief makers' in Caledonia – persons with their own agendas bring an added element of risk and will be held accountable for their actions." In court it would be revealed that the phrase "other legitimate stakeholders" was code language for Native protesters and the McGuinty government. Apparently, to the OPP, the residents of Caledonia are not "legitimate stakeholders." They are "troublemakers" and "mischief makers" who have their own illegitimate agendas.

The Ontario Provincial Police Association even got into the act when its president Karl Walsh issued a repugnant, bewildering release on January 19 accusing Mark and me of "promoting hatred, flaunting the justice system and inciting violence," a claim they would eventually retract in 2012 after we sued for defamation with the help of John Findlay. I cover Walsh's Caledonia role in more depth in Chapter 8 – *Cashedonia*.

In seven years, the "legitimate stakeholders," i.e. the Native protesters, have crossed police lines at every single event. Not one of them has faced arrest. Yet Fantino wanted to arrest non-Natives for doing exactly what Natives were doing, because, in his twisted worldview, Caledonia residents and those who support them are not "legitimate stakeholders." In other words, the Ontario Political Police has ceased to function as a legitimate police force, ceased to uphold its oath, and has been a blunt instrument used to uphold the will of its political masters. And its political masters, the Ontario government, wrote a letter instructing it to arrest anyone who is not a 'Land-Claim Protester' who tries to enter DCE. Apparently this allows the OPP to target non-Native people. Acting as the government's enforcers – its muscle – is how a police force operates in a totalitarian system. That's not how it is supposed to function in a free and open democracy like Canada.

Anyone who disagreed with the OPP was barred from the area. However, because they sided with the Natives, members of the Communist Party of Canada and CAW, CUPE and other unions have been allowed on DCE.[27] So have some Palestinian protestors who, on May 3, 2006, raised the Palestinian flag alongside that of the Mohawk Warriors.[28] Do you think Fantino would have the courage to call any of these people "mischief-makers" or "troublemakers"? Do you think the OPP ever once threatened to arrest a CAW leader or a Palestinian supporter who rallied in Caledonia? Do you think the OPPA or OPP issued news releases accusing Natives or their anti-capitalist supporters of inciting hatred and violence? Of course they didn't. The OPP would never dare touch anyone who supports the leftist view that, because Natives were once victims, they have every right to use violence and engage in crime against non-Natives; the leftist view also holds that only white people are capable of racism. Natives and other minorities are incapable of "racism" (even when they express what, clearly, are racist views) because they are seen as perpetual victims. Such thinking pervades Canada's "human rights" bodies. It is also the basis of Ontario's "new" approach to policing. If I, Gary McHale, had supported McGuinty's handling of Caledonia, the OPP wouldn't have dared arrest me.

But back to that day in Caledonia, with Fantino's Ninja Turtles massed against us coffee drinkers, and his OPP helicopter circling in the sky: Despite all that overkill and intimidation, I was able to raise a Canadian flag across from DCE by driving down the road with a friend and jumping out at the spot where I wanted it to go. As I raised it, a busload of OPP officers drove up and told me I was under arrest. After calling their command center, though, they let me go. I placed my flag beside the Canadian flag that had been put up the same day by Native protesters. It was their way of beating us to the punch so that we wouldn't have to raise ours. (Of course, the issue wasn't just the flag. It was also that non-Natives were not allowed to walk down the road and hoist the flag.) Two other flags flew beside the Canadian ones, an American flag and a Mohawk warrior flag.

Inspector Nichols was lead officer when the OPP got off the bus, and within a few minutes, he decided that one of the Canadian flags was there illegally, so he had it removed. Guess which Canadian flag it was. If you guessed it was the one the Natives raised, you'd be wrong. Nichols also had no problem with the other two flags. To recap: the one flag raised by non-Natives was "illegal." The three flags raised by Natives were well within the law. (The inspector never explained how Canada's Criminal Code applies to an object, for example how a flag is a breach of peace. Objects don't break the law; people do.)

The timing could not have been worse for Nichols. Fantino had told Caledonia residents concerned about the abundance of Native flags being flown that the

OPP could not remove them because to do so would violate an individual's Charter-protected right to fly a flag. Here was Nichols, though, removing our flag, in essence telling us that we did not have the same rights. Oops! Nichols claimed he was unaware of Fantino's statement, so I guess we'll have to take him at his word. It defies logic, though, to imagine such a senior officer being out of the loop, flag-wise, especially since Nichols was hardly a newcomer on the scene. By then, he had been at a few Caledonia events, and was the officer who spoke to me back on December 16, 2006 when the OPP arrested me. He knew full well that Natives and non-Natives have equal rights in Canada. He knew Native protesters had been raising flags for months while the OPP did nothing to stop them. Therefore, he must have known that raising a flag on a hydro pole was not illegal. However, he chose to blindly follow the racist OPP policies ordering officers to treat Natives and non-Natives differently.

To defeat this revolting systemic racism in a land that bills itself as "the true north, strong and free," we held approximately a dozen flag-raising and other protest events in Caledonia, Queen's Park, and even one at Julian Fantino's home [29] over the next two years until, on July 12, 2009, we were at last successful in forcing the OPP to respect our right to raise a Canadian flag across the street from the entrance to the occupation site.[30] The OPP had to be made to accept the principle given by God and enshrined in our Constitution that all citizens have the right to freedom of expression, and, as the Supreme Court of Canada had ruled, that included the right to place flags on hydro poles. Try telling anyone in Canada that you were arrested for trying to raise a Canadian flag on public property and they'll probably be incredulous. But I and others with me have been, so I know it's true. And I will continue to raise the Canadian flag because it is the easiest, most peaceful way to highlight the OPP's racist policing in Caledonia.

In a remarkably (dare one say a deliciously?) ironic turn of events, Julian Fantino, now a Conservative Member of Parliament and a Cabinet Minister in the Conservative-led federal government, has affirmed his love for the Canadian flag. His colleague, Conservative MP John Carmichael, introduced a Private Member's Bill – *National Flag of Canada Act* – in Parliament that would protect Canadians' rights to fly the flag. Cabinet Minister Fantino had his office issue a statement supporting the new law. "The minister has always been strongly supportive of demonstrative patriotism, which our flag represents," it affirmed.

Carmichael's bill had originally included a provision whereby anyone who broke the new law would be subject to up to two years in jail. The bill was subsequently amended to eliminate that provision before it was finally passed into law; however, before it was amended, SUN TV personality Brian Lilley offered this wry comment: "Hmm, up to two years in jail for stopping a flag from flying. How does Julian Fantino feel about spending two years in the slammer? See, a few years ago Fantino arrested Gary McHale for flying the flag at a counter protest for the illegal native occupation in Caledonia. That's the illegal occupation aided and abetted for six years now by Liberal Premier Dalton McGuinty. Fantino was Commissioner of the Ontario Provincial Police back then and didn't want an act as inflammatory as flying the national flag to happen on his watch. So he busted McHale. Have we mentioned that few native protesters have been busted for a whole raft of illegal activity? Often the cops just stood and watched."[31]

Christie Blatchford highlighted the outrageous injustices against non-natives in a 2011 *Globe & Mail* article after yet another failed OPP attempt to have me convicted of a non-crime (the Crown dropped a bogus OPP 'assault' charge against me before trial). After reviewing the testimony of Detective-Constable Wesley Barnes and witnessing proceedings in the Cayuga Courthouse she wrote: "…the law in Haldimand County operates as the law in America's Deep South once worked, where there was one law for the white man, who could break it with impunity, and another for the black man. In Haldimand County, since the occupation began, there has been one law for natives and another for non-natives.[32]

Exactly

---

1   Caledonia Victims Project, History of the Mohawk Warrior flag: a legacy of lawlessness, June 1, 2011. *
2   Photo, Venezuelan flag on occupied Douglas Creek Estates, 2006. *
3   Photos, Native occupiers destroy Canadian flag, 2006. *
4   CaledoniaWakeUpCall.com video, edited version of Chris Syrie video recorded Jan. 10, 2007, *Two Tier Justice By The Numbers.* *
5   Supreme Court of Canada ruling, *Ramsden v. Peterborough* (City), [1993] 2 SCR 1084, http://canlii.ca/t/1fs08.
6   Gary McHale photo, arrest of Bo Chausse, Dec. 2, 2006. *
7   Ontario Provincial Police, Professional Standards Bureau report, *Police Service Complaint for False Arrest* (re: Gary McHale arrest, Dec. 16, 2006), Oct. 18, 2007, Witness #12 – Chris Diana, pp.30-31. "Diana advised that Commissioner Fantino had emailed the Director of the Legal Services Branch, Ann McChesney, contacting his office on Sunday Dec. 3, 2006." *
8   Ibid, page 38.
9   Ibid, page 29.
10 Written statement by Assistant Crown attorney Andrew Goodman, Nov. 21, 2008. Statement made in response to subpoena issued by Gary McHale to force Crown to testify as a defense witness at McHale's preliminary hearing. Statement was entered as exhibit #21 at the preliminary hearing. *
11 OPP Occurrence Report # RM06136448, Dec. 16, 2006. *
12 The Estate of Martin Luther King, Jr., Stanford University, *Statement by Alabama Clergymen*, April 12, 1963. *
13 Dr. Martin Luther King Jr., *Letter from Birmingham Jail*, April 16, 1963. *

14 Ipperwash Papers project, March 14, 2007, www.IpperwashPapers.ca.

15 CBC, Dec. 25, 1962, 'The Eyes of Children' – life at a residential school (Christmastime at a residential school in British Columbia in 1962.). CBC video still available online. *

16 Mark Vandermaas, VoiceofCanada, VoC speech at 'Remember Us' March, Oct. 08, 2007 (Natives are victims of Two Tier Justice). *

17 Tekawennake News, Aug. 15, 2007: Band Council and citizens clash. Former Chief David General says "he does not consider Kanonhstaton [Douglas Creek Estates] sacred land, citing two reported rapes and several other unseemly acts which have been reported from the reclamation site." *

18 Ontario Provincial Police, Professional Standards Bureau report, Police Service Complaint for falsely pulling Gary McHale over on Hwy #6 on Dec. 16, 2006, Oct. 25, 2007. OPP audio taped their conversation with Gary McHale – transcripts of this conversation start on page 11 of the report. *

19 OPP news release, Dec. 16, 2006, Police Take Action To Keep The Peace In Caledonia Several Arrested. *

20 Ontario Human Rights Commission, Respondents Reply (OPP response to Vandermaas complaint), July 22, 2008, p2. *

21 Caledonia Class Action website: www.CaledoniaClassAction.com.

22 Gary McHale presentation, Lions Hall, Caledonia, Jan. 14, 2007, Why we come. What has been accomplished. Where do we go from here. *

23 Photos and videos of this event are available online. *

24 VoiceofCanada.ca, Jan. 21, 2007, OPP &OPPA vs. Supreme Court of Canada and the Charter of Rights & Freedoms. *

25 Dave Brown & Dana Chatwell Amended Statement of Claim, July 18, 2007, see paragraph 82 to 86. *

26 OPP news release, Jan. 18, 2007, RALLY IS IRRESPONSIBLE. OPP Press Release, Jan. 19, 2007, O.P.P. Police Line = Public Safety – Breaching It Isn't An Option. *

27 Photos available online. *

28 MostlyWater.org, May 3, 2006, Palestinian flag raised in support of Caledonia land claims dispute. "Representatives from the Niagara Palestinian Association today visited the site of the first nations land claims blockade. A Palestinian flag was presented…The Palestinian flag was raised by the head of security…It looks beautiful flapping in the sky on the same pole below the proud Mohawk flag. Palestinian hattas or scarves, a universal symbol of resistance, and food were given as gifts." *

29 Jeff Parkinson video, Canadian Advocates for Charter Equality, Flag raising protest at Julian Fantino's home, Woodbridge, Ontario, March 2, 2008. *

30 VoiceofCanada.ca, July 12, 2009, THE END OF THE BEGINNING!. *

31 Brian Lilley, Sept. 28, 2011, Quick, arrest Julian Fantino for stopping a flag from waving… *

32 Christie Blatchford, Globe & Mail, May 4, 2011, Caledonia activist free to drop by Canadian Tire. *

*See http://www.GaryMcHale.ca/book for additional information, links to documents, videos and photos

Chapter 4

Julian Fantino: The Gift That Keeps on Giving

There is little doubt that, while Julian Fantino was Commissioner, the OPP forcibly suppressed the rights of residents and business owners in Haldimand County because of their race. The OPP threatened the building industry, various trades, local shops, etc., with arrest if they exercised their rights to protect themselves and/or their property. During Fantino's term as Commissioner, Superior Court Judge J.A. Ramsay said the following in a 2008 ruling that dealt with the illegal occupation at a townhouse development in Cayuga, Ontario and the manner in which it was being policed. (Caledonia, Cayuga, Hagersville and Dunnville are the largest towns in Haldimand County):

> *The remaining defendants' [Native protesters] resort to self-help, taken with the authorities' refusal to defend the plaintiff's property rights, has put the plaintiff [developer] in a most unfair position. The same government that advises the plaintiff not to pay extra-governmental development fees refuses to enforce its property rights and threatens to arrest its agents if they try to enforce these rights on their own.*
>
> *I would be the last person to interfere with the proper exercise of discretion by the authorities. I do think that it might be helpful to clear up some misapprehensions that they appear to have.*
>
> 1. *The police have the right to remove unwanted persons from private property at the request of the owner with or without an injunction.*
>
> 2. *The police have the right to use their discretion in the enforcement of the law and private property rights. A blanket refusal to assist a*

> *property owner or a class of property owners, however, would be an*
> *abuse of that right.*
>
> 3. *The police have no right to prevent the plaintiffs [developer] from*
> *acting within their rights under s.41 of the* Criminal Code. *Their*
> *warning to the plaintiff that they would arrest anyone who is in-*
> *volved in a physical confrontation, regardless of the circumstances,*
> *is an abuse of the power conferred on them by s.31 of the* Criminal
> Code. [1]

Judge Ramsay accepts as fact in this ruling that the OPP was threatening the business owners with arrest if they exercised their rights under the Criminal Code to protect their property. For years the OPP had lied to residents and business owners, telling them, falsely, that Natives have "colour of right" to occupy private property during land claim protests, a legal defence that was rejected by the Attorney General of Ontario in a 2006 submission to the Ipperwash Inquiry that we discussed at length in our 2008 *Legalized MYTHS of Illegal Occupations* report.[2] Instead of enforcing the law, the OPP told business owners that they would refuse to honour land title deeds to private property and thus would refuse to remove trespassers.

During Fantino's leadership, officers continued to stand by and watch crimes taking place while at the same time threatening law-abiding business owners with arrest, which was illegal. In some cases OPP officers themselves engaged in criminal activity while trying to help Native protesters. In 2007, CanACE videographer Jeff Parkinson filmed two OPP officers, Det. Sgt. Rick Fraracci and Cst. Christopher Galeazza, helping Native protesters erect a barricade in Hagersville.[3] The barricade was intended to keep the legal owner off his property. This prompted our first use of Canada's private prosecution provisions, and, after a two-year legal battle in the groundbreaking cases of *R. v. Parkinson*, Superior Court Justice David Marshall ordered the two officers charged with mischief.[4] At no time did Commissioner Fantino denounce these or any of his officers' other criminal activity in Haldimand County.

Engaging in criminality, refusing to enforce the law, denying the legal merit of the Land Titles deed system, targeting non-Natives to be silenced: this was the OPP's approach to policing in Haldimand County. In service of that illegal policing, Fantino tried to control the public message; curtailed free speech; threatened elected officials; smeared ordinary citizens who dared to speak out; covered for Natives when they committed crimes; and misled the courts regarding the seriousness of the protesters' criminal behaviour. In all this, he was supported by his boss, Premier Dalton McGuinty.

In 2006-2007, Dave Hartless, an officer with the Hamilton, Ontario police department who lived a few doors away from the Caledonia occupation, was victimized numerous times by Native protesters. The OPP refused to do anything to stop these crimes. A few times Hartless helped neighbours who were being victimized. Again, the OPP stood by and did nothing. Once, Native protesters attacked Hartless as he was helping a neighbour. The OPP response was the same: the Natives could do what they wanted. There were other Hamilton police officers living in Caledonia, but they were too cowardly to speak out. Hartless was the only one who was willing to stand up and criticize OPP policing in public. In all his statements, he spoke not as a member of a police force, but as an ordinary resident of Caledonia. Once he saw that his neighbours were being victimized daily while the OPP refused to do anything about it, Hartless, whose home was very close to an OPP checkpoint manned around the clock, put 4 ft. x 8 ft. signs on his front lawn. One sign read, "NO CONFIDENCE Bring in the ARMY! Eject the Terrorists attacking Caledonia. OPP = 2 TIER Policing, No Protection 4 us."

OPP Insp. Dave McLean, the detachment commander in Haldimand, was the first to try to silence Hartless.[5] On December 5, 2006, McLean sent an email to Chief Supt. Bill Dennis and A/Supt. Doug Babbitt drawing their attention to an email from Hartless posted on "McHale's website". McLean's email stated: "As you are aware the OPP in the past has been victim to Hamilton Police Service Officer David Hartless and his direct verbal aggression as well as written slander by signs on his lawn and articles in the website of Gary McHale. We have in the past contacted his Chief, Brian Mullen and on several occasions he has been spoken to by their senior command." So let's see: Insp. McLean was detachment commander in Haldimand when Natives were committing numerous crimes with impunity while OPP refused to do their sworn duty and enforce the law. And yet, McLean believed that he and the OPP were the real victims in this scenario because a resident, who also happened to be a cop himself, had criticized their policing in signs posted on his private property. Either Insp. McLean is unaware of the laws on slander, or he doesn't care about misrepresenting them. The OPP itself cannot be slandered; only people can be slandered. Besides, the truth is not defamation. Hartless's signs weren't slander; they were his opinion about what was happening.

For months, the media had reported on two-tier justice in Caledonia. In fact, it was Karl Walsh, the President of the OPP Association, who had coined the phrase "two-tier justice" in a media interview in June, 2006. Walsh was concerned as to why so many OPP officers were being injured in Caledonia. He explained that OPP brass was allowing officers to be injured because it had ordered them to not wear protective equipment that would have prevented injuries. The *Toronto Sun* reported that Walsh said, "It's okay to have an officer walking around in tactical uniform at Wasaga Beach on a long weekend, but it's not okay in Caledonia...the president of the union representing 7,500 OPP officers says the Caledonia standoff indicates there's one law for aboriginal people and another for everyone else in the province. Our concern is basically that there is a two-tier justice system.'"[6]

McLean, in his anti-Hartless email, also said: "I feel the members of Haldimand detachment who have been very much victimized over the Native Reclamation by virtue of having to work in difficult circumstances as well as live in the community should not have to be further chastised by a fellow police officer who has a contact [Gary McHale] who also openly discredits the attempts of the OPP to maintain peace in a fragile environment." If OPP officers were victimized, though, it was because of decisions made by officers like McLean (who had already experienced Native insurrection during the Ipperwash crisis when he was "Sgt." McLean there).

While, legally, Haldimand Council has the final say on its detachment commander, Commissioner Fantino ignored this and forced Haldimand Council to accept McLean. McLean was well aware that Native thugs were terrorizing Haldimand families, but he too simply followed *The Framework* policy that was allowing the terrorization to occur. He pursued the OPP's racist policies, doing his best to silence anyone who dared to speak out. In a supreme irony, when McLean was first appointed commander, Dave Hartless told his neighbours to give him a chance. However, within months McLean was trying to have Hartless silenced.

In Canada, the Charter of Rights and Freedoms guarantees people "the freedom of association" – meaning that the government doesn't get to pick who your friends are. Apparently, though, McLean doesn't believe people have the right to associate with whomever they wish. In his less than eloquent email about Hartless he notes: "In addition Hartless' association to Gary McHale once again in my opinion is a breach of the code of conduct by virtue of McHale's position against the past and present commissioner and his inability to follow rules of law, create [sic] breaches of the peace and sponsor the Rally for Freedom this past October. Now once again he is attempting to rally the troublemakers in Caledonia against us to prove his agenda."

McLean's email is typical of how the OPP functioned. Two days after my first Caledonia rally, held on October 15, 2006, McLean phoned and thanked me for the peaceful gathering, and for following the agreed-upon plan he and I had created. He followed up this phone call with an email reminding me that he had thanked me for the way I had conducted myself at the rally. However, it was clear to me from his email about Dave Hartless that, behind the scenes, he was either lying to me or to his fellow officers. His email stated that I had an "inability to follow rules of law" and had "create[d] breaches of the peace"; he also called Caledonia residents who had spoken out "troublemakers." If that was so, then why, as detachment commander, did he not have me or them arrested? And why, if I have an inability to follow the rule of law, did he thank me? But that's how the OPP functions. It says nice things to your face while smearing you behind your back.

McLean sent his email on December 5, 2006 – three days after the OPP had illegally arrested Quintin "Bo" Chausse for allegedly trespassing on the property of Caledonia's Baptist Church. The OPP claimed that the church had phoned in a complaint about a trespasser, but the church denied doing so. Either way, Bo was not on church property at all, but on the side of the road. In other words, the OPP arrested him illegally on a trumped up charge.

Previously, on June 12, 2006, Bo Chausse and other residents and business owners filed a class action lawsuit against the OPP and the McGuinty government. (McGuinty paid $20 million to settle it in 2011[7]). It is thus not surprising that Bo became an OPP target. Two days after his arrest, two OPP officers apologized to him. However, the OPP's press release about the arrest shows how it really viewed non-Native protesters like Bo. It read in part: "As a result of the incident on Saturday one male party was arrested for Trespassing and released unconditionally. The male party, clearly frustrated with the ongoing occupation expressed regret for his action to police. The O.P.P. Criminal Investigation Unit is now looking into the Criminal Theft of the flags and charges are pending. The O.P.P. will not tolerate the actions of those willing to put their own self-motivated agendas ahead of the betterment of the community. The O.P.P. remains committed to keeping the peace and wish to remind everyone that there will be serious consequences for these types of selfish and juvenile actions."[8]

I was the one who picked up Bo after his illegal arrest. I can assure you that he didn't "express regret" to the OPP, because he knew he had done nothing wrong. The OPP release is typical; they loved to smear non-Native people. Of course, they would never dare accuse Native protesters, who were actually committing real crimes, of having "self-motivated agendas" or for acting in a "selfish and juvenile" manner.

What big crime had Bo Chausse and the other Caledonia residents committed on December 2? They had raised Canadian flags and placed yellow ribbons on hydro poles. Local MPP Toby Barrett stood right there as flags were raised, but I guess the OPP was too afraid to illegally arrest a provincial politician. Instead, they targeted someone else as a way of trying to intimidate and control others. In the end, Bo sued, and the government settled the case out of court. I don't know how much money the government has paid out to settle all of the OPP's illegal arrests in Caledonia, but I'm not counting on Fantino and/or McLean to tell us. It was clear at the time, however, that McLean was angry that non-

Native people believed they had the right to speak out and expose OPP corruption. His Hartless email went up the chain of command, and then was sent to Hamilton's Chief of Police in the hope that Hartless would be silenced. Senior police brass in Hamilton did speak to Hartless more than once, but he refused to shut up.

Since McLean had failed to silence Hartless, Fantino thought he'd give it a try. Here's the background. On February 17, 2007, Hartless emailed McGuinty and local council members an email posted on my website.[9] The email told McGuinty that he (McGuinty) had "allowed the OPP to operate outside of not only their mandate but the laws of this Country," and that McGuinty's suggestion that the people of Caledonia should be "patient" was "coming from a coward who hides from his responsibilities and avoids his duties as a leader." Hartless told McGuinty that he "displayed cowardice in the execution of his sworn duties and a betrayal of not only this town but the people and laws of this Province and this Country."

McLean immediately emailed Supt. John Cain, asking him to tell Hamilton Chief of Police Brian Mullan that Hartless had called McGuinty a coward. McLean then emailed Fantino to inform him, too. Fantino was outraged that an ordinary citizen, and a police officer to boot, would dare call the Premier a coward. He immediately emailed Chief Mullan, telling him: "Your man Hartless has gone over the top this time. I realize that he is also a private citizen and quite entitled to exercise freedom of speech, however, as a police officer, on or off duty, he is also held to a higher standard of accountability... I am formally taking exception to his latest mean-spirited and totally false accusation directed at the OPP that are very serious and about which I take exception. Bad enough that he slams the men and women of the OPP, refers to the Premier as being a coward on several occasions but then scatters his venomous email far and wide. If this isn't conduct unbecoming I don't know what is."[10]

At first, Chief Mullan, under pressure from Fantino, punished Hartless by ordering him to remain silent on issues pertaining to Caledonia. Hartless wouldn't allow himself to be bullied by Fantino or McLean, and hired lawyer John Findlay to challenge Mullan's order in court, citing his Charter right of freedom of speech. Hartless filed for an injunction against the order. Court papers show that the Hamilton Police Association also stepped in and told the Chief that the order was inappropriate. Less than a week after Hartless filed for the injunction, the order to silence him was lifted by Hamilton's Deputy Chief of Police.[11] At the same time, the Hamilton police had an outside police service investigate Fantino's complaint about Hartless. In the end, Hartless was cleared of any wrongdoing; apparently, Fantino's idea of what constitutes "conduct unbecoming" isn't shared by other police services.

The many statements made by Karl Walsh, OPP Association President, as recorded in Christie Blatchford's book *Helpless*, tell the real story about whose actions were unbecoming:

> *"I got numerous calls from members [OPP Officers] who will tell you that they were petrified of the repercussions of acting... they've got all these examples of people on the ground [Officers] who have already been persecuted, disciplined, had repercussions career-wise... I still don't understand why we took different approaches to law enforcement in Caledonia... I can't forgive them for a lot of the approaches they took to this and I think numerous officers got unnecessarily injured, I think people from the general public got unnecessarily injured, I think everybody that was involved in this suffered injuries that could have been avoided had they just stuck to their training, stuck to their policies and stuck to the law. You know, the law doesn't discern colour of skin or ethnic background, and it's not supposed to. Justice is supposed to be blind."* [12]

In her introductory *Author's Note*, Blatchford doesn't mince words in placing blame on those responsible for the law enforcement failures in Caledonia: " the front-line officers of the OPP were sold down the river, too, by their senior ranks, in particular by two commissioners of the force, Gwen Boniface and Julian Fantino, who either subjugated themselves to government will, held their tongues or respectively dreamed up the disastrous operational plan for Caledonia and then stubbornly held onto it for dear life.[13]" Clearly, the OPP brass should have been looking in the mirror to find the unbecoming conduct they were trying to pin on Dave Hartless.

Hartless isn't the only officer punished by Fantino for speaking out. In 2008-2009, Fantino attempted to silence a senior OPP officer who he believed had leaked information to the media about the Commissioner's actions. He failed.

* * *

In 2004, OPP Supt. Ken MacDonald headed up a probe investigating internal OPP police corruption. Insp. Allison Jevons was a senior investigator in that unit. The probe was investigating police response to a domestic violence complaint made against an officer. The investigation reviewed why supervisors in a town in eastern Ontario had looked the other way when a local officer allegedly took a baseball bat to his wife's car. When MacDonald and Jevons reported misconduct within senior brass, Fantino ordered a review of the findings. He then had these two senior officers charged with neglect of duty and deceit for their handling of the investigation.

The CBC reported that these officers claimed they were the victims of a witch-hunt inside the OPP being orchestrated by Fantino.[14] Part of the evidence against Fantino was an email from the Ontario Provincial Police Association (headed by Karl Walsh) stating the union wanted to "Take down MacDonald." Days before Fantino had had these officers charged, he asked another senior OPP officer, "Are you going to execute the disloyal one, or am I?" Various media outlets reported that Fantino's comment had been written down by the other senior officer, and that when Fantino learned of this (and that his comments were about to become evidence) he ordered the officer transferred to North Bay. The lawyers for the two charged officers stated in court that this amounted to witness tampering.

The CBC asked Fantino directly why he transferred the note-taking commander to North Bay. According to a CBC report, "At that point, Fantino became angry, calling the notes 'cheat notes'," adding: "'People who know me wouldn't hold onto those notes'."

Supt. MacDonald and Insp. Jevons filed a motion accusing Fantino of abuse of process. Fantino was forced to testify at the disciplinary hearing. The officers argued that, for political reasons, they were being prosecuted to appease the head of the OPP union. The hearing was adjourned after Judge Montgomery criticized Fantino for using a specific exhibit to refresh his memory, ignoring an order not to do so. Outraged by the criticism, Fantino called for the judge's removal and for the case to be stayed. The judge refused to remove himself, whereupon Fantino appealed to Divisional Court, which ruled against him. The three Superior Court Judges at the Divisional Court stated: "the adjudicator [Judge Montgomery] is a professional who understands his responsibility to be fair and impartial."

Fantino wasn't going to allow this court to tell him anything, so he appealed once again, to the Ontario Court of Appeals, Ontario's highest court. It, too, ruled against him, saying that while "the Commissioner states that his appeal relates to the unqualified and independent right of those appearing before administrative boards to be treated fairly..." it found the Divisional Court's "chain of reasoning" in ruling against him to be "perfectly acceptable." The reasoning in question: the Divisional Court held "the rulings of the adjudicator [Judge Montgomery] were reasonable, the comments of the adjudicator were understandable. Given this, a reasonable, informed, right-minded person would not think that the adjudicator was biased therefore, the adjudicator was correct in not recusing himself."[15]

The case was ordered back to Judge Montgomery, but the day Fantino was scheduled to appear in court in December 2009 to answer questions under oath, the charges against Supt. MacDonald and Insp. Jevons were suddenly dropped. Fantino thus escaped the hot seat he had been trying to dodge with all his appeals. The media reported that throughout this process Fantino was lawyered up with three high-priced government-provided attorneys, ultimately resulting in a legal tab of more than $500,000, picked up by the taxpayer, of course. This bill included the $60,000+ the government was ordered to pay to cover the legal costs of Officers MacDonald and Jevons.[16]

Remember, Fantino claimed that the cost of policing me in Caledonia in 2006 was $500,000. However, these costs related directly to measures taken by Fantino in a vain attempt to impose his will on residents and on me. It was Fantino, not Gary McHale, who called in the London Riot Squad to confront "threatening" coffee drinkers on Chris Syrie's property on January 20, 2007 (the squad remained for a total of five minutes, quickly disappearing once the media showed up). And it was Fantino who ordered up the expensive police helicopter on the same day. Think of the money he could have saved taxpayers had he decided not to try to intimidate us in such expensive ways!

* * *

As a result of efforts to silence opponents, Fantino left many victims, both ordinary citizens and police officers, in his wake. In 2007 I received an email from one of them, an RCMP officer named Bob Stenhouse. Stenhouse was part of the RCMP Gangs Unit when Fantino targeted him for making public comments about policing. Stenhouse had been following events in Caledonia and, upon learning that Fantino had threatened the town's elected council, emailed me the following:

> I am a former RCMP Staff Sergeant presently living in Edmonton Alberta. My name is Bob Stenhouse and I was dismissed from the RCMP in 2002 for being a whistleblower, and then re-instated by the Federal Court of Canada in 2004 due to the abuse of process on my disciplinary case... Mr. Fantino's apparent inappropriate abuse of power seems to be a part of his personal make-up, which I am deeply concerned may border on the psychological make-up of what experts in the field would call a chronic bully.

> I have read Mr. Fantino's e-mail to the town council and was struck by the similarities of his rhetoric in this e-mail with an anger fuelled letter he had written about me in 2000 when he was chief of York Regional Police and I had given media strategy documents to an author who had criticized Mr. Fantino in his book "Hells Angels at War". While I was critical of the policing response to organized crime I had not been critical of Mr. Fantino personally. This was left to the author who was quite scathing in his criticisms, thus fuelling an angry response.

> In a vitriolic letter written to the Commissioner of the RCMP, Mr. Fantino cited my actions as one of the most 'corrupt' he had witnessed in

his 32 years of policing. He then went on to demand what he termed "appropriate sanction" against the person responsible. This then had the domino effect leading to the abuse of process that was overturned at the Federal Court. My actions were taken for the greater public good and in his position of power he called it corruption.

I am deeply concerned about the state of policing in our country. I am concerned about police leaders appearing to believe that they are above accountability and above the law. I acknowledge the very difficult job they have to do while balancing competing interests and ideals, however, one thing I have discovered on my own journey is that personal frustration is never a legitimate excuse for abusing one's power...

In closing, I do not condemn Mr. Fantino, in fact I pray for him. However there comes a time and a place where one must stand against something that is wrong and unjust and in this case, at least with the facts I am equipped with at this time, it would appear that his actions are abusive and wrong and must be challenged. [17]

This seemed to be Fantino's three-part routine, and it happened over and over again: first, he pushed his weight around, next, he overplayed his hand, and, finally, he got his knuckles rapped by a court. For the most part, Fantino did whatever he pleased, and he left the taxpayer to pick up the cost of his arrogance. As of this writing, it has been almost ten years since Fantino was Toronto's Chief of police, and there are still cases in courts regarding his leadership there. Canadian taxpayers will likely never know exactly how many tens of millions of dollars this one man has cost them, never mind the traumatized lives left in the wake of his policing policies.

* * *

On April 7, 2007, Fantino's approach to policing and his desire to destroy my credibility got the better of him and he actually threatened elected officials – in writing, no less. On that morning, I phoned Mark Vandermaas and asked, "Is it Christmas or is today my birthday?" This was our way of saying that we'd just gotten an unexpected 'gift' from someone which created an opportunity to expose the injustices in Caledonia. In this case, the gift was an email sent by Julian Fantino (the gift that keeps on giving) in which he threatened the Haldimand County council, a mistake that would result in a Superior Court judge issuing process for a criminal charge against him after I used the private prosecution provisions of the Criminal Code to hold him accountable.

By late March 2007 I was becoming increasingly frustrated because local Caledonia councillor Craig Grice (who had been elected six months earlier because he had promised to be a lion, not a mouse) was doing nothing to help the very people who paid his salary. Grice quickly became like most politicians who were too afraid to speak out against the political correctness gripping and endangering his community. To draw attention to this, I shut down my website save for a message that said if local elected officials were unwilling to help, why should I, someone who doesn't even live in the area, fight day and night on their behalf?

The reaction was both immediate and expected. Residents contacted Grice to find out why he was doing nothing to help fight the injustice. Predictably, he responded by sitting on the fence, refusing to favour either side. However, he did say a few positive things about me to a resident in an email which I posted on my website. Fantino read this the same day and became enraged – apparently senior brass was reviewing my website daily. There was no way Fantino was going to stand for any person, business or elected official saying anything even remotely positive about me. After all, according to Fantino I was evil and had to be stopped.

By late 2009, the local newspaper, the *Regional News This Week*, had started publishing my weekly columns that kept residents abreast of events in Caledonia.[18] Throughout the previous two years, Fantino had waged a public war to smear me in the media, but by late 2009, his smear campaign was going down in flames. One notable sign of its failure was an editorial written by the owner of the *Regional News*: "I have had a couple of phone calls from people wanting to know why we are publishing articles written by the devil incarnate, Gary McHale. I wondered myself about McHale before I met him and found a pleasant, intelligent man with some strong views on law and order and the even-handed practice thereof, and not at all the rabid activist OPP chief Julian Fantino had painted him."

In her book, *Helpless*, Christie Blatchford sums up Fantino's reaction this way: "McHale, Dave Hartless, the Vanderwyks, AnneMarie VanSickle, Bo Chausse – anyone who criticized the government or the OPP had become the enemy." And now Fantino had a new enemy – Haldimand County council member Craig Grice. In an email[19] sent to Grice, Mayor Marie Trainer and Haldimand Council, Fantino expressed his outrage over Grice's positive words about me, and demanded he be punished for them. Fantino honestly believed that in a democracy elected officials are accountable to the police, and that he had the final say about which speech was and was not permissible. But that's how it works in a police state, not in a democracy.

Throughout the world, democratic nations have many things in common. One core principle they share is that police and the military answer to elected officials, not the other way around. In the province of Ontario, OPP Commissioner Fantino answered to an elected official, the Minister of Community Safety and Correctional Services. In defiance of the core principles of civilian over-sight, however, there was no way Fantino was going to allow a mere elected council member or mayor to speak out on issues of importance to the public, issues they had promised to act upon while campaigning for office.

Fantino called his threatening email the 'McHale Communication' and of course included his usual rant about officers being injured at Caledonia and the cost to taxpayers, without any mention of the cause of these problems. Fan-tino also stated: "And now, apparently, we have Councillor Grice commend-ing someone that he knows is a lightning rod for confrontation and potential violence. Just as troubling, Councillor Grice has now added another aggravat-ing political dimension to his previous "anti OPP" rhetoric."

Fantino also told Haldimand Council that he was prepared to punish the coun-cil in several ways. First, he would publicly hold Grice and Haldimand County accountable, along with me, for the ongoing conflict in Caledonia. Second, he would support any injured officer in the pursuit of civil redress. Third, he would transfer the policing costs to Haldimand County (by April 2007 they totalled around $30 million). Fourth, he would strongly recommend to his Minister that the OPP contract with Haldimand not be renewed.

These were powerful threats, especially since, one month earlier, 22 OPP of-ficers had filed that $7.1 million lawsuit against me claiming defamation. I wasn't concerned about the lawsuit, knowing it was really meant only to in-timidate me into silence, but others like Grice were easily intimidated. In the wake of the email, Grice's public message began to change. Fantino's effort to silence elected officials and control the message had, in this case, worked.

Very quickly, Grice appeared on TV to tell the public that he didn't support the Caledonia flag-raising rallies. That was a lie, and I could prove it. The day before the January 20 rally, I had phoned Grice and, not trusting politicians, had taped the conversation. The purpose of my call was simply to confirm that Grice would be at the rally, and to enable him, as the elected official, to speak to the media.

Not only had Grice supported these flag rallies, he had suggested ways to im-prove them. My approach to the rallies was simple – walk down the side of the road carrying the Canadian flag so that the media could videotape the OPP ar-resting us. From 2006 to 2008, we organized over a dozen Canadian flag rallies and related protests. Each time the OPP violated people's rights by preventing them from walking down the side of the road. Our logic was to follow in the footsteps of Martin Luther King Jr., who used non-violent "civil disobedience" to confront and expose the racist policies in society and government (except, in our case, we didn't need to disobey the law to be arrested). Grice wanted me to go further by walking in dangerous areas of the town. One area was the

Highway #6 bypass bridge which is a mile down a road that even the OPP simply refused to use at the time – this would clearly endanger people at my rally and thus I refused to follow Grice's suggestion. I asked Grice why he wanted me to walk to this bridge and he stated, "it would piss off the OPP."

Fantino concluded his threatening email to Haldimand Council by stating: "When I appeared before you several months back I came away believing that we had a mutual understanding about the detrimental effect that McHale and his followers were having on Caledonia. I know that Councillor Grice has some personal issues that he finds particularly aggravating, however, we never expected that he would fall prey to McHale's propaganda and it is now up to you as a Council to deal with the fall-out."

It is interesting that Fantino called it "McHale's propaganda" when virtually every major media outlet in Canada (TV, radio and newspaper outlets) had repeatedly said exactly the same things I was saying. The local mayor, local councillors, the local MPP and local MP have all criticized how the OPP – and in particular how Julian Fantino – failed Caledonia. Are we to believe that everyone in society had suddenly fallen "prey to McHale's propaganda," or did Fantino just want to focus attention on me in an effort to divert attention away from his own personal failure as Commissioner? It is hard for the OPP to pick on the CBC or CTV or a major newspaper. It is a lot easier to target someone small, like me who doesn't have the same resources with which to fight back.

Fantino's closing statement made another interesting point. He admitted that he – Commissioner of the OPP – had an "understanding" with elected officials about me and my followers. There didn't appear, though, to be any similar "understanding" re the ongoing peril of allowing thugs to control policing in Caledonia. Five months later, thugs attacked local resident Sam Gaultieri, almost killing him.[20] So it might have helped if Fantino had had an "understanding" of who the real troublemakers were, and "understood" that he needed to do something to stop them.

What Fantino wanted in Haldimand County was for the mayor and each council member to simply shut up while the OPP continued to ignore the Native protesters' crime. He didn't want any local government to expose the failures of the OPP and the McGuinty government, let alone the way he and his provincial police force were actually working with the very Native radicals who were behind the ongoing violence. He was proud that he never met with non-Native protesters, and proud that he met regularly with the very Natives who were attacking and hurting his officers and local residents. (In September 2009, Fantino refused Mayor Trainer's request to meet with her and 14 of the most aggrieved non-Native families in Caledonia saying he was too busy now, and would be in the "near future.")[21] Fantino wanted absolute control. In his world, no one was permitted to speak out without his permission, and only he held public officials accountable.

There were already glimmers of this mindset when Fantino was Toronto's Chief of Police. In May of 2003, Police Chief Fantino wanted every group that wanted to hold a demonstration to first get a permit from police.[22] He wanted to have the final say as to who was and wasn't allowed to protest in a democratic society. The Toronto Police Services Board and local councillors disapproved of turning over control of democratic protests to him. Fantino also wanted to require citizens to pay a bond before being able to gather and speak out on issues. (I guess if you make it too expensive for people to speak out, they might think twice about doing so.)

Of course, in Caledonia, these coercive measures were selective. They applied only to groups of which Fantino disapproved. Native protesters were not only free to walk down the road carrying Mohawk Warrior flags, they did so with an OPP escort! Meanwhile, Fantino took it upon himself to be in Caledonia on rally days, so that he could personally ensure that no non-Natives could walk down the same road carrying a Canadian flag.

In 2008 we tried to get advance approval to hold a march combined with a food event on public property (political protests do not require a permit, but 'entertainment' events do), but by then the OPP had control over the local council. The conditions of approval required us to purchase a $5 million bond and get written approval from the Natives occupying Douglas Creek Estates who had terrorized Caledonia and from Six Nations leadership. Can you imagine telling, say, black people that if they wanted to walk down the road they had to get the approval of area white people and official approval from the local KKK society? Using this "logic," it would be okay to force black people to first get permission from whites before finding a seat on a bus. Maybe black people should be required to allow whites to determine which schools their children can attend. Of course, such things would never happen. Black people would rightly point to their Charter rights, and lodge a complaint with Ontario's Human Rights Tribunal. However, police and the government are apparently allowed to treat non-Natives in Caledonia in a way they would never treat blacks or members of any other minority group. The racist polices of the OPP and the McGuinty government are clear for all to see. I cannot think of one reason why it makes sense to allow one person to assault and hospitalize another person without police intervention simply because of the perpetrator's skin colour or ethnicity or some other criteria.

To return to Fantino's threatening email: It didn't take much of an I.Q. to appreciate that, in a democratic society, Fantino couldn't go around intimidating elected officials, but it went further than simply trying to harass, intimidate and silence politicians; I believed Fantino's actions were criminal and so I launched a prosecution against him under the private prosecution provisions of Canada's Criminal Code. A two year court battle ensued and, on December 31, 2009, Superior Court Judge David Crane agreed with me that the email provided the evidence that established Fantino should be tried under section 123(2)(b) – influencing a municipal official by threats. At the hearing against him, Fantino had a government lawyer (Chris Diana) and two Crown lawyers (Andrew Bell and Anne-Marie Carere) arguing that he should not be charged. The two Crown lawyers attempted to argue that Fantino wasn't threatening someone in his/her official capacity. The judge disagreed and ordered the charge to be issued. (The Crown would quickly step in and withdraw the charge, which prevented the case from going to trial for a ruling on whether Fantino was guilty.)

During an earlier hearing with a Justice of the Peace, the Justice commented on Fantino's email, stating, "There is absolutely no doubt in my mind that this e-mail was perceived as threatening by the Mayor and by Councillor Grice and presumably by the other councillors... I would characterize this e-mail as threatening, ill-conceived and ill advised. Frankly, I found it shocking."[23]

Judge Crane, in his ruling, summed up the facts this way: "The evidence on the record is that Councillor Grice sent an e-mail to his constituent using the official communication facility of Haldimand County Council... The further evidence on this record is that Mayor Trainer and Councillors, including Mr. Grice, had appeared as Municipal officials at public rallies held or organized by Mr. McHale. These rallies broadly speaking involved Mr. McHale's critical views on the standard of policing and policing policies for the Town of Caledonia. The letter of Julian Fantino would be reasonably read as to enjoin and prevent further such support and appearance in the future."[24]

Long before Judge Crane ruled that there was sufficient evidence to charge Fantino with committing a criminal offence, the Ontario government had done everything it could to cover for its OPP Commissioner. Soon after Fantino sent his threatening email to Haldimand County in 2007, Merlyn Kinrade and I each filed an official complaint charging that Fantino had violated the law and acted in a way unbecoming an officer. Other residents – Steve Tong, Lenora Taylor and Sheldon Taylor – filed similar complaints. Mark Vandermaas had earlier filed a complaint against Fantino on April 2 for his false statements about us in the media, and would file another on May 1 for Fantino's role in violating our right to raise a Canadian flag.

MPP Toby Barrett reserved the media room at Queens' Park for us where, on April 17, 2007, the three of us (Merlyn, Mark and I) gave what we dubbed our 'FantinoGate' presentation to the media in which we recounted Fantino's threat to democracy.[25]

It was the first time in the history of Ontario that anyone had filed complaints against the OPP Commissioner, and the McGuinty government didn't know what to do because Fantino was doing exactly what the premier wanted. He had to make it look, though, as if he cared about these threats now that the public had been made aware of them.

A complaint made against an OPP Commissioner can be reviewed only by the Minister for Community Safety and Correctional Services, at that time, Monte Kwinter. Kwinter stepped in quickly and hired an outside lawyer to review what steps he could take. Since no one had ever submitted such a complaint, the government had no precedent to follow.

The lawyer wasn't hired to investigate the allegations, but to advise the province on the process of reviewing a complaint against a sitting OPP commissioner. Ontario Ombudsman Andre Marin publicly denounced Kwinter for hiring an outside lawyer, telling the media that, "the Liberal government is circumventing his office and squandering tax dollars by hiring outsiders to investigate public complaints because it wants to maintain control over the investigations... The government could have asked the ombudsman to investigate the complaint but instead chose to hire outsiders so it can dictate the scope of any investigation and retain some control over the results."[26]

As we would see, Andre Marin was correct to believe that the McGuinty government wanted to control the outcome of the investigation. The government had hired Rod McLeod from the firm Miller Thomson LLP in Markham, Ontario. McLeod would interview Mayor Marie Trainer, Mark Vandermaas, Merlyn Kinrade and me. He made it clear to me that he was not investigating the allegations, but was only advising the government about the process of handling a complaint against an OPP Commissioner.

Prior to McLeod's meeting with Mark, our lawyer, John Findlay, sent McLeod a letter questioning whether he really was independent when both McGuinty and Kwinter had repeatedly made public statements supporting Fantino. It thus came as no surprise when, a few months later and with no notice, Monte Kwinter held a press conference announcing the result of McLeod's report. The "independent" lawyer had cleared Fantino of all wrongdoing. What the public wasn't told was that, in fact, he was not "independent." According to Haldimand Mayor Marie Trainer, McLeod wrote the report he'd been ordered to write, the one the McGuinty government wanted.

Testifying in court, Mayor Trainer stated: "Rod McLeod, he was a lawyer and he had interviewed me previously in my office." Trainer asked the court that she be allowed to review the communications between her and McLeod that she had on her Palm Pilot. She testified to the following:

It was June the 28th [2007]. He called me in early in the morning and saying he was finalizing his report and he went over a few things – he was going to put in the report about things that I had said. And he said he wanted to soften the report a little bit so that Commissioner Fantino wouldn't look too bad. And that he would call me later in the day and go over what he, how he had quoted me to verify that it was okay with me.

So, I was on the way to the opening of the new RCMP offices here in Hamilton and Chinta Puxley from the Canada Press had called and wanted to know what I had thought of Minister Kwinter's announcement that Commissioner Fantino had been exonerated. And I said, "Pardon me?" And she repeated it. And I said, "But the report isn't even written yet, I just talked to the fellow who's writing the report." She said, "Oh, Rod McLeod?" And I said, "Yes." And she said, well, she was just at a press release with Minister Kwinter, and he had said that the Commissioner had been exonerated.

So meanwhile, Rod did send me an e-mail, sent me – left me a message, and I do have it here:

"Your Worship, it's Rod McLeod. It is just about 12:30 on Thursday the 28th. Thank you for the time this morning. The more substantive discussion that I referred to that you and I might, that I might be asking you to participate in with me today is not going to happen today as far as I know at the moment. I will get back to you when that can be re-activated. I hope that is okay. Thank you very much. If you need to talk to me I am at..."[27]

The Mayor continued: "He leaves the number of Miller Thompson Barristers. So of course, I called him back and said, 'what's going on, I didn't think the report was finished yet and yet Chinta Puxley had said Minister Kwinter had already made the announcement.' He had changed his whole tone. He actually seemed quite upset and said, 'I have to write the report as I'm instructed.'"

Of course, no media or member of the public has ever seen a copy of McLeod's report. Minister Monte Kwinter was McLeod's client, so the report is protected by lawyer/client privilege. Ombudsman Marin's warning about the McGuinty government using outside lawyers to protect their own interests by controlling the results of any investigation proved to be absolutely correct. What Kwinter and McGuinty may not have known is that we had a private meeting with senior officials at the Ombudsman's office in which Merlyn, Mark, me and Mayor Trainer discussed Fantino's threatening email. In the end Ombudsman Marin could not step in to review the process because the law exempts the police from being investigated by the Ombudsman.

The entire process overseen by Kwinter raises serious questions. We are not surprised when politicians like Kwinter and McGuinty lie to us, but according to Haldimand Mayor Marie Trainer's sworn statement, McLeod and the shield of lawyer/client privilege was used by the government, I would suggest, improperly, to cover up Fantino's actions in Caledonia. According to Kwinter, McLeod's report cleared Fantino of any wrongdoing – an amazing claim given that McLeod made it clear during his meetings with us that he was not investigating the allegations but merely advising the government on the proper process to follow in an investigation of an OPP chief.

To sum it all up: Fantino threatened elected officials because he wanted to control the message and because he didn't want the public to know the many ways in which the OPP and the McGuinty government were failing to respect the rights of non-Natives in Caledonia and refusing to uphold the law; the McGuinty government hired an outside lawyer bound by lawyer/client privilege to (allegedly) investigate Fantino; a report was written in the way the government had ordered it to be done, and Fantino was cleared of all wrongdoing beforehand.

I leave it to the reader to decide the level of corruption within the McGuinty government over this outrageous episode. One additional piece of information about this affair involves Crown lawyer Milan Rupic.

On December 31, 2009, Judge Crane ordered Julian Fantino to be charged with criminal behavior. The order was signed by a justice of the peace, and Fantino was ordered to appear in court on February 3, 2010. Before he had even been served with court papers, though, Crown lawyer Milan Rupic rushed into court to change the court appearance to January 15. Fantino wasn't even in the country at the time so dropping the charge before he was even served would save him having to respond to the media. It was thus clear that the Crown was rushing the case into court because it wanted to try to kill it before the media got hold of the story. While the Crown does have the authority to withdraw a case, standard procedure is to do so during the accused's scheduled court appearance. The Crown's Milan Rupic, however, moved to change the court date before he even had all the evidence. When I learned about Rupic's actions, I sent letters to him, Ontario's Attorney General and to the media.[28] In them I said that Rupic had not taken the time to talk to me – by law, I was both the informant and investigator of the case – or review all the evidence I had. In my mind, that confirmed that the government did not care about the evidence and wanted only to clear Fantino.

Thanks to my notifying the media, Rupic had a problem. The media knew he hadn't reviewed all the evidence since he hadn't talked to me. Several reporters from TV and radio stations and about a dozen newspapers were camped out at the courthouse on January 15 to find out from Rupic why the McGuinty government had rushed the case ahead. I was telling the media it had done so with the intent of having the charges withdrawn regardless of the evidence, which Rupic probably wouldn't bother to review anyway. On January 15, Rupic stood up in court and asked for the February 3 court date again so he would have enough time to speak to me and review my evidence.

CHCH TV approached Rupic in the parking lot of the courthouse, demanding to know why he rushed the case forward only to ask the court to change it back to the original date. Rupic refused to answer, but on February 3, he arrived in court with a written statement. In it he explained that he withdrew the charge against Fantino because he was satisfied that the Commissioner's email did not break the law. He further stated: "Fantino's remarks that he would send a bill to Haldimand County if police officers were injured, does not and cannot constitute an offence under section 123 of the Criminal Code. I say that because it is not an offence if you tell somebody that you might send them a bill for services." [29]

In other words, Superior Court Justice Crane and the Justice of the Peace were wrong. Both judges saw the email as a threat, and the Crown (both Andrew Bell and Anne-Marie Carere) accepted it as such when the case was before Crane, but suddenly it was not a threat. Obviously, sending a bill to someone for services rendered isn't illegal. But Rupic was conveniently highlighting the least offensive portion of the email and ignoring the crucial context in which it had been written. (If the mob sends you an invoice for their services protecting your business, that invoice could probably be used as evidence for a crime.) Fantino was threatening to saddle Haldimand County with a bill for tens of millions of dollars for services it had not purchased. Fantino wasn't just a businessman issuing an invoice to a customer. He was the Commissioner of the OPP, and he was threatening to withdraw all policing in the county and issue a bill that could have bankrupted the local government.

Rupic also failed to address the fact that Fantino was charged with "Influencing Municipal Officials." During the hearing before Judge Crane, the Crown admitted that Fantino's email was his way of influencing what the mayor and council members would say in public in their capacity as elected officials.

Finally, Rupic claimed that Fantino's email was not a threat as the Criminal Code understood it. However, that had already been dealt with when the issue came up in Judge Crane's court. During that hearing, Chris Diana, the OPP's top lawyer who was representing Fantino went into great detail about the exact meaning of the word "threat" in an effort to try to clear Fantino. Despite his best efforts, Judge Crane still ruled against Fantino.

Fantino's efforts to suppress free speech backfired big time in terms of his criminal charge and the widespread media coverage. The incident is recorded for history in Christie Blatchford's *Helpless*. Even the CBC, which had studiously – and shamefully – avoided covering the plight of non-Native victims in Caledonia in any depth, published two articles about some of Fantino's shenanigans directed against me, including one by CBC National News investigative reporter John Nicol entitled, *The two men who are putting a police chief on trial*.[30] His purpose in writing the story, he told Mark Vandermaas and me, was to show Canadians how we were using the system to fight back against injustice.

As we came to learn, Fantino's ego was surpassed only by his own arrogance. Like most bullies, Fantino lashed out when faced with opposition, and showed the public just how corrupt the justice system had become. Unfortunately for Fantino, even he, arrogant as he was, had to submit to the due process of the law.

The positive lesson here is that when citizens, police officers and court judges refuse to be bullied, the system works, and people like Fantino are eventually exposed.

1   *1536412 Ontario Ltd. v. Haudenosaunee Confederacy Chiefs Council*, 2008 CanLII 28041 (ON SC) http://canlii.ca/t/1x6s8.

2   Gary McHale & Mark Vandermaas, Canadian Advocates for Charter Equality, *Legalized MYTHS of Illegal Occupations, Myth #1 – Colour of Right*, pp. 4-11, May 13, 2008. *

3   Videos are available online. *

4   *R. v. Parkinson*, 2009 CanLII 729 (ON SC) http://canlii.ca/t/224jp.

5   Insp. Dave McLean's email on Dec. 5, 2006 at 3:43 p.m. was filed as part of an affidavit by Hamilton Deputy Chief of Police Ken Leendertse which was sworn out on June 13, 2007. *

6   *Toronto Sun*, June 16, 2006, Between a rock and a hard place. *

7   *KRP Enterprises Inc. v. Ontario Provincial Police Commissioner*, 2010 ONSC 901 (CanLII). http://canlii.ca/t/27x4t *

8   OPP Press Release, Dec. 3, 2006, *Compromising Peace in Caledonia – Not an Option*. *

9   Dave Hartless' email is contained in Hamilton Deputy Chief of Police Ken Leendertse's affidavit sworn out on June 13, 2007. *

10   Ibid,. Fantino's email is also contained in Leendertse's affidavit. *

11   Ibid., Leendertse's order silencing Hartless and the order lifting his silencing order are contained in Leendertse's affidavit. *

12   Christie Blatchford, *Helpless: Caledonia's Nightmare of Fear And Anarchy, And How The Law Failed All Of Us*, Doubleday Canada, 2010, pp. 143, 222. *

13   Ibid, p. IX.

14   *CBC News*, Oct. 17, 2008, Fantino calls allegations against him 'hysterical nonsense'. *

15   *Ontario Provincial Police v. Macdonald*, 2008 CanLII 63164 (ON SCDC) http://canlii.ca/t/21r56. *

16   *CBC News*, Nov. 13, 2009, OPP commissioner loses court appeal. *

17   See http://www.cbc.ca/news/canada/edmonton/story/2004/03/19/ed_stenhouse20040319. html and http://reports.fja.gc.ca/eng/2004/print/2004fc375.html.

18 Every story published in the *Regional News* by McHale is available on-line. *

19 Fantino's email to Haldimand Council, April 7, 2007 at 5:09 p.m., Subject: McHale Communications. *

20 *The Hamilton Spectator*, Feb. 28, 2011 , Beaten builder never fully recovered. *

21 *Dunnville Chronicle*, Oct 21, 2009: Fantino says no. *

22 *National Post*, May 14, 2011, Seize a street, all you need is a cause. *

23 Transcripts of Justice of the Peace David Brown's comments, Aug. 11, 2009. *

24 *McHale v. Attorney General of Ontario*, Dec. 31, 2009, ruling by Superior Court Justice Crane. *

25 Our presentation at Queen's Park is available on-line. *

26 *Toronto Star*, June 20, 2007, Ombudsman blasts province for bypassing him. *

27 Transcripts of Haldimand Mayor Marie Trainer's testimony at McHale preliminary hearing, Nov. 25, 2008. *

28 McHale's letter to Ontario Attorney General Chris Bentley, Jan. 10, 2010. *

29 Crown Attorney Milan Rupic's written comments to the Court stating why the charge against Fantino was being withdrawn – Rupic ensured he had copies to hand out to the media.*

30 *CBC News*, Feb. 2, 2010: The 2 men who are putting a police chief on trial. *

* See http://www.GaryMcHale.ca/book for additional information, links to documents, videos and photos

Chapter 5

The Fleming Rally: A Pivotal Event

There had been rallies held in Caledonia before December 1, 2007, the date of the rally organized by resident Doug Fleming of 'Doug's Smokes' fame, and rallies were held afterwards. But the rally that took place on that date was particularly important, not only because of the Native violence that was unleashed that day against non-Natives, including me, but because the OPP's reaction to the rally speaks volumes about its bizarre and illegal policing in Caledonia, and the shocking lengths it (and the Ontario government) will go to protect it.

The Lead-Up

I have already mentioned Doug Fleming, the Caledonia townsperson who, in response to the OPP's non-response to Natives setting up illegal smoke shops in the area, set up his own shop in a ramshackle truck. It wasn't that Doug wanted to go into the illegal tobacco business, it was his way of highlighting the problem: protesting police refusal to take any action in response to it (as a result of which smoke shop business was booming as more and more illegal shops kept popping up) and, yes, having a bit of fun at police expense. I didn't know Doug too well back then. He had attended a few events organized by my group CanACE (Canadian Advocates for Charter Equality), and I had photographed some of his protests. He was the one who called for a rally to be held on December 1, 2007 to protest illegal smoke shop activity at a shack that was selling cigarettes to the town's children, and he was the one who publicized it in local newspapers. When CanACE heard about it, we thought it sounded like a worthy protest, and decided to join in.

The OPP, of course, knew that a rally was scheduled to take place on that day. One of the first things the OPP did to prepare for it was try to figure out a way to get me arrested. As far as Fantino was concerned, Caledonia made both the OPP and McGuinty look bad and he knew that CanACE's involvement always brought media attention. If he could focus police attention on me – and at this stage, it is clear from court evidence I became aware of later, I had become Fantino's all-consuming obsession – he could keep the lid on how the media reported on Caledonia.

To that end, Fantino did his utmost to exploit the violence on December 1 by falsely and publicly blaming me – one of its victims – for it and ensuring I was thereafter banned from the town which, in turn, ensured the media would fall asleep and stop reporting on Caledonia. In one of the many emails he sent out leading up to that day he wrote:

> [...] I want every avenue explored by which we now can bring McHale into court seeking a Court Order to prevent him from continuing his agenda of inciting people to violence in Caledonia. We should be able to prove to the Court that McHale's forays into Caledonia have been planned and executed for purposes of breaching the peace which today also resulted in violence... To date, added policing costs are in the area of $500,000 solely attributed to McHale's forays into Caledonia. One final point, I don't want us to get side tracked by Crown lawyers on this. We need to be guided by the long established RPG [reasonable and probable grounds] criteria and not be constantly frustrated by timid Crowns who seem to only get charged up when they have a sure prospect of conviction.[1]

It is clear from this that Fantino saw me and CanACE's rule of law agenda, and not Natives and their ongoing criminality, as the biggest problem in Caledonia. The fact that Caledonia residents themselves were furious about the situation, and were themselves involved in protests, was more or less irrelevant to him. In Fantino's twisted view I was the pot-stirrer, the trouble-maker, the fellow who was interfering with the appeasement of Native protesters. What he wanted above all was to impose travel restrictions on me and members of my group so that we could not participate in future protests. The aim was not to convict me of a crime (I have yet to see an email written by a senior OPP officer indicating that police were looking for such a conviction), since that would require that I commit a crime which wasn't going to happen. And he didn't want his officers to listen to Crown attorneys (whose job it is to tell police when charges are likely to succeed in court). Rather, he was looking for something quick and dirty, something – anything – police could use to keep me out of town – permanently, if at all possible. So on November 16, 2007, well in advance of the scheduled December 1 rally, OPP Inspector Dave McLean ordered his officers[2] to prepare court papers in case police could come up with a charge that would stick.

December 1, 2007: A Day of Protest – and Violence

The beginning

It began quietly enough, with town residents, me and other CanACE members joining Doug Fleming near one of the Natives' illegal smoke shops. Soon enough, though, we became aware that there was something different, and more ominous, about police response to this rally. For one thing, there were far fewer police around for this event than were there at earlier (and, as it turned out, at later) rallies. It was standard OPP M.O. to send hundreds of officers to these events, and even, on occasion, to back them up with a helicopter, a police unit dressed in full riot gear, and an OPP video van to record any tumult. This time, however, the police presence was underwhelming, to say the least. No helicopter, no video van, no back up units dressed in riot gear. For that matter, there were not many police officers there at all. In fact, a scant 20 uniformed officers showed up with some supervisors. The situation was so unusual that even police at the scene thought it odd; by 8 a.m., two hours before the rally was scheduled to begin, some were writing in their notebooks that they were concerned that not nearly enough officers were there.

From the OPP's different approach to this event, one could easily conclude that senior brass wanted there to be trouble, violence that I and my group could be blamed for so that the public, disgusted by it all, would turn against us: Afterwards, some OPP officers privately admitted that that's how it looked to them.

At 10 a.m., we drove over to the rally site near the previously-destroyed hydro sub-station on Argyle Street, Caledonia's main thoroughfare and were supposed to march with Canadian flags to the smoke shop which was illegally built without permits on land controlled by Hydro One – which we began to do. By that time, though, Natives had shown up to meet us.

Violence flares – the assault on Mark Vandermaas

CanACE had participated in Caledonia rallies before, in none of which had there been any physical contact with Natives. All that changed in a big way on December 1, 2007. Five minutes after the Rally started, CanACE's Mark Vandermaas was swarmed by a group of Natives as he carried a Canadian flag down Argyle Street. One Native started chewing on Mark's flag, presumably as a way to tear it, as the others threatened him. The group shoved him around, and he fell to the ground. All this took place in plain view of the site commander OPP Sergeant Steve Sloan, who did nothing as it unfolded, and who ignored Mark and others when they tried to complain about it. Mark asked him to arrest the Natives who had assaulted him. Instead, he ordered Mark and the others to back off.

We know that's what happened because the entire chain of events was videotaped both by Natives and CanACE's Jeff Parkinson, whose filming skills once again proved to be invaluable. Sergeant Sloan was obviously unaware of the filming because what he records in his police statement isn't what the camera records him saying. I wonder, is it a criminal offence to make a false statement during a police investigation? Of course OPP officers are not going to record how they really treat non-Natives in Caledonia and they know the courts will automatically believe a police officer.

Sloan claimed, for example, that he saw Mark being pushed and shoved, and saw him "slipping to the ground," but that when Mark and the others approached him "demanding that the OPP arrest them [the Natives doing the pushing and shoving] for assault," he:

- told them "it didn't seem like an assault and was more of a consent thing" (whatever that means);
- called for the Emergency Response Team (He did? Then where the heck was it?);
- said they could complain to the local OPP detachment, but that "we [the OPP] weren't gonna proceed with it at this time." (That's pretty funny since it wasn't until 2012 that the OPP took any action on our complaints.)[3]

More violence, courtesy the Powless siblings, Camille, Clyde and Steve

At this stage, a trio of Mohawk siblings, Camille, Clyde and Steve Powless, took centre stage in the day's violent proceedings. (The Powless family owned illegal and very lucrative smoke shacks, so they had good reason to want to shut down a rally intended to bring this illegal activity to the public's attention. As well, Clyde Powless provided "Native Security," i.e. the muscle, for the DCE occupation.) Not long after the assault on Mark Vandermaas, Clyde Powless began taunting police, inviting them to fight him "man to man." He then threatened a female officer, shoving her with his chest. After that, he, unsuccessfully, tried to get something started with local resident and CanACE member Merlyn Kinrade, who was 72-years-old at the time.[4]

It was Camille Powless's turn next (Clyde wasn't done by a long shot). When she thought no one was looking, she came right up to me and screamed, "Don't you f***ing touch me" and then she pushed me.[5] Of course, I had done no such thing, it was pure 'street theatre' and it was all captured, from start to finish, by Jeff Parkinson. Now that Camille had made the accusation and all eyes were upon her, that was the signal for her brother Steve, owner of one of the illegal smoke shops, to jump me and punch my head. He did so again and again, whereupon two OPP officers pulled him off me and – wait for it – let him go.

So where was Clyde? Well, he had gone over to DCE to tell occupiers to pull the huge hydro tower they used to block Argyle street for weeks in 2006 across the highway. He returned fifteen minutes later, got out of his truck and screamed at the top of his lungs, "This is all on you, McHale." (You could say that Clyde, like OPP Commissioner Julian Fantino, was more than a little obsessed with me.) Still screaming, he walked right through the police line.[6] Waving to the crowd of Native protesters, he signalled them to come towards me and they started screaming, too. Then, Powless and the mob passed, unimpeded, through the police line.

Powless walked right up to me, with four OPP Officers standing no more than three feet away, and screamed, "F*** you, McHale, this is on you, McHale." One officer leaned in and said to me, "I think you should leave. Do you want to leave?" I said, "Yes." The officer said, "Whatever happens you just keep walking." As I tried to do just that, Powless made a move to grab me, but two OPP officers blocked his way. Since he couldn't get to me, Powless grabbed Officer Greg Moses and shook him.[7] Moses took hold of Powless who screamed, "Get your f***ing hands off me." Moses raised both hands and released him. Powless shoved Moses aside and strong-armed the next officer. Powless then broke through the barrier of officers and grabbed me around the neck from behind. Another Native took hold of my right arm and Lynda Powless (no relation to Clyde's family; she is the owner and editor of *Turtle Island News*) grabbed my left arm. Meanwhile another Native, Brian Skye, stood in front of me, punching me in the face. Clyde Powless was still behind me, punching me in the head. The attacks on me only encouraged the angry mob, which swarmed me, screaming "kill him, kill him" as they punched and kicked me to, and on, the ground. Doug Fleming – small, but tough and fearless – then tackled Clyde Powless to stop his attack on me.

After allowing this angry mob to walk through the police line in order to attack me the OPP did rush in, get me to my feet and lead me away. A *Hamilton Spectator* reporter captured the moment in an iconic picture that is included in *Helpless*. I walked away, bloodied, but unbowed, knowing that I had remained true to my commitment to Dr. King's methods by not responding with angry words or violence to the hate-filled rage of the Six Nations smoke shack supporters. A resident called for an ambulance that took me to the hospital. When the mob attacked me, an OPP officer grabbed our videographer Jeff Parkinson from behind, picked him up and threw him to the ground, rendering him unconscious. Police summoned an ambulance to take Jeff to the hospital and a Caledonia resident stayed with him until it arrived. He sustained head injuries that continue to plague him to this day. The OPP refused to admit that they had grabbed Jeff, but we had an eyewitness who saw it all. In addition, during sworn testimony, an OPP officer said that he, too, had seen an officer throw Jeff to the ground.

Meanwhile, back at Julian Fantino's OPP command post...

What was the OPP Commissioner doing as this flurry of activity was taking place? I would learn later, during the discovery phase of my prosecution for the charge Fantino's officers would eventually lay, that he was very busy sending emails. Lots of them. And so was his second in command, Deputy Commissioner Chris Lewis, the man who would go on to replace Fantino as OPP chief. In one of his first emails that day, sent just 20 minutes after the protest began, Fantino fumed, "At some point McHale has to go."[8] To which his #2, Chris Lewis, responded, "[Doug] Fleming too. Just sent a message to that very effect!"[9] Less than a minute later, Fantino emailed back, "If they get the opportunity they should go for it." Lewis replied, "I was careful to say 'soon as grounds are there'. They need a 'wake up call'." Fantino fired back, "Totally agree". (This and the information that follows in this section were revealed later on in court.)

Police officers at the scene did their share of emailing, too. They told their superiors exactly what was happening, as soon as it occurred. These emails, which went right up the chain of command, described, for instance, how such and such Native person had blocked the road with his truck and how, fifteen minutes later, someone else had moved his truck across the road. Emails coming down from on high, on the other hand, ignored what Natives were doing and focused exclusively on me. The Fantino and Lewis emails were all about how "McHale is blocking the road" or doing something else whether or not I was even doing what they claimed. At 12:30 p.m., for example, Deputy Commissioner Lewis emailed senior police brass to say, "I hope McHale was arrested!!!!!" (Please note that what I was doing was supposedly so bad that it earned five, count 'em, five exclamation marks.) At 1:00 p.m., Lewis sent an email that sounded just as angry, if not angrier: "If we aren't going to arrest the likes of McHale for blocking off the road on a Saturday before Christmas and causing total chaos that results in violence," he wrote, "we're going to lose all credibility."[10] It should be noted that at no time did I block the road, but they were not going to let facts get in their way.

Fantino received hourly updates about the rally from Inspector Dave McLean, who was the commander in Haldimand.[11] At 3:22 p.m., after the event was all over, Fantino issued an email that summed up events not as they were, but as he saw them. "Today," he wrote, "we had another flare-up in Caledonia spearheaded by McHale. As the event unfolded things turned ugly and some violence erupted. McHale and a few others continue to converge on Caledonia to basically create mischief. We had to call in resources to quell the aftermath of his nonsense once the occupiers began to retaliate by blocking off a public highway. All in all, but for McHale and his few supporters Caledonia is a relatively peaceful place..."[12]

A "relatively peaceful place," eh? Well, that would certainly come as news to many Caledonia townspeople who had watched Natives commit serious crimes for many months, ones that police refused to acknowledge or do anything about. And I highly doubt that, say, Sam Gaultieri, the Caledonia man who was building his daughter a home in a Caledonia subdivision, and who was attacked and almost killed by natives, sustaining permanent brain damage, would have described his neighbourhood as "peaceful." No, it seems clear that any "peacefulness" apparent in Caledonia existed solely in Commissioner Julian Fantino's mind, a function of his wishful thinking or delusions, or perhaps both.

But back to Fantino's emails: In his 3:22 p.m. email, the one in which he summed up the day's events, he wrote, "Today we had another flare-up in Caledonia spearheaded by McHale." An hour later, he and Lewis seized on the news of my non-existent "assault" on Camille Powless, thinking that that could be the "gotcha," and that at long last they would be able to charge me with a crime. In response to this "hidden gem" (the way a police officer described the purported assault in an email to his superiors),[13] a gleeful Fantino wrote: "Looks like McHale will be charged with assault." "Great," Chris Lewis chimed in. Fantino immediately called for a media release to be prepared blaming me and the other non-Natives for the violence. The release was being distributed as early as 5:40 p.m.[14] But even though the arrest order had gone out, police at the OPP Cayuga detachment had not yet heeded it, so Fantino had to hold off on making any announcement about my arrest. By the next day, he was so steamed about this state of affairs that he felt the need to take a "time out." As he wrote in an email to Chris Lewis, explaining why it had taken so long to respond to an email Lewis had sent him, "The reason I waited to get back to you was simply to cool off."

Not that he did. Fantino continued, apparently as hot and bothered as ever: "What are we doing in Caledonia?" he wrote, "We seem to be in an almost state of paralysis when it comes to proactively doing anything respecting McHale et al. If it isn't us being told what to do by feeble Crowns, it's our own lack of fire. It seems to me that we are reactive to the point that McHale is the orchestra leader while we are almost captive to his nonsense... Ahh, I can't believe this!!!!!"

After the Fleming Rally: The OPP Lays the Groundwork for My Arrest and Prosecution

Not to be outdone by his boss, Deputy Commissioner Chris Lewis wrote in an email: "I'm not comfortable that from a crime perspective we've been doing our best to be proactive in planning for such things as this [past] weekend. Incident Command, POU, media, roadblocks, etc., are always well coordinated, but the proactive thinking around taking out organizers and agitators like McHale just isn't there... Some of these guys should have been extracted yesterday in the early stages. McHale for one has release conditions that must have been breached very early on." Not so. I hadn't breached any release conditions because, up till then, police had not laid a single charge against me. The second highest-ranking police officer in Ontario was clueless about whether there were release conditions on me; exactly who was keeping these officers so badly misinformed?

The challenge now for the OPP was to change the perception of me in the eyes of the public and their own officers by charging me with a crime. To that end, and to speed the process forward, Inspector Bill Renton was assigned to lead the investigation against me. Renton knew how important it was for the OPP to find a charge – any charge, whether a conviction would occur or not. He knew it because OPP senior brass kept getting in touch with him, to let him know how crucial it was. (At one point during his investigation, Renton was ordered by Superintendent Ron Gentle to arrest me, an order supported by Deputy Commissioner Chris Lewis. Later on, the court would order Gentle and Lewis to face a criminal charge of obstructing justice because of this order).[15] Insp. Renton also knew it because in his media release issued after the Fleming Rally, Fantino had harped on the "interlopers" – meaning me and other CanACE members – who he falsely accused of being responsible for all the day's violence (never mentioning, of course, that there were plenty of "interlopers" on the Native side who had shown up in Caledonia from British Columbia, northern Ontario, Quebec and New York State). The release stated, "These incidents, where interlopers put their own personal agendas over those who are striving for a permanent and lasting resolution will not be tolerated."

(Some related and interesting facts about the "interlopers" issue: Fantino repeatedly told the public that non-Native "interlopers" had cost taxpayers $500,000 in extra policing for our protests. What he didn't mention was that this amount paled in comparison to what Native protesters were costing them. In 2006, at the height of Native violence in Caledonia (and prior to my activism there), the extra OPP policing cost taxpayers a whopping $2.6 million *per month.* In 2008, during those months I wasn't even in town, extra policing costs were over $800,000 a month. Ontario taxpayers should – but likely don't – know exactly how much they are out of pocket for policing Native protesters in Caledonia: a staggering $80 million.[16] Nor do taxpayers know the health care costs associated with treating 60 OPP officers, the victims of Native thugs, in hospital; some of these officers never returned to duty. Even these huge numbers seem small in comparison to the estimated $4.1 billion dollars in lost economic activity in the Haldimand Tract due to native lawlessness as stated in a report presented by Haldimand-Norfolk MPP Toby Barrett in 2008.[17] The reason Ontarians haven't been made aware of these numbers: it conflicted with the message of Fantino's propaganda.)

Haldimand Council reacted quickly and negatively to Fantino's "interlopers" media release and called a meeting to discuss its very different concerns. As outlined by Caledonia Councillor Craig Grice, they were:

> *The two-tier response in policing, the non-policing of 6th and 7th line, the failure of the OPP to respond to Dave, Dana and Dax being continuously harassed and threatened, the failure of the Federal and Provincial government to provide financial support for businesses and developers that experience occupations, that residents need confidence that their families are safe and that property values will not continue to decrease, the repeated by-law violations by Natives on provincially owned land and the need for the Council to replace the OPP with an alternative police force.*

These issues were not priorities for Fantino. And perhaps because of the tantalizing possibility of charging me with assault, nothing was moving fast enough for him. He said as much in an email he sent officers on the evening of December 2:

> *I believe that we are falling short on exploiting every possible proactive investigative strategy that could curtail the activities of McHale et al... Did we assign an arrest team dedicated to McHale if/when the opportunity presented itself to take him out? etc.? I believe you know where I'm coming from and when this 'post event' investigation is done, I trust we will not be relying on a Crown to tell us what RPG [reasonable and probable grounds] looks like. There has been far too much of that in the past. Our job is not to act only when there is an absolute likelihood of a conviction as often told by Crowns...*[18]

In other words Fantino's highest priority wasn't to ensure that a charge would stick in court. In fact, his top-of-mind concern was something considerably different:

I want us to take McHale to court to seek a Court Order to keep him out of Caledonia... And even if we are unsuccessful we will be able to publicly expose him for the mischief-maker that he is... I would like to see a chronological outline of events that we can draw upon to show a consistent pattern of activities intended to escalate conflict and confrontation that have now resulted in violence that can be directly attributed to McHale.

He wanted to use the courts, not for any crime I had committed, but as a public relations exercise to convince the public that I was a public menace. Even more revealingly he wrote:

I don't want us to get bogged down with legal nuances." (In court testimony later on he would not explain what he meant by "legal nuances," so we don't know if he was, say, telling his officers to overlook, or to ignore the law while preparing court paperwork against me.) We know what information needs to be pulled together to make the case why a Court Order is well justified as a way of preventing future violence in Caledonia. I would like to see such a brief asap following which I will deal with getting the matter on to a Judge.

So Commissioner Fantino, the highest-ranking police officer in the province, was personally going to see to it that a judge issued a Court Order barring me from going to Caledonia? That was his number one priority? Wasn't there, perhaps, some biker gang violence he could have been more concerned about? Any rapes, murders or organized crime shenanigans that were potentially more threatening to public safety than the sight of little old me toting a Canadian flag down a dusty road? That, from Fantino's standpoint, there didn't appear to be anything remotely as menacing as a flag-carrying McHale speaks to what I can't help but see as the OPP chief's bizarre, all-consuming obsession with me. (If I didn't know better, I might have thought that his name, a la Victor Hugo's *Les Miserables*, was Julian Javert.)

Insp. Bill Renton, who was in charge of the OPP's McHale investigation, wrote an email that gave Fantino and his crew hope that they could finally get me. The email reported that Lynda Powless (no relation to the Powless siblings), the owner of *Turtle Island News*, had come forward to say that she had seen me assault Camille Powless. Lynda claimed her TV crew had caught it in photos and on video, which she had promised to turn over to the OPP. She provided the names of the crew, along with the names of four other individuals who had supposedly seen the assault. One can only imagine how overjoyed Fantino, Lewis and other senior brass were when they learned that, not only had I supposedly assaulted Camille, but at least seven individuals were prepared to come forward to say they had seen it. How delighted Fantino and the gang must have been to know that, finally, they had a shot at nailing me for a real crime. (As opposed to all those make-believe crimes they'd wanted to pin on me over the years).

Alas for Fantino, that hope was short-lived. On December 3, OPP Deputy Commissioner Chris Lewis and Superintendent Ron Gentle sent an email in which he acknowledged that, while plenty of people had video showing me being assaulted by Clyde Powless, as yet no video had surfaced showing me assaulting Camille (there was an excellent reason for that, of course: no such assault had occurred).[19]

On December 4 I posted part of Jeff Parkinson's video[20] showing Camille Powless assaulting me, irrefutable proof that she had lied to police. His great instincts in deciding to film her as she first began walking purposefully towards me saved me from being charged – and likely convicted – of her bogus assault allegation.

The OPP charged Camille with public mischief for filing a false police report… eventually. In fact, it took them a leisurely three weeks to get around to it – two weeks after they arrested me. (A number of obvious questions arise here: Why did it take police so long to arrest Camille? And what about Lynda Powless's claim that she and others had seen me commit an assault? Who were these people? As for why Lynda was never charged with public mischief for making a false statement to police, that will become clear in a later chapter.)

Poor Julian Fantino. With all the video evidence that did – and did not – exist, it looked as though he was not going to be able to see me charged with anything. And, almost as upsetting for him, he learned that local MPP Toby Barrett had booked the media room at Queen's Park for December 4, so Caledonians and members of CanACE could expose OPP antics. Scrambling to counter such exposure, Fantino issued these orders:

> *ASAP, I want a canned strongly worded rebuttal to McHale's diatribe that sets out the following. During his self serving forays into Caledonia McHale has escalated the conflict, violence has resulted, and police officers have been injured in efforts to protect him and his followers and to keep the peace. OPP bring in police officers from other communities in Ontario policed by the OPP as well as assistance from neighbouring police services. [McHale] caused in excess of $500,000 in added policing costs to the taxpayers of Ontario. When he doesn't get his way he resorts to self serving verbal diatribes against the OPP and engages in frivolous law suits, the cost of which will also be downloaded on the taxpayers of Ontario.* [21]

Our media conference went ahead as scheduled on December 4.[22] Fantino made sure an OPP officer was there to record our every word. Two days later,

Fantino learned that the OPP had decided to lay a criminal charge of 'counselling mischief not committed' against me for allegedly telling Doug Fleming to block the road during the December 1 rally. The next day, December 7, 2007, police arrested me at my home.

Of course, Fantino truly wasn't concerned by the cost to taxpayers – after all, he was receiving an extra $80,000 bonus per year, and the police cost in Caledonia had reached $80 million. During the 30 months I was barred from Caledonia the police cost was an extra $800,000 per month, but Fantino never, even once, publicly targeted the Native protesters that were causing these expenses to taxpayers.[23]

Furthermore, the public should be aware that so-called Land Claim occupations are a big money maker for Native protesters. Time after time the provincial government invited to its negotiation tables the very protesters who assaulted police and residents, and paid them to "negotiate." Both Clyde Powless and Jesse Porter (the one who pulled the hydro tower across the road on Dec 1) received money from the McGuinty government. In one year alone Porter received $131,000. In three years he received over $300,000. Ex-Premier David Peterson negotiated a deal to give 297 acres of land to Six Nations in order to get Clyde Powless and others to remove a six-week blockade of the main road in Caledonia. Look at the list of names of Natives receiving money in 2006-2007 from the McGuinty government and you have the list of names of many of those directly involved in crimes committed in Caledonia. Your tax dollars at work.[24]

In Ontario, if you are a Native and block a road for weeks, the government will pay you to stop. If, however, you're a non-Native who merely walks down the same road carrying a Canadian Flag, you will be arrested. Racism is alive and well within the OPP and the McGuinty Liberal government.

Fantino's emails to officers often talked about us having an agenda to incite people. He would say similar things to reporters. Fantino was interviewed by AM640 radio host John Oakley in April 2008 (to respond to the news that Mark Vandermaas and I had filed complaints against him with the Ontario Human Rights Commission) and used similar language to what he had used when emailing his officers over a year and a half earlier. The email had stated that I had an "agenda of inciting people to violence" and that my rallies were "planned and executed for the purposes of breaching the peace." When he repeated almost those exact words on radio over a year later, Mark Vandermaas and I launched a defamation suit against him.[25] The suit was filed in July 2008 and took 2½ years. It was ultimately dismissed on the grounds that Fantino had also stated in the interview that he didn't know if we realized what we were doing. In the narrow context of our defamation suit, Fantino won, but in doing so he ended up exposing his own lies about our motives. Or rather, his own lawyer did!

In order to win the suit, Fantino's lawyer told the court: "The Plaintiffs have indeed, as you see from the evidence, never advocated violence, but through demonstrations, websites, media and court cases, hoped to draw public attention to the issues that concern them... not to provoke violence. The evidence is clear on the record that certainly was not the intention of these plaintiffs... I mean, by this point in time as you'd see in the evidence the plaintiffs have been active with their websites, with other demonstrations, trying to raise profile of these things. But, when given the opportunity to say their agenda is one of violence, [Fantino] didn't say that. And, of course, if he had that would be completely contrary to the evidence that Mr. McHale through all of his publications never made any kind of statements to that effect."[26]

So Fantino's lawyer told the court it was clear that Mark and I had no agenda to incite violence, that we wanted only to draw the public's attention to the issues. So why had Fantino said exactly the opposite to his officers? It's amazing that a small claims defamation lawsuit against Fantino that cost each of us $75 to file would result in him finally admitting the truth. Fantino's campaign to paint us as people with an agenda of inciting violence was pure propaganda. He had knowingly lied to both the public and his officers.

Fantino wasn't the only senior OPP figure who misled officers about the facts. On the scene in Caledonia during the Dec 1, 2007 riot starring the violent Powless siblings, Sgt. Phil Carter and Insp. Dave McLean had sent out hourly updates to top brass. Despite this information Chris Lewis sent an email next day in which he said, "Yesterday McHale's planned and so-called 'peaceful march' got ugly as you are aware. It appears that only one arrest was made [that being of a non-Native quietly drinking a coffee!][27] and now videos taken and interviews being conducted are being examined by investigators as to charges against organizers and agitators. It doesn't look like any of our uniformed officers on scene can give us enough evidence at this point as to what McHale... did or didn't do..." Lewis's account is remarkable for its bias and what he left out. Not one mention of the Native violence against us, or the fact that I had not responded to it. He, too, is either misinformed or deliberately misrepresenting the fact that CanACE (and I) had absolutely nothing to do with planning the protest. Lewis, seemingly, didn't care at all about the facts or the non-Native victims, only about supporting the Fantino party line of blaming Caledonia's troubles on us instead of those actually responsible.

The December 1, 2007 riot, combined with Fantino's obsession with stopping non-Native activism at the expense of the truth, would mark the beginning of 30 months of prosecution against me that would have profoundly negative consequences for the OPP's credibility, not to mention the two senior officers who would eventually face Obstructing Justice charges in connection with my case.

1   Fantino's emails, Dec. 1, 2007 3:22 p.m., Exhibit #38 from McHale's Preliminary Hearing. *
2   Insp. Dave McLean's email, Nov. 16, 2007 at 11:33 a.m. *
3   Sgt. Steve Sloan's police interview statement, Dec. 2, 2007. *
4   Jeff Parkinson's video, Dec. 1, 2007 - Clyde Powless confronting Merlyn Kinrade; also, Lisa Parent's video, Dec. 1, 2007 of Clyde Powless pushing and threatening female OPP officer. *
5   Jeff Parkinson's video, Dec. 1 ,2007 – Camille Powless walks up to Gary McHale and then pushes him as she screams out "Don't you F**king push me". *
6   *Turtle Island News* video, Dec. 1, 2007 – Clyde Powless leads a mob through police line and fights with OPP officers in order to attack Gary McHale. *
7   Ibid.
8   Fantino email to Deputy Commissioner Chris Lewis , Dec. 1, 2007, 10:20am: "at some point McHale has to go" (protest began at 10:00 a.m.). *
9   Lewis' email, Dec. 1, 2007 10:30 a.m. responding to Fantino's email. *
10 Chris Lewis' emails, Dec. 1, 2007 3:22 p.m., Exhibit #35 McHale's Preliminary Hearing. *
11 Hourly December 1, 2007 Protest Update provided by Insp. McLean to Commissioner Fantino *
12 Fantino's email, Dec. 1, 2007 3:22 p.m. *
13 OPP Officer Rick Barnum's email, Dec. 1, 2007 2:24 p.m. *
14 OPP Dave Ross' email (re: news release blaming McHale for smokeshack violence) to Fantino and Lewis, Dec 01/07, 5:40 p.m.
15 Email from Supt. Ron Gentle sent to Deputy Commissioner Chris Lewis, Dec. 3, 2007 at 9:37 p.m. *
16 Ontario Aboriginal Affairs' website provide regular updates regarding the costs related to the occupation in Caledonia. *
17 MPP Toby Barrett, Feb 22/10: How much are these land disputes costing us? ($4.1B). *
18 Fantino's email, Dec. 2, 2007 at 9:31 p.m. *
19 Email from Supt. Ron Gentle sent to Deputy Commissioner Chris Lewis, Dec. 3, 2007 at 9:37 p.m. *
20 Jeff Parkinson's video is available on-line. *
21 Fantino's email on Dec. 4, 2007 at 7:06 a.m. *
22 Our Queen's Park presentation is available on-line. *
23 Police cost documentation is provided on-line. *
24 Native protesters being paid is documented on-line. *
25 Statement of Claim (defamation), Feb. 2, 2009: *McHale & Vandermaas v. Fantino*. *
26 Transcripts of statements made by Chris Diana on behalf of Fantino. Nov. 18, 2010. *
27 VoiceofCanada.ca, Dec. 12, 2007: Kyle Hagan: arrested for 'Protesting While White.' *

   * See http://www.GaryMcHale.ca/book for additional information, links to documents, videos and photos

Chapter 6

Desperate Measures: A Long, Drawn Out Prosecution

Interloper. Outsider. Trouble maker. Rabble rouser. Enemy and undermin-er of *The Framework* (the OPP document sanctioning race-based policing while turning a blind eye to Native criminality, all in the name of maintaining peace and quiet at all costs). That's how I was viewed by the McGuinty govern-ment and Ontario Provincial Police chief Julian Fantino. And that's the reason they seized on me and my activism in Caledonia, and made it their priority to shut me down. As we have seen in the previous chapter, Fantino and the OPP thought they had proof that I had assaulted Camille Powless, a Native agita-tor, on December 1, 2007, the day of the Fleming Rally. When that failed to pan out, police had to come up with some other charge. And so they did. They arrested me on a criminal charge of "mischief." And even though the charge was ridiculous and the evidence supposedly substantiating it was, in a word, pathetic, it was enough to subject me to a prosecution/persecution that was to last for 30 long months which required me to appear in court on 50 separate occasions.

Ultimately, I was vindicated when the charge was dropped after a 15 day pre-liminary hearing without ever making it to trial or even a decision by the judge. Nonetheless, the message to me and other activists in Caledonia was loud and clear: Oppose the glaring injustices there at your own peril. If you insist on do-ing so, you, too, can count on losing at least two years of your life answering ridiculous charges in court in the hope that the process will so grind you down that you will run screaming from the scene, never to oppose the great Fantino and his forces again.

That was the idea, anyway, behind the mischief charge, and for the next 30 months the OPP and the Crown did their utmost to make the charge stick. That they failed to do so is a good indication that the charge and the evidence used to back it up were fatally flawed from the outset. It is also a testament to my own innate belief that truth and justice would prevail if I refused to be cowed by those who were using their positions of power in an abusive way.

The OPP Invent a Charge Just for Me and Back It Up With Questionable Evidence

Orders had gone out to arrest me within seven days of the December 1 rally, which meant that the OPP had to come up with something to charge me with – and fast. As discussed in Chapter 5, the whole idea was not necessarily to find a charge that would result in a criminal conviction (although, if they could find a charge that would have that effect, that would be all the better for them – and all the worse for me). The real aim was to keep me out of Caledonia and put an end to my rallies. The events that unfolded on December 1 during the Fleming Rally gave Fantino the opportunity he was looking for to put such a plan into effect.

Since an assault charge wasn't going to pan out now that Camille Powless's bit of street theatre had blown up in their faces, OPP investigators scrambled to find something else that would do the trick. In their haste, the only thing they could come up with was a criminal charge of "mischief." That charge was based on a 20-second piece of film in which I suggested that a road be blocked. Because it was so rushed, the charge was not well thought through, and ended up being changed not once, but twice. Finally, it became a criminal charge of "Counselling Mischief Not Committed," meaning that I had "counselled" someone to block a road, but since he had failed to heed my "counsel," no mischief was actually "committed."

'Not Committed' charges are laid for serious crimes such as conspiracy to commit a murder that never takes place. Such a charge for a minor offence, as the only charge against someone, is unique in Canadian law. It appears the charge is normally used against organized crime groups in conjunction with other charges like extortion and the unlawful possession of explosive substances and firearms. In a pre-trial conference held July 2, 2008 an experienced judge, who claimed to have done over 1200 pre-trials, questioned the Crown as to why it was even bringing the case to trial. The judge stated, "Court time in Hamilton is at a premium. We have an incredible number of crack-cocaine fueled crimes, violence, bank robberies, child sex assaults… a lot of murders, a lot of aggravated assaults. Very serious charges. […] Okay. You tell me what's so serious about this."[1]

You can be sure that, no matter how many times Native leaders in Caledonia call for roads to be blocked (as they often have), because of the double standard in Ontario policing (as articulated in *The Framework*), these leaders will never be hit with the McHale charge, no matter how many times the "mischief" they "counsel" is "committed." How many times on TV have you heard Native leaders calling for blockades of roads, etc., and yet, have you ever heard any of them being charged with counseling to commit a crime?

The Evidence: 20 Seconds of Video

As I've said, the sole piece of evidence against me was a 20 second video clip. Here's the background to it: At one point during the December 1 Fleming Rally, a Native used his truck to block Caledonia's main road. Seeing that police, in keeping with *The Framework*, had no intention of doing anything about it, Doug Fleming decided to park his truck in the middle of the road, too. Because Doug was not a Native and, therefore, was not seen by police as having the same rights that Natives did, he was told by an officer to move his truck. Doug said he would, but only if a member of OPP senior brass would come to where he was to discuss a number of serious issues; Caledonia residents had been making the same request, and had been ignored, throughout 2006-2007.

This is where those crucial 20 seconds come into play. At this point, I told Doug to keep his truck where it was until a senior OPP official arrived on the scene to discuss our concerns. (Hence the "counselling mischief.") I further suggested that he get others to park their vehicles there as well. (There was no danger in any of this, since traffic had already been brought to a standstill by the hundreds of people milling about on the road.)

My mischief-counselling – all 20 seconds of it – was captured on tape by a videographer working for Lynda Powless, owner of *Turtle Island News*. It was contained within an hour-long videotape of the Fleming rally. (Lynda, you will recall, had made a false statement to police claiming that she and seven others had seen me assault Camille Powless. More about Lynda later.)

The Bail Hearing: OPP Resort to Dubious "Evidence"– A Doctored Transcript of a Taped Conversation

The OPP did dredge up some other evidence which was unrelated to the charge and was even more questionable than the film clip and would never have been allowed to be used against me during a trial. However, the rules governing a bail hearing are not nearly as stringent, so the OPP was able to use this "evidence" – such as it was – to smear me, even though it amounted to hearsay and came from a dubious source. Again, the primary aim here was to find a way to keep me out of Caledonia. And if, to do that, the OPP had to tarnish my name and destroy my reputation, they were perfectly willing to do so, and there was little I could do to challenge it.

The source of the evidence used at the bail hearing was a partial transcript of an OPP interview with an odd character named Jon Sabin. A Native and a private investigator, Sabin lived in New York State. Sabin seemed to be immensely interested, though, in the goings on in the Caledonia area. He was being sued by Ken Hill, part owner of Grand River Enterprises (GRE), a local Six Nations cigarette manufacturer. Sabin claimed to have had information about GRE involvement in various illegal activities, including cigarette smuggling, and supposedly had the goods (bank records and police records) on Native protesters in Caledonia who had run afoul of the law in the U.S. Sabin claimed to be the source of a series of articles that had run in the *Hamilton Spectator* exposing the illegal Native cigarette trade.[2]

I didn't know Sabin very well when he approached me before my very first Caledonia rally on October 15, 2006 with two requests: First, he wanted me to deliver a speech he had written. In the speech, he named a number of Natives who he said were committing crimes. (Obviously, he hadn't read *The Framework* which, in effect, gave them permission to do so.) Next, he wanted me to give him $10,000, money he said would help pay for a lawsuit against GRE. I refused to turn over any money (not that I could have afforded to do so even if I wanted to), but did allow my wife to read his speech at the rally (after editing out unsuitable portions).

Sabin didn't take my refusal to give him money too well. Unbeknownst to me, in December of 2006, he taped one of our telephone conversations. I should have known that something wasn't right because Sabin seemed extremely worked up – somewhat unhinged, even. He said that things were about to boil over in Caledonia and claimed that Natives were going to riot, burn down houses and kill people, including me. I tried to calm him down. I told him that I was pretty sure his dire predictions wouldn't come to pass because the situation was too high-profile, the media were on the scene, and because of the large police presence there.

That's what I said. However, those words, in the sequence and context in which I spoke them, would be twisted into something drastically different after Sabin turned over the tape of our conversation to the OPP. Police got to work, and, via some creative editing and redacting, they reshaped the conversation into something else. The result of their handiwork: a transcript in which I appeared to be completely cavalier about the possibility of violence breaking out in Caledonia.

Even though the transcript was tainted from the outset because it had been blatantly tampered with, the OPP used it as the "ace up its sleeve" (even though, in reality, it was more like a Joker) because it supposedly proved that I wanted violence to break out in Caledonia, thereby giving the bail court the ammunition it needed to ban me from going there.

Now, here's where it gets weird – or should I say weirder? On December 28, 2006, two OPP officers paid Sabin a visit in New York. I don't know what was said during their discussion, which was tape recorded, portions of which were later used against me in my bail hearing. (On six occasions I wrote up a request asking the Crown to reveal the tapes' contents, and on six occasions my request was denied.) I do know that, the day after the OPP-Sabin conversation, Sabin launched a campaign on the Internet that aimed to destroy my name and reputation. He left comments on various blogs claiming we were associated with white supremacy. Pretending to be me he also set up a neo-Nazi website in my name, GaryMcHale.blogspot.com. Sabin did a great job making it appear that I was the website's creator. Using my name, he posted various items, including photos of me, my wife and Mark Vandermaas along with hate symbols – swastikas, pointy white hoods and the like. At the same time, Sabin claimed, on a number of other blogs, that he was working with the OPP to expose me.

As soon as I became aware of the phony hate site that had been set up in my name, I contacted York Regional Police. Following an investigation, the YRP confirmed that Sabin was behind it. Was Sabin working for the OPP? He says he was, and I have no reason not to believe him.

As for the taped OPP-Sabin conversation repeatedly denied me by the Crown Attorney: since my 30 month prosecution came to an abrupt end only days before my application to compel the OPP to release the tape was to be heard, thereby terminating my legal right to make such a demand, the tape's contents will likely remain forever shrouded in mystery. However, there had to be reasons why the OPP didn't want me to hear what their officers said to Sabin and why they didn't want the court to hear it either.

The Evidence: What I Discovered During The Disclosure Process And Why the OPP Wishes It Had Remained Hidden

If the charge against me was eventually dropped before making it to trial, it wasn't only because the evidence backing it up was, to vastly understate it, underwhelming. It was also because of what I was able to learn during the Disclosure phase of the process. Disclosure, for those unfamiliar with how the legal system operates in Canada, occurs early on in a criminal proceeding and continues until the trial, when the Crown must turn over all the evidence it has against the person who's been charged, whether or not it hinders the prosecution's case. The requirement to do so is enshrined in the landmark 1991 Supreme Court of Canada case of *R. v. Stinchcombe*. Neither the Crown nor the police are allowed to hide evidence that helps the defence. However, the defence is under no obligation to disclose anything: you are innocent until proven guilty and no one has to help the Crown convict them.

In practice, the Disclosure phase is often where the Crown does its utmost to try to prevent the defence from gaining access to information that will help its case. Few can afford to pay a lawyer enough to ensure they get all the evidence regarding a case because the process requires countless hours of document review, cross-checking police and witness notes for references to undisclosed evidence and other witnesses and, possibly, applications to the court to force full disclosure once that missing evidence is identified. Police hide evidence (though that's illegal) so that a Crown attorney can say truthfully in court that the Crown is unaware of any other information that could prove helpful to the defence (not knowing that police are keeping it hidden).

You might refer to it as the "too little information" tactic. On the other hand, the Crown can resort to a "too much information" tactic, too – inundating the defence with an enormous amount of material. That's certainly what happened to me, as the Crown dropped a mountain of information in my lap. It began with two huge volumes containing the photocopied notebooks of around 70 OPP officers, only a few of whom were involved directly in the December 1, 2007 rally. They gave me, for example, the notes of officers directing traffic kilometers away who never saw me, but not those of the officer who had ordered my arrest. The Crown provided me with two more volumes of documents and then repeatedly told the court that there was no further evidence that needed to be disclosed. By the time my case was over, however, the Crown would turn over an additional 20 volumes of evidence where much of the key information was contained in the last few volumes.

With the initial four volumes it seemed clear that the Crown was hoping I would be so daunted by the sheer volume of information that I would throw up my hands in despair. Instead, I took it as a challenge. And because I was acting as my own attorney, I did something that a real lawyer would never do (because a lawyer's time is so expensive that it is not cost-effective to do so): I pored over each and every page I was given. Like someone panning for gold in a vast river who squints at every shiny pebble, I examined every handwritten scrawl, every tiny and seemingly innocuous notation at the bottom of a page. In so doing, I was able to extract a few gold nuggets and this information, in turn, gave me clues as to where I should hunt for more. (The Crown, you probably won't be surprised to learn, objected whenever I asked for approval to see more material.) My biggest find was a short notation revealing that officers had been ordered to arrest me even *before* an investigation had started. That led me to an email written by Julian Fantino which showed that he had become involved in my case. That one email resulted in my uncovering what you might call the mother lode as the Court ordered Fantino to turn over all emails that he had written about me regarding December 1. Once Fantino's emails were disclosed, it was clear that many senior officers were directly involved in my arrest.

What I discovered thanks to Disclosure proved to be hugely embarrassing to the OPP. Thanks, especially, to the key evidence contained in the last two volumes, two of the OPP's top officers would face criminal charges, and give me the opportunity to possibly obtain even more evidence that could well prove direct interference from politicians within the McGuinty government. The Disclosure process also showed that there is often a glaring disconnect between how the OPP claims to operate, how it's *supposed* to operate, and the reality of how it actually functions. Here are some examples of the disconnect that became evident during the course of the prosecution, ones, I'm sure, the OPP wish had never come to light:

Claim: OPP officers on the ground in Caledonia assess the situation and, using their personal discretion, lay charges on the basis of their own assessment.

Reality: Most of the time it's a top-down affair as police on the ground are told what to do by superiors who are pulling the strings from another location.

If the claim were true, then, on December 1, the day of the Fleming Rally, police on the scene in Caledonia would have waited to see how events unfolded and, had they thought it necessary, would have laid charges based on what they had seen at the scene. It became evident, however, that, even before the rally, Julian Fantino was looking into ways to achieve his long-held goal of arresting me to obtain bail restrictions that could prevent me from going to Caledonia.

I'd call that a top-down effort, wouldn't you?

When no legitimate reason could be found to keep me away, the push was on by Fantino and his senior officers to find some charge they could pin on me. (Recall the email exchange mentioned in the previous chapter, the one in which Fantino asserted that "At some point McHale has to go" and his #2, Chris Lewis, said that I needed "a wakeup call.") After Fantino and his senior officers (who were not on the scene) were apprised of my run-in with Camille and Clyde Powless, OPP senior brass issued an order to arrest me for assault on December 1 before they had even had a chance to interview me or even investigate.[3]

Again, as top-down as it gets.

The reason I know about the December 1 arrest order is not because OPP senior brass came clean about it at the outset – why would they, when they knew that issuing such an order before they had a witness to the incident was a criminal offence? – but because in the Disclosure documents, I found a small notation in an OPP officer's notebook mentioning that an order had been issued. In court, Detective Sgt. Murray, my arresting officer, had the unenviable task of sticking to the OPP talking points – the blather about ordinary police officers on the scene exercising personal discretion to make arrests (ha!) while their superiors stayed out of it. He declared in court that he had no knowledge that an arrest order had been issued on December 1 or that two officers had been dispatched to find and arrest me on that date. "I never heard that order," he said when I questioned him about it in court.[4] Such a claim is more than a little difficult to swallow, given that Murray was the lead investigator in my case, and was working alongside Insp. Renton, his superior in charge of the overall investigation, as well as with the other officers who played a direct role in issuing and passing along the order. (Murray mentioned that he had spoken on December 1 with Supt. Ron Gentle and Supt. John Cain, the two senior officers who had ordered my arrest. Odd that, during the course of that discussion, the arrest order didn't come up.)

Sputtering and spinning, Murray further declared during questioning that if he had been aware of such an order, he would have ignored it, knowing that at no time was there sufficient evidence to warrant it.

As for officers being dispatched to arrest me on that day Murray said that on second thought he did recall "that there was some discussion about somebody having been sent out, but that never got completed. Or it was stopped." Funny that the two officers who went looking for me didn't seem to get that memo. In fact, they recorded the order in their notebooks. I wonder who got it wrong here – the officers, or their superiors? Or is Murray perhaps implying that these officers were exercising – now, what was that overused phrase again? – oh yes, their "personal discretion." This also established that Murray wasn't being completely truthful in his previous testimony about not hearing anything about officers being ordered to arrest me.

Claim: OPP investigators took their time after the December 1 rally, so that all the evidence could be collected and assessed in a professional manner, and so that the charge that was eventually laid would be the result of a thorough and unrushed analysis.

Reality: The post-December 1 investigation was rushed and chaotic; senior brass wanted me charged no matter what; and when investigators couldn't pin an assault charge on me they scrambled to find some other charge (hence the creative charge of "counseling mischief not committed").

Having disavowed knowledge of the December 1 arrest order, Murray said in court that, following the December 1 rally, he, as lead investigator, took his time, conducting an extensive and thorough probe. However, he tripped himself up when he let it slip that, upon his arrival in Caledonia, he could sense that there was a rush to arrest me; it was in the atmosphere at the police station. Once he said that, the door was open for me to ask about the atmosphere, and who had created it. Murray then tried to back track via some embarrassing verbal contortions. He said that, while there definitely was a rushed atmosphere, he could not explain what that meant. All of a sudden he couldn't recall any officer saying anything that contributed to the rushed atmosphere, or being privy to any orders, text messages or emails that would lead him to believe that there was a rush to charge me, and that it affected the atmosphere. Somehow it was just there. Like a gentle breeze (or some hot air) blowing in from some unknown source. (In fact, senior brass was texting and phoning to ensure I was charged, something Murray could not admit on the stand.)

In court, Inspector Renton, the man in charge of the overall investigation (and Murray's superior) concurred with that assessment. When asked about the email from Julian Fantino, instructing officers to go about "exploring every avenue" to find a charge to pin on me, Renton (who was also devoted to the "there's no top-down policing" narrative), said that he took that to mean he was to conduct a "thorough investigation. When I asked if he was told to wrap things up "as quickly as possible," he said, "Yes; they wanted it assigned and investigated immediately…However, my direction upon getting there is we'll take our time and we'll do all the investigation we have to, interview all the people, review all the videos, and we'll do that in as timely a manner as we can. But I certainly didn't rush out my investigation to, to that suggestion."[5]

The facts suggest otherwise. OPP top brass wanted the investigation wrapped up, with me arrested, by the weekend following the rally. Initially, there were high hopes that they could get me on an assault charge – hopes that, of course, the OPP wanted to keep hidden. Thus, Renton claimed that he "couldn't remember" receiving a call from Supt. Ron Gentle on December 3 instructing him to arrest me for assaulting Camille Powless. But the contents of the phone call – including Gentle's observation that I had a "long history as a public safety risk whereas Clyde Powless and Jesse Porter, another Native protester, were "non-instigators" and "mediators" who "assisted in crisis resolutions" – was right there in black and white, in Renton's meticulously-kept notes, and I was looking right at them!

When the assault charge didn't pan out, and with the deadline to arrest me for something fast approaching, another charge had to be found – and quickly. That's when the "mischief" charge was chosen. In testimony, Renton claimed that there was no rush, that it took him a good one to three hours ((downgraded to a mere 45 minutes after my questioning) to review the Criminal Code, talk to the Crown, look at the video clip, and mull it all over. It was only then that he decided that "mischief" it was to be. According to Insp. Renton, it was he and he alone, who came up with charge, in a leisurely, unrushed way. When I burst that bubble by pointing out that, during those totally laid back and unhurried 45 minutes he had had a conversation with senior OPP officials Det. Insp. Dave Cardwell and Supt. Ron Gentle, Renton insisted that he had made up his mind to go with "mischief" *before* that conversation, and that his discussion with his superiors had nothing to do with it. Suddenly, Renton was testifying that his supposedly "unrushed" investigation had actually lasted no more than a few minutes.

When asked to clarify this discrepancy with his earlier testimony, Renton, of course, could not. Clearly he didn't review the Criminal Code or consult with the Crown because the charge Renton issued against me had to be changed twice in the two weeks that followed.

Furthermore, within a few hours of my arrest on December 7, Chris Lewis sent out an email that summed up the OPP attitude toward investigating the events of December 1 – Lewis calls it the "McHale investigation" and states the following:

> *Hi Guys. This past week has been a challenge for all of us and even more so for our people, given the concerns and sensitivity around the McHale investigation... We've put extraordinary pressure on them to do what is right as quickly as possible, due to the political and public perception issues... The Commissioner and the Provincial Commanders need to know what is happening in a timely way... Then he [Fantino] asks questions of various commanders and gets conflicting info, which further frustrated him and hampers his ability to keep the DM [Deputy Minister] properly apprised...I realize that there may be disclosure issues as a result of such communications, but we'll deal with those hurdles as they arise.* [6]

This was the second reference I found regarding Fantino's communications with the Deputy Minister; on Dec 3, Commissioner Fantino emailed Lewis and others, saying he wanted a boardroom meeting for OPP brass before speaking to her.

Thanks to the "disclosure issues" we now know the investigation into the rally wasn't really about who committed the numerous crimes of the day, but was primarily a "McHale investigation" in which the Deputy Minister of Community Safety And Correctional Services, Deborah Newman, was directly involved. Senior brass was applying pressure on their officers because of both the political and public issues.

Claim: When OPP officers on the scene are assaulted, they can exercise "personal discretion" and call for the assaulter(s) to be arrested.

Reality: If Natives are behind the assault, OPP officers do not have discretion to lay a charge.

Here is a blatant example of just how far the OPP will go not to arrest Natives who assault their officers: during the December 1 rally, a Native protester drove his van, twice, into OPP Officer Paul McDonald. Here's how Officer McDonald recorded the incident in his own notebook, most of which was read out in court:

At 12:19 pm I arrived at the detail location and set up a dual police cruiser blockade at the intersection. We were asked to stop and prevent all vehicles from entering onto Argyle Street, and to divert them to another route into Caledonia.

At 1:25 pm a red van approached our blockade. I approached the vehicle and the driver and occupants looked to be of native descent, the driver said he was going through the blockade. I told him he would have to drive around to another location to get into Caledonia, and that I had orders not to let anyone through the intersection. The driver told me where to go and started forward. I positioned myself in front of the van and the driver continued to drive his vehicle into my legs. I placed my hand on his hood and told him to back up and that he just assaulted an officer. He then drove forward into my legs again. I then told him that if he made any more movement towards me with his vehicle I would pull my firearm out and use force if I had to. He then stopped the vehicle and placed it in park. His passenger jumped out and ran over to the smoke shop at Argyle Street and Highway 6. At this point the driver got out of the vehicle and started verbally abusing PC Sean Nichols and myself. A short time after the driver's passenger arrived with 10-13 other natives from the smoke shop and protest, they proceeded to bump and push us away from the van.

At 1:36 pm ART [Aboriginal Relationship Team] member [OPP Officer] Atkins arrived on scene and took the driver and the rest of the people away and told them. The extra members that arrived kept yelling back telling PC Nichols and myself to do our jobs or we would get hurt. The situation was then calmed down, and PC Nichols and myself [sic] returned to our cruisers. At 3:05 pm PC Nichols and myself [sic] were relieved from our post to return to Caledonia to meet with Command Staff. [7]

In court, Officer McDonald testified that he wanted the Native who hit him to be charged. I asked him specifically – because I wanted it to be crystal clear –

whether he was exercising his personal discretion when calling for the arrest, and in filing a report about the assault. He replied, "Yes."[8] Although other officers were on the scene, they too chose not to exercise their discretion to arrest. Neither did Sgt. Murray, the lead investigator of the OPP's rally probe who simply noted the assault in his notebook but failed to investigate this crime. In fact, Officer McDonald's "personal discretion" went exactly nowhere. Once the assaulters were released at the scene by OPP Officer Atkins (that's how *he* exercised *his* discretion) the matter was essentially dead. A year had passed between the time of the assault and the time I questioned Officer McDonald about it in court. In all that time, he had not been "debriefed." That is, no one had ever come to ask him about the assault or his report. And, of course, the Native who intentionally struck him with the van (never mind those who assaulted McDonald and his partner afterwards) was never charged. As we know, that's because he was a Native. Had a non-Native done the same thing, you can be certain that the outcome would have been completely different.

There were numerous assaults on OPP officers by Six Nations smoke shack supporters on Dec 1. Not one resulted in a charge.

Claim: OPP officers record facts in their notebooks in an unbiased way.

Reality: You must be joking. What officers choose to record – and, perhaps even more crucially, what they decide to omit – is highly selective, and conforms to the OPP's *Framework*.

After I was released from hospital on December 1, I went to the Unity Road command center in Caledonia with Mark Vandermaas and my wife, Christine: the OPP had rented an unused school on Unity Road to house all the extra officers needed to police the Natives' occupation in Caledonia. After police there refused to do anything about Clyde Powless's assault on me, we went to the Cayuga OPP detachment, where I met with Detective Sgt. John Murray. I wanted to know why police had not arrested Powless, who had assaulted and injured me. My plan was to pursue a private prosecution if, as I suspected, police refused to take action. As it turned out, that was the case. Police had no intention of arresting Powless; however, they had no such hesitation when it came to me. In fact, because of my supposed assault on Camille Powless, they had already been ordered to arrest me, something I didn't know at the time. Sgt. Murray merely told me there was an allegation. Murray then audiotaped my statement in which I twice named Clyde Powless as the man who had assaulted me, and said the reason I wanted to pursue a private prosecution was because I was so disgusted with the way Premier Dalton McGuinty and OPP Chief Julian Fantino were handling things in Caledonia and, therefore, had no faith in the OPP's willingness to lay the charge.

A year later, in court, Murray testified that I never named my attacker, referring to his notebook to support his claim. Murray's notebook contained various allegations against me including Insp. McLean's spurious claim that I had blocked the highway into town. His notebook recorded my statement against McGuinty and Fantino, but nothing about me naming Powless as my attacker. Murray testified that when I gave him my statement my shirt was ripped and bloodied and that my face had cuts, etc., but these details, too, were not in his notebook. It was only because the OPP audiotaped my statement to Murray that I had the proof I had identified Powless as my attacker. According to the transcript of the statement I gave on December 1, Murray assured me over and over again that he planned to conduct his investigation in a fair and professional way. He said he would not be swayed by politics or by the desires of his OPP superiors. His notebook methodology, however, says a lot about the biased way in which Murray actually conducted his investigation: an experienced detective made sure to record my views about the premier and OPP commissioner, but not the fact that I was injured and could identify my attacker. Were I asked to describe it, I'm afraid the words "fair" and "professional" would have to be, yes, omitted.

Another example of purposeful omission: when Officer Paul McDonald was twice assaulted by a Native who hit him with his van, no OPP officer, including McDonald, bothered to record the Native's name, his license plate number, or a description of his appearance. After all, that would be evidence of a crime, and would conflict with *The Framework*'s recommendation that crimes committed by Natives be ignored whenever possible.

Then again, it isn't always about what police choose to leave out; it can be about those "little extras" they decide to put in. Take the case of Sgt. Ben Gutenberg, for example. In his notebook, he recorded a number of things I allegedly said and did – things I have never said or done. For instance, he wrote in his notebook that I carried signs bearing certain messages, a claim that is contradicted by five different videos filmed by both Natives and non-Natives showing no such thing. "Fair" and "professional"? Not so much.

Claim: You can trust the OPP to be forthcoming with important evidence as required by Canadian law and by Supreme Court of Canada rulings.

Reality: The OPP will do what it can to stonewall the release of important evidence if it believes doing so is to its advantage, and if it thinks it can get away with it.

The *Stinchcombe* ruling required the Crown to provide me with Lynda Powless's videotaped statement to police. As mentioned earlier, Lynda, the owner of *Turtle Island News*, told police that she had seen me assault Camille Powless during the December 1 rally. She further claimed that seven others had seen it too and might be willing to come forward to say so.

In making that false statement, she committed a crime. So, too, did Camille, when she told police that I had assaulted her. So here we see two women, both of whom lied to police about the same incident (which never took place). Yet, only one of them – Camille – was ever charged by police. Why? And why did the OPP not disclose Lynda's statement to me?

Here's why: The OPP's charge against me, and the Crown's case, hinged solely on that 20 second clip of me telling Doug Fleming to leave his truck in the middle of the road, and encouraging him to ask others to do the same. That clip was part of an hour long videotape of the rally made by Lynda's employees for the *Turtle Island News*. If I knew about her statement to police, and how she had lied to them, it would likely cast doubt on the credibility of her video and, therefore, on the key piece of evidence contained within it. Had that occurred, I might have been spared the 30 month long prosecution, one that would have been financially ruinous had I not represented myself in court, and taxpayers would have been spared the million or so dollars it must have cost to prosecute me.

It took me two years and six written requests to persuade the Crown to turn over Lynda's statement to police. After that, the Crown declared it "an important piece of evidence," a piece of evidence the OPP would likely have sat on forever, if not for my persistence. (There's more to this story, as will soon be revealed.)

OPP Commissioner Julian Fantino Takes the Stand at my Preliminary hearing

During the course of my defence, I called Julian Fantino to the stand on three memorable occasions over the course of the 15 days of the preliminary hearing: Nov. 26, 2008, April 22, 2009 and April 28, 2009. Being grilled by the man he despised must have been excruciating. Although he had made many wild claims about me in various emails to his officers – emails designed to whip them up against me – under oath, suddenly, he couldn't remember anything about them. Nor could he recall the names of any officer injured due to any of my events. Nor could he describe a single example of how any officer got injured. Nor could he remember a single lawsuit he claimed was frivolous, or even whether I had filed any lawsuits.[9] In other words, he could remember nothing to support the wild allegations he had made.

And while Fantino and the OPP had repeatedly told the public that police do not treat Native protesters preferentially, his testimony revealed that he had many meetings with Native protesters, that they had his cell phone number and that the OPP "never" used negative terms to describe Native protesters. I got him to admit that he'd never met with a single non-Native protester, that no non-Native protesters had his cell phone number, and that he and other officers regularly used negative terms about non-Native protesters. It was disgraceful, with worse to come.

On December 6, Supt. Ron Gentle sent Fantino an email informing him that a criminal charge of mischief would be laid against me, and that Clyde Powless would be charged with "assault, assault PO, mischief," and a press release was prepared for his approval, listing those charges.[10] An hour later Fantino emailed back revisions to the press release – omitting the criminal "assault PO" [assault police officer] charge against Powless.[11] When I questioned his revisions, he couldn't explain why he had given such an order. In fact, he did everything he could to avoid admitting he had done so. When I asked him to read the charges for Powless listed in the email, he read them as "mischief, assault, and mischief," which was incorrect on two counts (dropping the assault "PO" and repeating the mischief charge).

When I asked him to read it again, he did so, very slowly – "Powless – assault, assault PO, mischief." I asked him what "assault PO" meant. He said, "I just know about the assault, I don't know what 'PO' means." In other words, Fantino, who had been a police officer since 1967, was claiming to be unaware of the commonly used short form for…police officer. (Over the years, I have told this anecdote to several police officers. Each time, they looked at me as though I had three heads. Obviously, "PO" does not mean, say, "Pink Orangutan." Or "Person Overboard." Or "Pickled Onion.") When I suggested to Fantino that it meant "assault police officer," he said, "Could be, yes." Then I asked, "You were informed that Clyde Powless was gonna be charged with assaulting a police officer, is that not true?" He replied, "It appears so, yes…" While he wanted no stone unturned to have me charged, even if his officers had to overlook "legal nuances" to make it happen[12], Fantino made the only "assault police" charge – out of the many that should have been laid against Native protesters that day – disappear with the stroke of a pen.

Fantino's atypical "top down," "hands-on" approach (usually, a police chief does not involve himself in the minutia of what's happening on the ground), an approach which often bypassed his own senior officers, resulted in confusion for at least one of them. Unaware that Fantino did not want Clyde Powless to be charged with assaulting a police officer and had taken it upon himself to get rid of the "assault PO" charge, Supt. John Cain, who was responsible for policing in Western Ontario (which includes Caledonia), swore out an affidavit about the same assault, the one Fantino had expunged. The affidavit noted that a Native man (Clyde Powless) was charged with assaulting an officer as a result of what happened on December 1, 2007. The officer Powless assaulted was under Cain's command. Now, either Cain believed that the charge had been, and should have been, laid, or he perjured himself in his affidavit.

Fantino's bully-micromanager style, combined with his reckless disregard for the truth, led to Fantino's campaign to smear and arrest me in order to keep me from speaking out about Caledonia, but it was about to leave him and his officers with egg on their faces.

The Prosecution Ends – or Should I Say Runs Out of Steam? – Abruptly

As I've said, the Crown's only piece of evidence against me was a 20 second video clip, part of an hour long documentary made by employees of Lynda Powless, owner of *Turtle Island News*. But there was another piece of evidence that, for two years, the OPP and Crown had sat on – Lynda Powless's statement to police. When, after a two year fight, I finally persuaded the Crown to let me see it, I saw for myself that Lynda Powless lied to police when she said she saw me assault Camille Powless at the December 1 rally. Her lies cast doubt on the veracity of her hour long documentary, the one containing that 20 second clip, the one she admitted in the taped police statement that she had had a hand in editing.

Had Lynda's statement to police been disclosed at the outset of the discovery process, it would have cast doubt on the only piece of evidence, the 20 second video clip, and, in all likelihood, I would have been spared the entire 30 month ordeal. As it was, the police statement was withheld, and the court proceedings went ahead. Now, two years in, and after an adjournment lasting several months, my preliminary hearing was set to start up again, only to come to a sudden and, might I say, a hilarious conclusion five days after it resumed.

Here's what happened: Because I had finally seen Lynda Powless's statement to police, and I knew she had lied in it, I asked the judge, on September 22, 2007, to allow me to question her about it. I wanted to cast doubt on the Crown's only piece of evidence, and wanted the court to go back and reconsider it in light of her lies. The judge ruled against me, I think because he was growing weary of a seemingly endless preliminary hearing arising from a charge that should never have been laid in the first place.

I had expected this ruling to come, and knew exactly what to do. I carefully prepared an application of Certiorari, that is, an application to overturn a judge's ruling. Such an application is rarely filed during a preliminary hearing (although one certainly has the right to do so). Because I wasn't a "real" lawyer, though, I didn't worry about what was usually done. So, unbeknownst to anyone, during the lunch hour, I filed the application with Superior Court, essentially asking it to overturn the judge's ruling because he had denied my right to call Lynda to testify in court. In so doing, I contended, the preliminary hearing could not be allowed to continue.

Just before court reconvened, I handed a copy of the application to the Crown attorney and delivered another copy to the judge's chambers. With the court

116

now in session, the judge asked the Crown attorney if he had received a copy of the application. He answered yes. The judge asked me whether I had already filed the application with Superior Court. I said yes. The judge then asked the Crown what he thought we should do. The Crown said that the document had little bearing on the case and that court should proceed and hear the remaining witnesses. What the Crown didn't know was I had done my homework. I knew that this judge had been hit with a Certiorari application at least once before, and would know exactly what it was. He did not disappoint. In fact, he seemed to enjoy the opportunity to bait the Crown attorney, thereby exposing his ignorance.

The judge repeated his question: what did the Crown attorney think the court should do? Once again the Crown said that the document had little bearing on the case and the hearing should continue with the remaining witnesses.

At this point the judge said, "This court is bound by the law. I have only received two of these as a judge and this is one of them. I am functus." Meaning that, by law, he had no further jurisdiction in the case until the Superior Court could rule on my application – essentially, he was now without authority. As if to underscore the point, he stopped paying attention to the court and began typing on his computer keyboard. After a while he glanced up and said, "Oh, by the way, Mr. McHale, you can leave any time you like." The Crown attorney's jaw seemed to drop to the floor. Obviously, he'd been completely blind-sided. (Because the Crown attorney was a "real" lawyer who knew the way things were usually done, he probably thought I was crazy to file my application when I did, and was certain the judge would disregard it. Also, I am sure he had never seen the accused in a criminal case being allowed to leave court without being bound to a future court date. When does that ever happen? Oh, it was tasty. Since it happened, I've replayed it in my mind a thousand times.) Nearly six months would pass before the Superior Court was ready to hear arguments re my right to question Lynda Powless about how she had edited the hour long videotape, the one containing that 20 second clip. (In her police statement, she admitted to the editing.) That hearing would never take place due to even more legal action outside the preliminary hearing that destroyed any remaining prospects the Crown had for a conviction, slim as they were.

Supt. Ron Gentle sent out an email on December 3, 2007 informing Lewis that while there was little evidence against me, they did have clear video evidence proving that Clyde Powless led the swarming attack that put me in the hospital. That posed a big problem for the OPP since, given their affinity for Native protesters (and in keeping with their beloved *Framework*), they would have preferred not to charge Clyde at all. Gentle referenced unnamed others who said it might be "counter-productive" to charge "Bullet" (Powless) although he himself disagreed. His solution – approved by Lewis in a follow-up email at 11:28 p.m. – was as follows: "We want to ensure when we arrest and charge Bullet we do the same with McHale to eliminate any of the usual issues."[13] What were those "issues"? Later emails would reveal that they included a fear of a backlash by Native protesters when they learned that one of their own had been charged but no charges had been laid against me.

Consider what had taken place between these two senior OPP officers: they had just together decided, at a time when they had no viable evidence against me, that I was to be criminally charged with…something, anything…in order to appease native radicals. I began a private prosecution of Lewis and Gentle and, on March 16, 2010, Justice of the Peace Lillian Ross accepted their emails as sufficient evidence to order the two to face criminal charges of Obstructing Justice.[14] I had recently succeeded, on December 31, 2009, in winning the two year legal battle to have Commissioner Fantino charged for illegally Influencing Municipal Officials over his 2007 email threat to Haldimand Council about me, so this now meant that the top three OPP officers in Ontario had all been charged under the Criminal Code in connection with Caledonia.

In light of the emails showing that Fantino was in contact with the Deputy Minister, I was also asking the court to order the OPP to turn over copies of all correspondence between them and the Deputy Minister's office, which I fully anticipated would eventually lead to the Minister and, possibly, to the Premier's office. The Crown refused my request and so, I was forced to submit an application to Superior Court for an order compelling them to give the material to me. As with my applications for orders to compel the Crown to turn over the tape of the OPP-Sabin interview, and to allow me to recall Lynda Powless to the stand, this request would never be heard. On April 21, 2010, just days before the court was to hear my arguments, and only four weeks after the charges of Obstructing Justice were issued against Lewis and Gentle, the Crown suddenly dropped its charge against me.[15] That rendered my requests to Superior Court null and void, and brought the whole 30-month ordeal to an end. It was over.

According to my log books, it took over 1,450 hours and $9,200 in out of pocket expenses to fight against the false charge the OPP had cooked up. Can you imagine how much a lawyer would have charged for my case? This is exactly what the government tried to accomplish, which was to create such a financial burden that I would plead guilty and then stop speaking out against injustice. Dozens of OPP officers and Crown lawyers were involved in this 30 month prosecution. Can you imagine the cost to taxpayers simply because Fantino ordered officers to find a way to charge me?

Was it worth it?

This was the first criminal charge against me in Caledonia and, as such, was exhausting and highly stressful, especially for Christine, who sat beside me in court every day helping in my defence as I was forced to take on the full weight of our judicial system alone, save for her. Technically, I faced up to five years in jail, although it would be highly unlikely to receive such a severe sentence if I was convicted. Some readers might ask if the fight was worth it; after all, the Crown, early on, offered me a deal that involved no jail time and no fine if I pleaded guilty. So what was the point of fighting?

First of all, it was important for me to refuse to plead guilty for the sake of convenience to a politically-motivated charge intended for no other purpose than to silence me. Had I pleaded guilty the government would have scored an enormous public relations victory in their quest to damage my credibility and effectiveness. But it goes much deeper. As with so many experiences during the fight for justice in Caledonia that others (especially those without a Christian viewpoint) might view as negative, I see the government's prosecution of this case – without a doubt – as one of the single greatest contributions to my/our mission against race-based policing for a number of reasons.

It enabled me to become privy to a mountain of evidence of yet more glaring examples of how far OPP officers were prepared to go to subvert the justice system for politically-correct ends, evidence that would otherwise have remained hidden; evidence that will be needed for any future official inquiry. This evidence proved conclusively that OPP Commissioner Julian Fantino and many other officers, along with at least one senior official in the McGuinty government, were involved in the "McHale investigation." As well, the evidence helped me convince the court that senior police officers should face criminal charges for interfering in the case; it showed how rotten the system is when it comes to political persecution cases such as those against non-Natives in Caledonia, and it showed how deeply Julian Fantino was implicated in the corruption.

This case, and those before it, provided me with a practical and invaluable legal education about our criminal justice system that has helped us send a powerful message to the police and government that we will not roll over and play dead, that they can expect a full-out legal battle when they cook up bogus charges against us, not to mention the negative media coverage of their antics. The OPP unwittingly helped me bring even more media spotlight on Caledonia's injustices thanks to the ongoing coverage of my case, and Fantino's failed prosecution against me was highlighted in Blatchford's bestselling *Helpless* for all to read.[16]

At a time in our history when people are losing faith in our system because of government willingness to appease potentially violent radicals, perhaps the greatest outcome from *R. v. McHale* is that the OPP helped me prove that an ordinary guy without money, a lawyer or legal training, could use the system, flawed as it is, to defend himself against the full weight of the state, and hold powerful government officials accountable at the same time.

1   *R v. McHale*, Judge's comments, July 02, 2008, transcripts p2. *
2   The *Hamilton Spectator*, Oct. 3, 2006, Tobacco Kings Part 2: Tobacco's billion-dollar empire. *
3   While Sgt. Murray was testifying there was never sufficient evidence to support issuing a charge of assault against me, OPP officer Tom Henry, who interviewed Camille Powless on Dec. 1, 2007, would write in his notebook that there were grounds to arrest me. In another officer's notebook it states that two officers were ordered to find me and arrest me. All this occurred within 5 hours after the rally was over. *
4   *R. v. McHale*, transcripts of Sgt. John Murray's testimony, Sept. 16, 2009, starting at page 64. *
5   *R. v. McHale*, transcripts of Insp. William Renton's testimony, Sept. 16, 2009, starting at page 1. *
6   Deputy Commissioner Chris Lewis' email, Dec. 7, 2007 11:41 a.m. sent to several senior OPP officers. *
7   OPP Paul McDonald's 'will say' statement, Dec. 1, 2007. *
8   *R. v. McHale*, Transcripts of Officer Paul McDonald's testimony, Nov. 25, 2008. *
9   *R. v. McHale*, Transcripts of Commissioner Fantino's testimony, Nov. 26, 2008, April 22, 28, 2009. *
10 Email to Supt. Ron Gentle, Dec. 6, 2007 at 4:23 p.m. *
11 Commissioner Fantino's email, Dec. 6, 2007 at 5:52 p.m. *
12 Commissioner Fantino's email, Dec. 2, 2007 at 9:31 p.m. telling officers not to get "bogged down with legal nuances" as they are to "exploit every possible proactive investigative strategy that could curtail the activities of McHale et al." *
13 Email from Supt. Ron Gentle sent to Deputy Commissioner Chris Lewis, Dec. 3, 2007 at 9:37 p.m. *
14 *Hamilton Spectator*, Daniel Nolan, March 16/10: McHale brings allegations against two more officers. *
15 *Globe & Mail*, Christie Blatchford, April 21/10: Charges stayed against relentless critic of Ontario Provincial Police in Caledonia occupation. *
16 Christie Blatchford, *Helpless: Caledonia's Nightmare of Fear And Anarchy, And How The Law Failed All Of Us*, Doubleday Canada, 2010. *

* See http://www.GaryMcHale.ca/book for additional information, links to documents, videos and photos

Chapter 7

Cop Assaulter Clyde Powless Gets a Sweetheart Deal

So far we have seen how Fantino and other senior OPP officers ordered their officers to focus all their resources on arresting me. In fact, before my arrest on December 7, Fantino was getting so frustrated by me not being charged with something that he had to take a time-out to cool off.[1]

In sharp contrast to the heavy-handed treatment I was receiving, the OPP and Crown were working to cover for the criminal behaviour of Native protesters. They focused their attention on us while ensuring Native protesters would not face justice in court or, if they did, that they received sweetheart deals.

OPP Encourage Criminal Charges against Non-Natives

Within hours of the December 1 rally the OPP were repeatedly calling Camille Powless to encourage her to file criminal charges against me. She was told that they would offer her brother a deal if she rushed into the OPP station to lay a charge. Once she complied with the OPP request it became an illegal act so the OPP was forced to charge her with public mischief because of the false allegation of assault she filed against me. In a courtroom in Welland, Ontario, Camille faced prosecution for her illegal behaviour. She testified that the OPP phoned her several times offering her brother a deal if she filed a charge against me.

What gave Camille's story some credibility is the fact that Insp. Renton had let slip in testimony that the OPP had "entered into negotiations with Clyde Powless for his arrest." The word negotiation implies a give and take. Exactly what was the OPP offering Powless in return for them arresting him? OPP emails showed they were concerned about the possible reaction from Natives to news of his arrest. Insp. Renton testified he didn't know the details of any deal with Powless but did state that Supt. John Cain had ordered negotiations with him.[2] Meanwhile, Fantino had ordered an arrest team be put together in order to take me out – in fact, the OPP sent an officer to stay throughout the night in his car outside my home in Richmond Hill to ensure the arrest team would know when I was home. They certainly didn't engage in any negotiations with me.

At the same time, the OPP repeatedly approached Tim Sywyk (a.k.a. 'Timmer') to encourage him to lay criminal charges against Ruth-Ann Chapman, a Caledonia resident who was present at the rally. During two separate visits the OPP wrote in their notebook that Timmer did not want to lay a charge. The OPP continued to contact him and, finally, he did file a charge of assault against Chapman.

Timmer was a staunch supporter of those responsible for the Caledonia lawlessness who prided himself in confronting people, swearing at or otherwise provoking them while filming any angry reaction so he could show how 'evil' the victim of his provocations was. Naturally, he edited his own role out of the tape. At the December 1 rally I was attacked twice in 15 minutes and each attack resulted in my being bloodied. Timmer, a registered nurse, responded as a vampire drawn to his victim. (Timmer worked at the Six Nations health centre and was disciplined by the College of Nurses of Ontario in 2007 for sexually abusing a patient.)[3] As my wife was crying due to me being injured, Timmer rushed up to her with his camera and started harassing her – waiting for a response. Chapman stepped in and told Timmer to stop and when he wouldn't she pushed his camera away resulting in the charge of assault against her.

While the OPP overlooked Clyde Powless assaulting at least a dozen officers throughout the rally (as well as assaults on other officers by other Native protesters) they were not about to overlook this minor incident and thus repeatedly asked Timmer to file a complaint.

OPP lay Charges that Demonstrate their Racial Bias

The OPP laid a Counselling Mischief charge against me for merely suggesting that someone pull their vehicle across the road which they didn't do. Clyde Powless ordered a hydro tower to be placed across the road where it did block the main road in Caledonia for 6 hours. He also instructed Native protesters to join him when he led them through the police line to attack me. Officers recorded in their notebooks that Clyde Powless instructed Native protesters to attack OPP officers and get their guns as he screamed at officers. Cst. Jeff Bird testified at my preliminary hearing that Powless and another woman were yelling, "Get the whites out of here!" and "Get their gun belts, you cops are ours."[4]

Based on this alone Powless had counselled people three separate times to commit criminal acts and twice these acts were carried out – the assault on me and blocking the road with the hydro tower.

However, the OPP didn't charge Powless with counselling to commit a crime. Powless was charged with mischief and the Crown prosecuted it as a summary offence – meaning he faced a maximum of 6 months in jail.

(Thinking the charge would never be laid, I intended to pursue my own prosecution, but the OPP avoided this embarrassment by charging Powless themselves, without any complaint filed by me. The fact that the video showing Powless assaulting me was being shown on television in all its incriminating detail may have had something to do with it.)

Meanwhile, I was charged with counselling and prosecuted as an indictable offence which meant I faced a maximum of 5 years in jail. Furthermore, the Crown stepped in and dropped the mischief charge against Powless within a few months while continuing to prosecute me for 30 months. So the person whose counselling resulted in real crimes being committed was let off the hook by both the OPP and the Crown's office in Cayuga.

Furthermore, the OPP had the court put travel restrictions on me banning me from Caledonia during the 30 months of my prosecution whereas there were no travel restrictions placed on the Native protesters – Clyde Powless, Steve Powless, Camille Powless and Brian Skye – who faced criminal charges. This fits exactly with what Fantino wanted to occur: for officers to use the court system to get travel restrictions on me and my supporters, but not on Native protesters.

Fantino Orders 'Assault Police Officer' Charge Dropped against Powless

While Powless had assaulted numerous officers at the December 1, 2007 rally the OPP were only going to lay just one 'Assault Police Officer' charge due to his assault on Officer Greg Moses. Other officers would record, either in their notebooks or in video statements, that Powless had assaulted them, but no one cared enough to even start an investigation into these assaults.

As we have seen in the previous chapter Fantino received a draft press release stating Clyde Powless was going to be charged with assaulting a police officer. Fantino's response was to send out an email ordering the charge not to be issued. Even one charge against a Native protester for attacking his officers was one too many.

Crown Attorney Intervenes to Prevent Charges against Powless

Even before the Clyde Powless case came to trial the Crown was intervening to ensure Powless didn't face true justice in court. After the OPP had refused to lay charges for the many crimes he committed I filed four charges as a private prosecutor against him: assaulting police officer Tracy Adams; being a member of a riot; 2 counts of obstructing police; and an assault causing bodily harm.

Crown Attorney David Foulds appeared at the pre-enquete (private prosecution hearing) to argue against the charges being issued, and was able to persuade the Justice of the Peace to go along with him. This was the same Crown lawyer who was prosecuting Clyde Powless for his assault against me and who would ensure he got a sweetheart deal as discussed below. Of course, there is a conflict of interest if, in one courtroom, David Foulds is arguing that Powless shouldn't be charged while in another court room he is prosecuting him.

I filed a Mandamus (Appeal) application to have Superior Court examine the evidence. During the hearing in front of Judge C.S. Glithero, Crown Lawyer Anne-Marie Carere attempted to persuade him not to issue the charges against Powless. She didn't present any legal argument why the charge should not be issued, she simply told the court that if the charges were issued, the Crown would withdraw them. While the Crown certainly did have the authority to do this, it wasn't a legal argument on whether charges should be issued.

While a pre-enquete is closed to the public, a Mandamus hearing, like all courts, is normally open to the public unless the Crown seeks a publication ban. Repeatedly, Carere attempted to read off the Crown's statement which explained to the court why they planned to drop all charges if the court issued them. Each time, I stopped her, informing the court that any statement read out by the Crown must be done while the public were in the courtroom. I wanted to ensure that, if the Crown was going to drop the charges against Powless, they were going to do it in open court in front of the public. The judge repeatedly asked Carere whether she wanted a publication ban but Carere kept avoiding this and simply tried to read her statement. After several interruptions by me the judge allowed the public into the courtroom, but instructed everyone there may be a publication ban at the end of the proceedings. Carere finally got to read off her statement and the judge ruled against a publication ban.

Judge Glithero disagreed with the Crown's argument about why the charges should not be issued and ordered Clyde Powless to face the additional charges: assaulting a police officer; being a member of a riot; obstructing a peace officer; and assault causing bodily harm.[5]

The Crown immediately dropped all charges. Part of the reason the charges were dropped was because, by this time, Powless had already pleaded guilty to assaulting me as part of a sweetheart deal with Crown lawyer David Foulds, and it is almost impossible to retry someone for related charges after a deal has been reached. One of the ways the OPP and Crown's office help Native protesters is simply to delay court cases until too much time has passed. Instead of the OPP laying the correct charges against Powless right at the outset, I was forced, as a private citizen, to file charges with the Crown who then intervened to obstruct the process. Two years had passed by the time the charges were issued, then the Crown dropped them, partially due to the time frame.

Fantino Meets with Powless to Discuss Helping in the Defence of Native Protesters

On May 29, 2008 *Turtle Island News* published a photo of Fantino laughing it up with Clyde Powless and Floyd Montour, another Native who was facing criminal charges. According to the newspaper, Jessie Porter (charged with blocking the road with the hydro tower on December 1, 2007) had called the meeting, the purpose of which was to get Six Nations chiefs' support in court regarding Porter's criminal trial. Fantino attended the meeting and spoke with three Natives who wanted his help with their own criminal cases. This is unheard-of behaviour by any police officer, let alone the force's own Commissioner.

(Floyd Montour and his wife, Ruby, led or participated in illegal occupations in Caledonia, Hagersville, Cayuga, Brantford and, more recently, at the Enbridge pumping station in Westover, Ontario.[6] I was able to convince a judge to issue nine charges of Extortion, Intimidation and Mischief against them in connection with their Cayuga lawlessness after a townhouse developer sought CanACE's help when the OPP refused to enforce the law. Families live in the homes today.)

With all his years of experience, Fantino cannot possibly have failed to appreciate how inappropriate it was for him to be even seen to be involved in helping in the defence of a criminal case. He had already made the "assault police officer" charge disappear against Clyde Powless, so what else did these Native protesters want from him? And, what deal did the OPP make with Powless to get Camille Powless to rush in and file charges against me?

Finally, can anyone imagine what justification Fantino could have to meet and work with someone he knew had assaulted his officers?

Fantino and Supt. John Cain Support Powless in Court

Fantino wasn't the only officer willing to help Clyde Powless. Although Supt. John Cain had sworn out an affidavit[7] that a Native protester had been charged with assaulting a police officer – referring to Powless – this didn't stop him from issuing a letter of support for Powless to be used by the Defence in court.[8] As we will see, Fantino would also come to the aid of Powless with his own statement to the court on his behalf.

Videos going back to 2006, prior to my involvement in Caledonia, showed Powless assaulting police officers. It is hard to imagine that Fantino and Cain did not know Powless had directly been involved in serious crimes in Caledonia. In the May 2006 Haldimand Council meeting with the OPP the mayor and councillors had informed the OPP that Powless had ordered the destruction of the power station which knocked out hydro for several days.

Instead of Powless being prosecuted for terrorism and for the numerous times he assaulted both police officers and residents, he received direct support from senior OPP officers. He was also receiving money directly from the Ontario government for being involved in so-called negotiation meetings.[9]

Fantino waited until December 4, 2008, the day before Powless would plead guilty in court, to email a letter of support blaming me (the victim of the assault) for the violence on December 1, 2007. He conveniently neglected to illuminate for the court how Powless had assaulted several officers that day. Instead he wrote:

> *Much of the conflict, confrontation and provocation has occurred during the times that Mr. Gary McHale and his followers have converged on Caledonia that invariably resulted in heightened tensions and conflict that has required an extraordinary deployment of police resources in our efforts to preserve the peace. Although I am not in a position to address the specific circumstances that resulted in criminal charges being brought against Mr. Powless, I do feel that but for Mr. McHale's mischief-making forays into Caledonia, the very volatile situation that exists there would not have escalated time and again as it has virtually every time Mr. McHale came to town.[10]*

This did not go down well in certain quarters. A few weeks later, Ken Hewitt (who would become Mayor in Haldimand in 2010) wrote Fantino a public letter in response to his public support of Clyde Powless:

> *Mr. Fantino, unlike you, I have been involved with the ongoing land claim in Caledonia from the time the OPP botched up the removal of protestors from privately owned land known as DCE. I saw with my own two eyes, protestors pushing back the OPP and breaking many laws as we know them. I saw the actions of men such as Clyde Powless exhibit very little concern for the people of Caledonia and much less concern for the misguided OPP officers on the street. Who were mostly un-prepared for the situations that they were put into...*
>
> *I was thoroughly offended when you came to meet with business leaders through the local Rotary, to listen to you lay blame on the citizens of Caledonia for injuries sustained by your police force in several confrontations. To hear you justify the lack of arrests made with respect to the many crimes committed by protestors around Caledonia. To hear*

you continue to use the phrase that you're only the 'meat between the sandwich' yet laws continue to be broken under your watch. These are laws that have nothing to do with land claims but your fear and your mismanagement has created a fear amongst your officers in knowing when to apply the law and when not to.

On several occasions, to hear you comment on the ongoing costs of policing in Caledonia, and that it is not related to your inability as Commissioner to contain the criminal elements that still continue to exist, but to lay blame on those that choose to challenge you and the government of Ontario, how you have let the community of Caledonia down in what I would call an abysmal failure of leadership.

Most of all, however it is this most recent letter of support that you submitted in defense of Clyde Powless, that has finally brought me to this point in writing you, along with petitioning for your resignation as Commissioner of what was once known as an exceptional police force, the OPP.

You were not there that day that Clyde Powless lead the protestors to block Argyle road for a month, you were not there when on his direction, the same road was dug up, you were not there when Clyde Powless and his associates specifically told me three days prior to the hydro station being destroyed, that should there be any resistance from the people of Caledonia, that the services such hydro or water could be targeted.

Instead, you allow your personal conflict with Gary McHale to cloud your judgement, and as such use your position of power to sway the courts in seeing Mr. Powless as a good man, a man who cares about his neighbours, and a man that would do everything to diffuse tense situations rather than the truth as already mentioned.

In football, they call this play the "Flim-Flam"; you have been played sir, and the confidence in your ability to lead and make the right decision without reservation is diminished...[11]

Hewitt would later draft a petition against Fantino which was signed by over 5,000 Haldimand County residents (from a community of only 40,000) and delivered to the Ontario Legislature by MPP Toby Barrett. The petition was signed by Barrett, MP Diane Finley and Caledonia Councillor Craig Grice, and stated:

Commissioner Julian Fantino has proven through his own court testimony and published documentation that he is no longer unbiased or neutral. Along with giving native leaders exclusive access to his personal cell number, he also uses his position to support native leaders in court against charges by his own police force... We, the undersigned, petition the Legislative Assembly of Ontario as follows: 1) To request the Premier of Ontario to immediately launch a public inquiry into the actions and decisions made by the Commissioner of the OPP Julian Fantino and impose his immediate suspension without pay and upon confirmation of the facts, his immediate resignation... [12]

Fantino disgraced himself by covering for the criminal actions of people because of their race. He also ordered officers to target others because of their race. Had he targeted Natives the same way, he would have been fired immediately. Instead, Premier McGuinty was publicly proud of how Fantino was handling Caledonia, which just happened to suit the Premier's political agenda.

The Crown Misleads the Court, Ensuring Powless Gets his Sweetheart Deal

So far, we had seen Fantino and the Crown stepping in to stop charges against Clyde Powless. We had seen him facing a less serious charge filed by the OPP and prosecuted by the Crown than the charge issued against me. We had seen Fantino attending a meeting with Powless and other native protesters facing charges that was called to help the defence and, we had seen senior officers writing letters to the court to help Powless.

All Powless needed now was for the Crown to ensure the judge didn't give a harsh sentence for assaulting me. In stepped David Foulds again, this time he was the Crown during Powless' guilty plea at trial. Whenever someone pleads guilty the court still hears a summary of the case in order for the court to understand the seriousness of the offence in order to determine sentencing. Foulds made a decision to ensure the court didn't have all the information needed to understand exactly what Powless had done.

During the sentencing hearing Foulds stopped his presentation three times to walk over to me to ask me what video contained which evidence. Clearly Foulds wasn't prepared to present the case before the court. In addition, I had written up a victim impact statement to make sure the judge would know two important points: First, Powless had crossed through the police line in order to lead the mob to attack me. Second, Powless had assaulted several officers in the process of fighting his way through to get at me.

The judge directly asked Foulds whether these points were true. While Foulds thought about how to reply, the defence lawyer told the court the police line wasn't established at the time Powless attacked me. Foulds told the court there was no evidence to support the fact that Powless had assaulted officers to get to me.

Both statements are a lie. Before the judge asked about this I had directly explained to Foulds which videos showed Powless crossing the police line and which video showed Powless assaulting the OPP to get to me. In fact, I told Foulds that the officers that were assaulted were sitting in the courtroom and could testify to being assaulted. However, Foulds refused to call the officers to testify but he did state to the judge, "Mr. McHale has asked to take the stand, but I will not be calling him." As my wife likes to say, "Clyde Powless had two defence lawyers in court during his trial – his own and the Crown."

On paper the OPP and Crown can tell the public how they charge and prosecute Native protesters but the facts remain that at each step in the justice system those who are entrusted to ensure equality before the law are the very ones institutionalizing racist policies that future generations will have to deal with.

Crown Attorney David Foulds was also the Crown involved in prosecuting Brian Skye, Steve Powless and Camille Powless – all of whom were charged with assaulting me. The trial of Skye and Steve Powless had to be adjourned due to Foulds' errors. As I watched him it became apparent that all these cases would be handled the same way as the Clyde Powless case, so, I wrote Alexandra Paparella, Acting Director of Crown Operations, to try to ensure that Foulds would never be allowed to handle any case where I was the victim:

> Ms. Paparella your office had a duty to ensure the proper Administration of Justice which includes the whole process from pre-enquette to trial. I ask that you request the OPP to launch a criminal investigation into the actions of Mr. Foulds on the charge of Obstructing Justice. Mr. Foulds has directly interfered with two pre-enquettes, failed to present the evidence in court regarding Clyde Powless, failed to administrate the above case [Brian Skye and Steve Powless assault trial] which may directly result in two cases being thrown out. Failing this you should remove Mr. Foulds from his position until an investigation can be done. In short, your office needs to demonstrate that Mr. Foulds' actions are not condoned by your office. I ask that you provide me with a reply to my request.

As far as I know no police investigation was ever started but I did receive a letter from Paparella which supported Foulds, however, he was immediately removed from all cases involving me – I never saw him again.

Our justice system was completely reversed: those committing the crimes had the system working to protect them while those who believed in the rule of law and equality were being viciously targeted with the full weight of the state. Not only were Native lawbreakers getting the sweetheart treatment from our justice system, they and those sworn to protect the innocent from them were laughing – literally – all the way to the bank.

1   Julian Fantino's email to Deputy Commissioner Chris Lewis, Dec. 2, 2007 at 2:19 p.m. *

2   Transcripts of Insp. William Renton's testimony at Gary McHale's preliminary hearing, Nov. 16, 2009. see pg. 45 line 26-28 and pg. 48 line 17-23. *

3   College of Nurses of Ontario, *Discipline Committee Results of Proceeding* (*vs. Timothy Sywyk*), heard Jan 8-May 25, 2007. *

4   Ontario Court of Justice transcripts, OPP Constable Jeffrey Bird, testimony April 24/09, p. 36. *

5   Transcripts of Superior Court Mandamus Applicant, March 25, 2009. *

6   Various photos, video and news stories are available on-line. *

7   Affidavit of OPP Supt. John Cain, Dec. 14, 2007. *

8   Court documents show the Crown withdrew the mischief charge after OPP Supt. John Cain wrote the Crown a letter supporting Clyde Powless and Jesse Porter. Commissioner Fantino's letter supporting Clyde Powless was sent to the defence lawyer a week before Powless' trial was to begin. *

9   Throughout 2007 and 2008 *Turtle Island News* reported that both Clyde Powless and Jesse Porter received money for being part of the negotiations that Ontario held with Six Nations. Porter received $300,000 in two years.

10 OPP Commissioner Julian Fantino email to Clyde Powless lawyer, Joseph Di Luca, Dec. 04, 2008. *

11 Open letter to OPP Commissioner Fantino from Caledonia resident Ken Hewitt who is now Mayor of Haldimand County. *

12 Residents' petition for inquiry into OPP: *Dunnville Chronicle*, Jan. 17, 2009: Petition asks for inquiry into Fantino and OPP. *

* See http://www.GaryMcHale.ca/book for additional information, links to documents, videos and photos

Chapter 8

"Cashedonia": A Town Where Officers Get Rich

We should never forget that it is the rank and file officers who enforce the racist policies on the residents of Caledonia. While it is the sworn duty of every officer to assist victims of crime and to prevent criminal offences, each one decides for themselves whether they are willing to watch innocent people being victimized because it is politically-incorrect to stop Native protesters from committing crimes. Each OPP officer takes the following Oath of Office; each should be held to account for refusing to uphold this oath:

> I solemnly affirm that I will be loyal to Her Majesty the Queen and to Canada, and that I will uphold the Constitution of Canada and that I will, to the best of my ability, preserve the peace, prevent offences and discharge my other duties as a Commissioned Officer, faithfully, impartially and according to law.[1]

Officers swear to uphold the Constitution of Canada; the Charter of Rights and Freedoms is Section 1 of the Constitution. Thus, officers swear to uphold the Charter rights and freedoms of all Canadians, not certain ones at certain times. Section 15 of the Charter states unequivocally: "Every individual is equal before and under the law and has the right to the equal protection and equal benefit of the law without discrimination and, in particular, without discrimination based on race, national or ethnic origin, colour, religion, sex, age or mental or physical disability." That being so, it is hard to see how any officer who has spent any time in Caledonia over the past seven years can honestly believe they have satisfied the Charter's requirements to provide "equal protection and equal benefit of the law" by consistently favouring one group of people – the Natives – over another group of Canadians – the non-Native residents.

Please note that the Oath of Office doesn't say that officers must follow orders from their superiors. Officers commit, as individuals, to uphold the Constitution, preserve the peace and prevent crimes. Preserving the peace cannot possibly mean standing by and watching crimes being committed. Preserving the peace is directly connected to "preventing offences," which is critical to preserving the peace.

The Ontario Police Services Act is legally binding on all officers in Ontario. According to the Act, officers' duties include (my emphasis):

(a) preserving the peace; (b) **preventing crimes** and other offences and providing assistance and encouragement to other persons in their prevention; (c) **assisting victims of crime**; (d) **apprehending criminals** and other offenders and others who may lawfully be taken into custody; (e) **laying charges** and participating in prosecutions; (f) executing warrants that are to be executed by police officers and performing related duties; (g) performing the **lawful** duties that the chief of police assigns...[2]

While OPP officers in Caledonia repeatedly say they are just trying to preserve the peace, the Police Service Act binds each of them to do more than just stand around. They are legally required to "prevent crimes" and to "assist victims" while they "apprehend criminals" and "lay charges," so they can "participate in the prosecution" of those who violate the law. The Police Services Act doesn't bind the officer to blindly follow orders. They are obligated to perform "lawful" duties assigned to them. That gives them the latitude to decide for themselves whether or not an order is lawful. There is no legal defence for an officer to state, "I had no choice. I was only following orders." That defence lost all credibility when Nazi officials were tried in Nuremburg at the end of the Second World War. Since then, we have expected our military and police officers not to blindly obey when ordered to do something they know to be morally or legally wrong.

Is it legal – and further, would it be right – to order officers to stand by and watch white people attack blacks, or Christians attack Jews? If any officer who has served in Caledonia can honestly say that such an order would be legal or right, then I suppose I could see how they could think that it's okay for Natives to victimize non-Natives. However, I doubt that there is a single officer willing to say so.

This book would have to be at least 1,000 pages long in order to include all the actions – and inaction – of all the officers involved. History must record that those in charge, Commissioners Boniface, Fantino and Lewis, weren't the only ones who made decisions that corrupted the justice system. Each individual officer also played a role in creating and justifying a two-tiered system of justice.

Police officers are duty-bound to resist and expose policies and practices that corrupt the justice system. RCMP Sgt. Bob Stenhouse did just that when he blew the whistle on police response to organized crime. After then-Chief of the York Regional Police, Julian Fantino, worked to have him fired for speaking out, the court sided with Stenhouse. In its 2004 ruling ordering his reinstatement to the RCMP, the Federal Court of Canada declared:

> *The freedom of a public servant, including a police officer, to speak out against the interests of his/her employer or supervisor about an illegal act or an unsafe practice or policy is protected in the common law and the Charter of Rights and Freedoms and is commonly called the "whistleblower" defence.... the Supreme Court of Canada has established the bounds of permissible public criticism of government policies by public service employees. Chief Justice Dickson (as he then was), at page 470 of that decision, identified two situations where freedom of expression prevails over the duty of loyalty, namely, where the government is engaged in illegal acts, or if its policies jeopardize the life, health, or safety of the public... Where a matter is of legitimate public concern requiring a public debate, the duty of loyalty cannot be absolute to the extent of preventing public disclosure by a government official. The common law duty of loyalty does not impose unquestioning silence."[3]*

Has government and OPP policy in Caledonia jeopardized the life, health or safety of the public? Any honest assessment would have to answer "yes." Yet, as of this writing, to the best of my knowledge, not one OPP officer refused to obey the orders they were given in Caledonia, and not one has voluntarily come forward to publicly defend the Charter right of non-Natives, including the right not to be attacked. In 2007, Cst. Jeff Bird became the first officer, under my subpoena, to confirm the existence of racial policing under oath,[5] but it wasn't until 2010, when *Helpless* was released (four and a half years after the lawlessness began), that any OPP officer publicly condemned the force's policing policy as it related to non-Native members of the public.

People wonder why officers were so compliant. There is no doubt that any whistle-blowing OPP officer would have been persecuted by the brass (this should not have prevented them from doing the right thing), however, there is another reason why officers might have decided to remain silent and why they would not want to blow the whistle on policies which, clearly, were racist. It is because OPP officers who served in Caledonia were very well paid. So well paid, in fact, that, by mid-2006, they took to calling Caledonia "Cashedonia."

All OPP officers are employed by Ontario's Ministry of Community Safety and Correctional Services (which also pays jail guards and various bureaucrats). In 2005, that ministry's "sunshine list" (of employees earning over $100,000 annually) included 669 names for a total of $79 million. Those figures would nearly double in one year. In 2006, the same ministry had 1,357 employees making over $100,000 for a total of $155 million – that is, a 106% increase in "sunshine" membership in one year, and an extra $76 million. As of 2012 the ministry listed 3,834 employees making over $100,000, for a total of $437 million in additional payouts.[6]

Before the issues in Caledonia started in February 2006, OPP Commissioner Gwen Boniface was paid $185,906 which then jumped to $220,378. Under fire for her handling of Caledonia, Boniface fled Canada in 2006 to get a job in Ireland in the middle of her contract which had been renewed right after the occupation started.[7] She was suddenly given $326,210.

The next year (2007), Julian Fantino earned $250,047 in the same post (a 35% increase over Boniface's pre-Caledonia salary and a 42% bump up from what he'd earned the previous year as Ontario Commissioner of Emergency Management – $176,240. By 2008, Fantino was being paid $265,776, but his successor Chris Lewis would not be so fortunate. As OPP Commissioner, Lewis' salary reverted to Boniface-era levels ($200,191 in 2011, his first full year in the post), showing that the job of OPP Commissioner doesn't normally pay a quarter of a million dollars. In 2006 Fantino was only the OPP Commissioner for 2 months (November and December) but received $250,047. So, why was Fantino earning a premium for the years he was involved in Caledonia and why was Boniface paid over $300,000 when she broke her contract to go to Ireland?

Karl Walsh became president of the OPP Association that year, making it onto to the sunshine list at $141,947, meaning that he received, at minimum, a 42% increase in salary. (Is this why, after his initial burst of candor about "two tier justice" in how his officers were ordered to dress,[8] that he fell silent on his sworn duty to expose any policies that threatened the safety of the public? Paradoxically, Walsh was paid not by the Association's membership but by the very ministry he was representing his members against.)

It may surprise you to learn how many front line officers suddenly joined the Ontario government's sunshine list as well. Those making less than $100,000 in 2005 saw their salaries jump to between $120,000 and $140,000 the next year. A lot of officers have made an extra $20,000 to $40,000 every year because of Caledonia. The gravy train had arrived in the station, whistles blowing! And don't think the public didn't notice. I started receiving emails from people across Ontario upset because an officer they knew, flush with all that extra "Cashedonia" money, was suddenly remodelling their kitchen or building a new deck.

An extra $20-40,000 annually for seven years, it would appear, is just about the right amount you need to buy submission and silence. The fact that they were duty-bound to uphold the Constitution and blow the whistle on faulty policies did not seem to bother these officers enough to act, even though we know that a lot of them were privately very disturbed about what was going on. Nor were their consciences pricked because they knew that this was blood money – literally: not only were non-Natives being arrested for non-crimes such as wanting to raise a Canadian flag, law-abiding people were being battered, bloodied and sent to hospital as a direct result of OPP policing. Non-Natives weren't the only victims: at least two Native women were raped on the un-policed DCE, in addition to the various assaults and gun violence committed against other native victims.[9]

In Caledonia the policing cost is normally approximately $5 million per year, however, according to the McGuinty government, policing costs increased by $50 million in the 18 months beginning in February 2006. The $50 million is most likely a low number considering how McGuinty liked to low-ball expenses (i.e. gas power plant cancellations during the 2012 election). Only the individuals involved know the true extent to which pay raises influenced their actions, but you can pay a lot of officers to keep silent with $50 million.

I had heard about the "Cashedonia" tag, but it wasn't until after the December 1, 2007 smokeshack riot that I would get (thanks to Disclosure) official proof, in the form of an audio recording, that officers were using it. After Clyde Powless led the angry mob that swarmed and attacked me, the OPP radioed for backup from the Town of Simcoe, Burlington and other near-by areas. The dispatcher told officers to go to "Cashedonia," and no one questioned where that was.[10]

Other key OPP players in Caledonia

As of this writing, CanACE legal work has convinced the courts to order criminal charges against the following officers: Commissioner Julian Fantino; Deputy Commissioner Chris Lewis; Supt. Ron Gentle; Detective Sergeant Rick Fraracci; and Constable Christopher Galeazza. Each time, however, the Crown stepped in and all charges were immediately dropped.

What follows is a list of only a few of the other OPP officers who played a role in Caledonia. Many of them observed crimes being committed and did nothing. Some were very pro-active in targeting non-Natives. Some were outright stupid and/or they blindly followed their superiors' illegal orders. Some of them lived in Caledonia or in Haldimand County, and watched their own neighbours being victimized. And yet, some of these officers are also the nicest people you will ever meet, which is why it is so difficult for a lot of people to blame individual officers for what happened.

Sergeant Ben Gutenberg

On December 16, 2006, Sergeant Gutenberg was brave enough to question what authority the OPP had to hold me in jail overnight.[11] Unfortunately, in December 2011, he was not brave enough to disobey an order to arrest eight non-Natives – the 'Caledonia 8'[12] – one of whom was me, for supposedly trespassing on a county road. As an experienced officer he knew it was perfectly legal for people to walk down a public road or sidewalk, not an act of "trespassing."

Here's what happened: On December 3, 2011, we walked on Surrey Street, which leads into the DCE sub-division. I knew we were well within our rights to do so because, more than a month before, I took the time to pull all the land title deeds in the area so that I knew exactly which property was owned by Dalton McGuinty (i.e. by the province) and which property belonged to Haldimand County. I also wanted to know whether the roads on DCE had been transferred to the county, and found that they had been. (In December 2005, two months before the beginning of the illegal occupation on DCE, the developer transferred the roads to Haldimand County. They were never purchased by McGuinty's government.)

As such, McGuinty did not have the authority to order the OPP to stop us from walking on property that the Ontario government didn't even own. I would argue that the government never has the authority to segregate sections of Ontario based on one's race, skin colour, etc. but, beyond that, it was quite clear the OPP had no authority to prevent citizens from using a public road. (It wasn't until February 2013 that an OPP official testified in court that the roads were, in fact, county roads that could be legally used by the public.)[13] And, even if the Ontario government does own the road (as it owns the 401, for example), police cannot stop citizens from using it. Imagine if the OPP obeyed orders that prevented certain classes of people from driving on the highway 401! British Common Law is clear that roads are open to all. A key point of the Caledonia Class Action lawsuit was that the OPP failed to keep the roads open for public use. By law, the police cannot shut down any road for more than two days without a special motion being passed by the local municipality.

That day in 2011, when Gutenberg stopped me on Surrey Street and ordered me to leave, I asked him, "Can you tell me who owns the property I am standing on?" Gutenberg refused to answer and ordered my arrest for trespassing. My seven non-Native companions (Merlyn Kinrade, Bonnie Stephens, Mark Vandermaas, Jeff Parkinson, Randy Fleming, Doug Fleming, and Jack Van Halteren) then lined up, one at a time, to take their turn refusing to leave so they, too, could be arrested. At no time did he order any Native protesters to leave the area. After being handcuffed, taken to the police station and receiving a trespassing ticket, I returned to Surrey Street and handed Gutenberg the legal paperwork I had showing exactly who owned the road: the county, not the province.

Instead of respecting the legal title deeds to the property, Gutenberg rejected them outright. He told me that if I walked on the street again I would again be arrested and would be held in jail overnight to face bail court in the morning.

My conclusion: when officers follow orders blindly – especially after being given proof that their orders are illegal – it is evident that they have become robots and that all discretionary ability has been programmed out of them. Maybe Gutenberg lacked the courage to disobey illegal orders. Maybe he was earning a lot of overtime pay, and was thus disinclined to do anything to put an end to it. Only Gutenberg can tell the public and his neighbours why he chose to disregard the evidence and blindly follow orders from above. Ironically, Ben Gutenberg would testify, as a Crown witness on July 3, 2013, that the roads on DCE were open to the public – the very thing the legal title deeds proved if he had only read them.

The upshot of it all: the Crown was forced to withdraw all the illegal tickets issued to the Caledonia 8, telling the court there was "no reasonable prospect for conviction," and offering by way of excuse that the "OPP has a difficult job to do." And, so…police did not have to accept responsibility for arresting law-abiding Canadian citizens – again.

Detective Sergeant John Murray

Officer Murray has appeared in a previous chapter. To recap: he's the OPP officer who promised to investigate crimes and lay charges, should the evidence support it, relating to the smoke shack rally/riot of December 1, 2007. Murray ended up turning a blind eye to many crimes. One of the most serious involved the Native protesters who repeatedly struck an OPP officer with a vehicle forcing the officer to threaten to draw his weapon. As you may recall, the officer wanted the Natives charged and filed a report to that effect. A year after Murray concluded his investigation, the officer testified at my preliminary hearing that no one had spoken to him about what had happened.[14]

An OPP officer being struck by a vehicle driven by Natives didn't warrant Murray's attention, but he spent an awful lot of time trying to find a way to arrest and charge *me*. (Only after 30 months of prosecution did the Crown finally drop its ludicrous "counseling mischief not committed" charge against me.) Murray was so biased in his "thorough investigation" that he failed to write down my attacker's name, even though I gave it to him twice. He *did* record my political views and my statements about Fantino and McGuinty. But, apparently, the name of the native man who assaulted me and caused me to be taken to the hospital by an ambulance wasn't important enough to record, nor was the fact that I was cut, bruised and bloodied. In court, he remembered my injuries, but for the life of him he could not recall my attacker's name.

It is impossible to imagine that any experienced investigator wouldn't think the name of an attacker or the fact that the victim was visibly injured, was noteworthy – clearly Murray made a decision simply not to include it in his notebook. Officers know that most judges are going to automatically believe them when they testify, especially when the officer refers to his notes. Murray would have known, by failing to record the name of my attacker and then telling the court I didn't give him the name, that the judge would believe him. Thanks to the OPP's own video, however, Murray was shown as not being truthful in his testimony.

Sergeant Brad Moore

Sgt. Moore is one of the nicest people around and can sweet talk you into anything. He makes this list because of his willingness to watch crimes being committed and then releasing the perpetrators. This M.O. ensures that more assaults will occur.

Some background to just one of my experiences with Moore: On February 27, 2011 we organized a 'Truth And Reconciliation Rally' in Caledonia to dramatize our position that true healing could only begin after Six Nations, the OPP and the Ontario government apologized to the people of Caledonia.[15] We modelled the idea on the efforts of the Canadian government to heal their relationship with native people via Prime Minister Harper's apology in conjunction with the Indian Residential Schools Truth and Reconciliation Commission.[16]

The idea of demanding apologies for the terror and vandalism inflicted on innocent people by Native militants was too much for the anarchists; anti-capitalists; Israel-haters (the Palestinian flag was raised alongside that of the Mohawk Warrior flag on May 03, 2006 by the Niagara Palestinian Association w/other Palestinian groups watching) [17]; terror group supporters (including the Tamil Tigers); and radical unionists who had been supporting the lawlessness in Caledonia since nearly the beginning in 2006. [18] One of the key organizers for this coalition is a union leader from York University's CUPE (Canadian Union of Public Employees) 3903 named Tom Keefer [19] who had once been kicked out of Concordia University in Montreal after he threatened a security guard who had caught the son of a Syrian diplomat spray-painting anti-Israel slogans on a wall (both were allowed to return after apologizing). [20]

Keefer had bussed in people on other occasions to disrupt our rallies while the OPP watched and did nothing, so it was no surprise when he did the same on February 27 to oppose our effort to seek apologies for the victims of his allies. We were forced to move our planned rally from the Lions Park where we usually held them to private property beside DCE (with permission from the owner). Keefer's goons swarmed and harassed us on the road, screaming at us from inches away, bumping us, making false claims of assault and making it impossible for us to walk down the road with our symbolic plywood monument, all while police watched. Al Gretzky and Mary-Lou Ambrogio from the International Free Press Society were present, and Al said afterwards, "I didn't think I was in Canada." They also harassed us on the private property we were using, and the police refused my requests to remove them.

Instead of arresting Keefer the OPP arrested me, claiming that I had assaulted Keefer. While the video did show that I had pushed him, the OPP refused to acknowledge the fact that, at the time, Keefer was trespassing on private property and engaging in the criminal behaviour of mischief. Since property owners and their agents have the legal right to use reasonable force to remove trespassers, the Crown was forced to eventually withdraw its false charge against me.[21]

One year later, several days before a rally planned for July 7, 2012 during which we planned to walk down the road through DCE, I went to the OPP detachment to swear out charges against Keefer. It was there that I spoke to Sgt. Moore. He persuaded me not to lay charges because, according to him, the OPP had supposedly "developed a new relationship" with me and my group, so there was no need to rehash old issues. He said I should forget how, a year earlier, I had been arrested, and prosecuted for months simply for trying to remove a trespasser.

Four days after our "friendly" conversation, it was Sgt. Moore who, based on our "new" relationship (presumably), stood by and watched as a Native protester assaulted me with a lacrosse stick. Even though he was standing a mere 10 feet away and there were only three protesters in the whole area, Moore refused to arrest my assailant, refused to prevent additional assaults, and refused to assist me, the victim of the assault.

Since Moore refused to do his duty by upholding his sworn oath, and honouring the Police Services Act, I placed the Native protester under citizen's arrest. When another protester assaulted a member of my group and stole our property, I placed him under arrest as well. Our videos and photos show that Moore watched these events unfold, and when I arrested one man and delivered him to Moore, he simply released him. The Native then got a baseball bat and returned to confront us. Moore's solution: he arrested me and two other members of my group in order to prevent the Native protesters from committing more crimes. As well, Moore stood not more than 30 feet away from a pickup truck into which the Native protester had placed the stolen property, but refused to walk the short distance to gather evidence.[22]

After Moore arrested me I was handcuffed and taken to the Cayuga OPP Detachment, where I was held for a few hours on their standard 'prevent-a-breach-of-the-peace-by-arresting-the-victim' rationale. I was asked whether I wanted to file any criminal charges. The only person I asked to be charged was Sgt. Brad Moore because he had illegally released a person in custody and refused to gather evidence of a crime. The detachment officer refused to take down my statement. I told him to remove my handcuffs so that I could track down Moore and arrest him myself. The OPP almost went into panic mode, and I was told by several officers that arrest warrants would be issued against the Native protesters who had assaulted me. Not once did I ask the OPP to charge any Native, but for the next few days they phoned me several times to tell me the steps they were taking to arrest Native protesters.

I emailed OPP lawyer Chris Diana to tell him that Moore had illegally released someone in custody (the subjects of my citizen's arrest). I quoted the relevant sections of the Criminal Code and asked Diana what authority Moore had to release these people. He emailed me on two occasions, promising to reply. Both times he failed to do so. Diana, who's a smart lawyer, could have resolved the matter quite easily by quoting the pertinent section of the law. That is, if such a section had, in fact, existed.

According to the law as written, all Canadian citizens can arrest someone whom they believe has broken the law. Section 494 authorizes citizens to perform such an arrest. These arrests carry the same weight as those performed by a police officer. Any arrested person who then flees can be charged with escaping custody – the Supreme Court of Canada has been clear on this point[23]; the Supreme Court has also convicted police officers of obstructing justice for refusing to gather evidence of a crime[24].

Section 498 of the Criminal Code of Canada contains four directives for police officers regarding how to deal with a "citizen's arrest." All four options require the officer who takes the arrested person into custody to ensure that that individual appears in court to answer the charge(s). Section 498 does not provide an option whereby an officer can declare the arrest invalid and release the person. And, according to s.146, "Everyone who permits a person whom he has in lawful custody to escape, by failing to perform a legal duty, is guilty of an indictable offence and liable to imprisonment for a term not exceeding two years." That means that if and when a court considers Officer Moore's release of the man I arrested, it will have to decide whether he committed a criminal act by releasing the individual, and by refusing to gather evidence of a crime.

On July 24, 2012 the OPP issued a news release announcing that they had laid charges against the three protesters involved in crimes against us during the rally.[25] Sgt. Moore would testify at the trial of one of the accused in February

2013 where, ironically, he became the first (but, not the last) OPP officer to testify that non-Natives did have the right to walk down public roads in Caledonia – including the road through DCE. It had taken seven years of non-stop activism, including numerous arrests of innocent non-Native volunteers, to force them to admit it.

Sergeant Rick Zupancic

It is hard to know whether Sgt. Zupancic is – or is not – a nice guy. Every time I've met him, he has been angry and aggressive. There seems to be little doubt that Zupancic is one of these officers who has no problem exerting power over citizens, whether or not he has the authority to do so.

Zupancic first came to my attention in 2012 when we put up signs reading "No Jews Allowed by Order of McGuinty", "No Whites Allowed by Order of McGuinty" and "No Blacks Allowed by Order of McGuinty," and he was the only police officer who took offence to them. (Of course, McGuinty never gave any such orders, but then, he didn't have to. Declaring a public space "Natives only" has the same effect.)[26] For six years in Caledonia, the OPP had repeatedly targeted non-Natives for arrest. We were simply posting signs referring to McGuinty's racist policies. Many officers saw the point of our political statements, as did our Jewish friends from the Never Again Group in Hamilton,[27] but Zupancic, sadly, did not. He became angry and warned me more than once that I would be arrested for posting the signs. Apparently, Sergeant Zupancic believes that he has the right to interfere with free speech, a Charter-guaranteed freedom.

Zupancic ordered officers to tear down the signs from one hydro pole and, when I went to a second, he had me arrested "to prevent a breach of the peace." He wanted people to believe that our signs were provoking Natives, and that he had to step in and arrest me in order to prevent violence (which was, supposedly, all but certain because the signs were so "provocative"). But even Zupancic realized that no laws had been broken. And, unfortunately for him, the video showed that Native protesters did not become angry. In fact, the video shows them holding the ladder steady as signs were posted, while never saying anything negative about them.[28]

Other than Sgt. Zupancic the only ones who looked angry were Tom Keefer (the CUPE 3903 leader) and his union friends who tried to claim that the signs were racist. By contrast, the OPP officer who said he was in charge that day was far from angry when, standing right beside Zupancic, he told me it was okay to put up the signs. That was after Zupancic had ordered them torn down. Less than ten minutes later, Zupancic ordered my arrest.

Several months later, on April 21, 2012, Sergeant Zupancic was the officer in charge when we held another rally at DCE. This time he was videotaped instructing officers to target us for arrest.[29] When I demanded that he issue the same instructions regarding Native protesters, he refused. He stood less than ten feet from me as I was repeatedly taunted and threatened by Natives. He took no steps to stop them from crossing police lines to confront me, let alone arrest them 'to prevent a breach of the peace.' (Not one Native protester has ever been arrested to prevent a breach of the peace in Caledonia since 2006; it is an arrest justification used solely for non-Natives)

At that event I asked Jeff Parkinson, our cameraman, to get the names of every officer in the police line. Jeff very politely went down the line, asking each officer for his or her name. They all complied, until Jeff got to Zupancic. The video shows that, even though there wasn't a single native within 50 feet of us, Zupancic refused to give his name, and ordered Jeff to back up. He did identify himself when Jeff asked a second time, but when Jeff said he was going to continue down the line and get the names of the three remaining officers, Zupancic had him arrested.[30] (When SUN TV's Michael Coren saw the video of Zupancic ordering officers to arrest CanACE's camera man because he'd asked officers for their badge numbers, he called Zupancic a "little fascist."[31])

Only an hour earlier, Ken Green had rushed over to stop Mark Vandermaas who was all alone as he started walking down the road carrying a sign that said, 'HEALING BEGINS WITH APOLOGIES.' Green jumped in front of Mark, swore at him, chest-butted him and, just as Mark was telling Green to stop assaulting him, Zupancic had Mark, the victim, arrested, in order to – you guessed it – "prevent a breach of the peace."[32] For the next two hours, Green repeatedly walked up to me and, with Zupancic watching, threatened me. Zupancic did nothing.

Green isn't seen around Caledonia these days. He skipped town when the OPP was finally forced to issue a warrant for his arrest. Four years earlier, Green had been charged with 14 criminal offences[33] in connection with another blockade of Caledonia's main street, and convicted on several. But you never saw Zupancic attempting to control Green at any of our events, even when Green was threatening and assaulting people.

Sergeant Dan Michaud

Sergeant Michaud is another officer who is a very nice guy, but he became famous for what appears to be wilful stupidity. I believe he has a conscience, and he finally did transfer out of Caledonia, but while he was there it became clear that he was a man who would obey orders even if they were objectionable. Officers like Michaud caused many property owners to be victimized by their refusal to do anything to prevent Native protesters from trespassing on people's private property. These residents knew it was futile to call 911 when that happened, because Michaud and his ilk were not about to protect them unless ordered to do so by a superior.

Officer Michaud lived in Caledonia but he did little to assist his fellow neighbours when they called for help. He allowed crimes to occur as long as Natives were the ones committing them. The best example of this kind of behavior: Michaud was site commander at a development in Cayuga where five Natives completely shut down construction by blocking access to the site. Fed up with OPP inaction, the developer had me and my group designated his legal agents so we could make arrests and file charges on his behalf. Jeff Parkinson videotaped my conversation with Michaud in which he told us that the Ontario Land Title Deed system was insufficient to enable him to determine who owned which property. He also could not explain why Native protesters in other parts of Ontario were being arrested and going to jail for doing exactly what these five Native protesters were doing in Cayuga. Nor could he explain why the Criminal Code was different in Cayuga than anywhere else in Ontario. Equally shocking are his repeated assertions that he would not charge anyone until the Crown told him to. So much for "officer discretion."[34]

Michaud may have told me that these five protesters were committing no crime, but the courts saw it differently. I took the two key Native protesters, Floyd and Ruby Montour, to criminal court and got the Justice of the Peace to issue a total of eight criminal offences against them in relation to the Cayuga occupation.[35] Charges included one count of intimidation and extortion and multiple counts of mischief. (The Crown & OPP later dropped my charges and replaced them with one count each of mischief.) Referring to the Cayuga construction site, Superior Court Judge J.A. Ramsay stated in an injunction sought by the owners: "The police have the right to use their discretion in the enforcement of the law and private property rights. A blanket refusal to assist a property owner or a class of property owners, however, would be an abuse of that right."[36]

How is it that Michaud was unable to see crimes being committed in Cayuga? Unfortunately, Officer Michaud is all too typical of OPP officers in Caledonia. We have him on video making it clear that OPP officers don't care what Ontario's Land Registry system says, that he would disregard private ownership of property if any Native protester claimed ownership. Most officers, Michaud included, do not use individual discretion or consider what courts are saying; if top brass tells them that Land Title Deeds mean nothing, then that is what they believe, no questions asked.

In fact, every single court has upheld Land Title Deeds, and has disagreed with the OPP opinion regarding ownership.[37] The OPP and its lawyers know this, but officers say that Title Deeds do not give them authority to arrest people for trespassing. As of the date of writing, however, four non-Natives are currently before the court on trespassing charges and the Crown has provided the Title Deeds to the Douglas Creek Estates in order to establish the OPP's authority to arrest non-Natives for trespassing. Furthermore, in 2006 Ontario's highest court, the Court of Appeal for Ontario, ruled that all Native protesters on DCE were subject to arrest by the OPP and prosecution by the Crown.[38] That was before the McGuinty government got around that ruling by buying DCE and allowing Native protesters to occupy it and control who is allowed to enter. These protesters have been allowed to remain on DCE for the past seven years only because the new owner, the Ontario government, authorized it, and not because the Land Title lacks authority. This proves, of course, that the ownership of DCE was never in question. It used to be owned by Henco Ltd.; it is now owned by the Ontario Government. Despite the claims of OPP officers, the enforcement of trespass laws there – or anywhere – is not in question. These laws are absolutely enforceable based on the authority of the property owner; the only reason they are not being enforced by the OPP officers like Sgt. Michaud is because of the race of people committing the crimes.

Inspector John Periversoff

Inspector Periversoff, too, is as nice a person as you will ever meet. Keep your guard up, though, because he can say things with great passion that he knows to be utter lies. While some officers have a conscience and have difficulty following orders blindly, Insp. Periversoff is not one of them.

Inspector Periversoff sat in my home and told Merlyn Kinrade and me that he had great respect for the rule of law and that he had served in the Canadian military. He told us that under his watch things were going to be different in Haldimand County. He told us that he wasn't going to allow crimes to be committed with impunity. He said that much of what had happened up to that point had taken place when he wasn't around, so he couldn't really address those issues. Later on we learned that he had been the acting commanding officer in Haldimand when some of the serious crimes occurred, including when the power station was attacked.[39]

When Haldimand Mayor Marie Trainer and her Council confronted Inspector Periversoff back in 2006 with what they considered a "double standard of law enforcement," his response was to blame the Federal Government. (Apparently, it is okay for police officers to stand around and watch crimes being committed as long as officers believe some other level of government is to blame). According to Periversoff, the attack on the power station and assaults on police officers and residents were not criminal issues, they were land claims and were, therefore, federal issues. Of course, the Criminal Code is federal legislation, as anyone – and certainly, any police officer – knows. Periversoff seemed to be implying, bizarrely, that the OPP had no business enforcing federal laws.

Native protesters knew the OPP would do nothing to prevent them from committing crimes. They knew that, instead of upholding the law and maintaining the peace, the OPP was blaming all the problems on the federal government. From what I saw back in 2006, it is clear that the OPP wanted to pass the buck to the federal government so that it would be compelled to reach an agreement with Native protesters, and so that the OPP would be excused from having to uphold the law.

Periversoff did his utmost to blame others for the OPP's poor public image. Here's an example: In 2010, OPP Constable Vu Pham was killed in the line of duty, shot after stopping a truck in Seaforth, Ontario, hundreds of kilometers from Caledonia. Constable Del Mercy, who arrived in a different vehicle, returned the truck driver's fire, hitting him six times. Periversoff knew full well that this incident had nothing to do with Caledonia, that the driver, who died four days later, was distraught because his wife had left him, and that he had threatened to kill her and himself. Nonetheless, Periveroff issued a press release in which he tried to link Officer Pham's death to Caledonia:

> [...] this week with the tragic murder of Constable Vu Pham of the OPP Huron Detachment. There is little in life that prepares us for the loss of a police officer. While there are those out there in our society that criticize police to further personal agendas... The litmus test in any action should be how is this going to help the community heal...While a variety of self-serving agendas continue to manifest and inject unnecessary discord into our community, perhaps as a community it is time to reflect on the need, appropriateness and true agenda of those groups and what is really occurring...[40]

The "personal agendas" Insp. Periversoff laments includes the "agenda" of upholding the principle that all people are equal before the law, and the "agenda" of saying that police have no right to create a two-tier justice system in which one race is exempt from prosecution. Inspector Periversoff swore an oath to uphold the equal rights of all, but now sees that as part of "self-serving agendas" which "inject unnecessary discord into our community." Imagine if Inspector Periversoff had said the same thing to black people or to Natives demanding equality. In fact, police and government officials reacted in the same way when Dr. Martin Luther King Jr. demanded equality, accusing him of having a self-serving agenda that was responsible for the discord between blacks and whites, and refusing to acknowledge that the law was unfair and that black people were being victimized and often killed by whites.

As for healing the community – Insp. Periversoff was well aware of our desire to bring about healing through justice and truth; we met with him prior to our planned anti-racism rally set for March 21, 2010 to explain our position. Unfortunately, our rally had to be cancelled for safety reasons because his officers refused to stop native protesters and Tom Keefer's gang from disrupting it. Mark Vandermaas had planned to give a speech that day in direct response to Periversoff's insulting comments about us; unfortunately, he would not be able to deliver it until our Truth & Reconciliation news conference at Queen's Park one year later where he concluded his *'Healing In The Absence of Justice'* presentation as follows:

> *If the OPP truly want to help "heal" this community they would begin by apologizing for the shameful conduct of their force. Then, they would help us find a credible partner from Six Nations who would be willing to help convince THAT community to apologize for THEIR role in victimizing Caledonia. Until the apologies are forthcoming from those responsible for Caledonia's misery, I will continue my 'self-serving agenda' of promoting healing by speaking out for innocent victims of native extremism and racist policing policies[...]*[41]

I closed by saying:

> *[...] the people of Haldimand County cannot be bullied into accepting the distasteful propaganda by the guilty parties that they should just get over the injustices done to them, or that the crimes were somehow justified in a 'land claims context.' There is no escaping the truth: true healing, whether the victims are aboriginal or non-aboriginal, begins with a sincere apology, not with denying truth and fundamental justice.*[42]

Unfortunately, Insp. Periversoff and the other OPP brass would rather smear, obstruct and arrest those of us who believe in a meaningful process of reconciliation than help us bring it about.

Inspector Dave McLean

What can I say about Inspector McLean? He was the OPP officer in charge when Caledonia residents were being terrorized, and he did little to bring that terror to an end. Even though he had been a police officer in Haldimand County for 22 years, he did not come to the aid of his neighbours when they needed it. The OPP knew McLean would be a useful and obedient officer when they forced him on Haldimand County. Years earlier, as Sergeant McLean, he led the 16-officer public order unit and emergency response team during Native unrest in Ipperwash, Ontario (he says he wasn't on duty the day Dudley George was killed).

Ipperwash residents first warned us about McLean in 2006. They told us that our biggest enemies would not be Native protesters, but the OPP. At first, Caledonia folks had a hard time believing such a thing, but that would change soon enough as they saw how OPP allowed Native protesters free reign to commit crimes.

Under McLean's leadership, there was an appearance of law and order, with several 24/7 OPP checkpoints throughout Caledonia, but officers there would not and did not take any steps to prevent crimes or to assist crime victims. McLean stationed a police car in Dana Chatwell and Dave Brown's driveway, but officers remained in their car, even as Natives committed crimes against these homeowners.

I believe McLean attempted to entrap me so that I could be charged with a crime. While I was very open about exactly how and why we did our protests, McLean encouraged me to raise Canadian flags at night in the dark. I don't believe in sneaking around in the dark to do something that is perfectly legal by the light of the day, so I wasn't about to take the bait. (The OPP had already arrested me for trying to raise a Canadian flag during the day.) After I exposed McLean's attempts to entrap me, he filed a lawsuit for defamation against me and the local newspaper. I refused to settle and demanded my day in court. McLean dropped the case against me.

Inspector Phil Carter

As I write this, Inspector Phil Carter is OPP detachment commander in Haldimand County. He is another nice officer with a conscience, but like the others, he has done little to halt Native criminality. As then-Sergeant Carter, he stood by and watched Native protesters illegally occupy a construction site in Hagersville. We videotaped him telling the public that he was dealing with an "illegal occupation," but he made no arrests. As well, he was present at this construction site when two OPP officers helped Native protesters build a barricade to keep the legal owner out of his property.[43] While the court would later order both these officers to face criminal charges of Mischief thanks to Jeff Parkinson's pioneering private prosecutions,[44] Carter did nothing to stop these officers from committing a crime.

Carter was videotaped telling people it was illegal for them to put up Canadian flags, but he couldn't explain why he allowed Natives to put up Native flags. When questioned about it by Jeff Parkinson, Carter, instead of answering, told Jeff that he hadn't given permission to videotape him and that he would contact his lawyer if Jeff posted any video without his consent.

I have been arrested nine times, six of those during Carter's service as Haldimand commander. These included the various occasions I and other CanACE supporters were supposedly "trespassing" by walking down a public road or arrested "to prevent a breach of the peace" because we were, or might be, victims of assault. Under Inspector Carter's command, two of his officers, Sergeants Moore and Zupancic, targeted non-Natives and made numerous arrests, too many to recount fully in this book.

* * *

None of the officers I have mentioned should be remembered for their friendliness or 'niceness.' They should be remembered because each played a role in what most reasonable people would see as the racist policing of a Canadian community. The law is abused not only when governments establish an unjust policy, but also when individual people who work for the government choose to enforce these policies. Ontario Premier Dalton McGuinty should not take all the blame for the victimization of Caledonia residents. The individual officers who swear an oath before God to uphold the law regardless of race, skin colour, etc., and to provide all citizens with equal benefit and protection of the law, also bear responsibility.

The officers mentioned here chose to watch crimes being committed and, in most cases, chose to arrest the victims of the crimes instead of the criminals. In my view, they have violated their own consciences, violated their oath before God, violated their duty to the community and violated the very foundation of what a democracy is supposed to be. They did this knowing that people were being harmed by their inaction. Each officer had the option to stand firm, to denounce injustice, to expose corruption, to be the whistleblower that the Supreme Court acknowledges is supported both by common law and the Charter of Rights and Freedoms. But each officer chose not to stand for justice. Instead, they allowed unjust OPP policies to jeopardize the life, health, and safety of the public. They made their choices and history should remember them accordingly.

* * *

The Lawyers

Before I end this chapter I'd like to say a few words about the various government lawyers and Crown attorneys who have been involved in Caledonia-related legal efforts. Earlier in the book, I wrote that OPP lawyer Chris Diana, Crown Attorney Alex Paparella and Assistant Crown Larry Brock were involved in a little scheme to use the criminal court system to force travel restrictions on me even though I hadn't broken the law. In my view, their actions violated the Criminal Code because these individuals knew, or should have known, that they were aiding the OPP in my illegal arrest and my illegitimate overnight imprisonment. I presented the facts to a court with the aim of having Diana and Paparella charged with a crime. Just before the Justice of the

Peace would have ruled on my charges, another Crown Attorney stepped in and ordered the case stayed, thereby preventing the judge from ruling. I was, of course, not surprised.

We will never know if an independent justice looking at the facts would have ruled that the evidence supported laying criminal charges against these lawyers.

Central West Region Director of Crown Operations John Pearson

John Pearson appeared in the Cayuga courthouse several times during 2008 and 2009, each time to ensure criminal charges against police officers and Native protesters did not proceed. Since then, he has moved up the ladder and now works in Toronto. As you can see from his high-falutin' title, he wasn't just any old Crown lawyer, which begs the question: why did such a high-ranking Crown attorney show up to stop criminal proceedings in small town Cayuga?

What is interesting from all the transcripts of the cases in which Pearson was involved is that he focused on trying to tell the court just how abusive "Gary McHale and his group" were. In every case, Pearson attacked the character of the people laying the charges rather than addressing the evidence for the alleged crimes. In case after case he simply declared me to be someone who was abusing the court system. Believe me, when a high-ranking lawyer for the Crown appears in Court, almost every Justice of the Peace bends over backwards to do anything he suggests. In every single case involving our group, the Justice of the Peace agreed with Pearson. Fortunately, we had the right to appeal these rulings. Both the Superior Court and the Ontario Court of Appeals rejected Pearson's assertion that we were abusing the courts.

In one case, Pearson attempted to prove that Jeff Parkinson (Pearson made sure to identify him as my associate) was abusing the courts. Jeff's alleged abuse consisted of filing the charges against the two OPP officers he had videotaped helping Native protesters build a barricade to keep the legal owner off his own property. The Justice of the Peace agreed with Pearson, but Superior Court Judge Marshall questioned how the videographer's "bias" changed the facts that the police had done something wrong, and that their acts had been recorded on video. He ordered the officers to face charges. Judge Marshall didn't have to comment further, but he felt compelled to deal with Pearson's attempt to smear Jeff. In his ruling he stated:

> ... as I have said, the incriminating evidence or intent, is virtually all in the video of the police helping to erect the barricade. It is hard to see how animosity in the informant could taint the video... We should look – except in the clear case – at public benefit not private demons... I

note, in reviewing the transcript there is evidence of good motive in Mr. Parkinson.[45]

On another occasion, Pearson tried to declare that I, too, was abusing the courts. Once again, Judge Marshall reviewed the case, and once again disagreed, describing the issues raised in my case as being "very important" and pertaining to the "bulwark of democracy." The Crown appealed Marshall's ruling, but the Court of Appeals for Ontario ruled against Pearson. This ruling is now case law throughout Canada. It was recently quoted extensively by the Quebec Superior Court.[47]

Ontario Provincial Police Association President Karl Walsh

Karl Walsh is quoted at length in Christie Blatchford's book *Helpless*, her bestselling account of the Caledonia crisis. As head of the police union, Walsh was furious that top brass had forced officers to depart from standard procedures. He told Blatchford:

> *I got numerous calls from members [OPP Officers] who will tell you that they were petrified of the repercussions of acting... they've got all these examples of people on the ground [Officers] who have already been persecuted, disciplined, had repercussions career-wise... I still don't understand why we took different approaches to law enforcement in Caledonia... I can't forgive them for a lot of the approaches they took to this and I think numerous officers got unnecessarily injured, I think people from the general public got unnecessarily injured, I think everybody that was involved in this suffered injuries that could have been avoided had they just stuck to their training, stuck to their policies and stuck to the law. You know, the law doesn't discern colour of skin or ethnic background, and it's not supposed to. Justice is supposed to be blind.* [48]

Walsh was quickly silenced in June 2006 after he spoke out against what he called "two tier justice" in Caledonia.[49] He didn't speak out again until January 2007, by which time he had done a complete about face. No longer did he criticize OPP policies or McGuinty government tactics. Instead, his new messaging criticized *us* because we were continuing to expose racial policing and OPP corruption. I think someone in the OPP and/or government ordered Walsh to shut up about the OPP, and he heeded that command. He knew that when his job as OPPA president ended, he was subject to discipline as an ordinary officer.

Initially at least, Walsh may have been outraged by the OPP's handling of Caledonia, but that didn't mean he thought members of the public had an equal right to be angry. And he did not think too highly of us, the group exposing OPP corruption and standing with the people against injustice. On January 19,

2007 the OPPA issued a press release that included the following:

> *"The people behind these protests are not from the area," said OPPA President Karl Walsh. "They are, however, acting on a sustained basis to push an aggressive political agenda that includes promoting hatred, flaunting the justice system and inciting violence."*

Aside from his bizarre 'hate' and 'violence' accusations that had no basis in reality whatsoever, Walsh never told the public exactly what our "aggressive political agenda" was. Was it that we believed all people are equal under the law and must receive equal protection? Officers like Walsh are the reason the Rule of Law broke down in Caledonia in the first place. He was willing to target peaceful non-Natives in public – and so unwilling to publicly demand an end to police policies that he knew were injuring police and members of the public. It may be true Walsh was little more than a tool the OPP used to defame us, but that doesn't excuse the way he abused his authority as head of the OPPA to attack ordinary people whose rights were being violated.

Mark Vandermaas and I sued Walsh and the OPPA for defamation. We filed the suit in 2007, but it was not settled until June 2011, eight months after the release of *Helpless*. (We were deposed by the OPPA's defence lawyers the day after the book was released in October 2010, and were amused to discover they had no idea that their client, Karl Walsh, was Blatchford's key source about OPP wrongdoing in Caledonia.) We can't disclose terms of the settlement, but I can tell you that Walsh and the OPPA were required to issue this statement:

> *On January 19, 2007, the OPPA issued a Press Release concerning protests in Caledonia. It has been suggested that the Press Release was critical of Gary McHale and Mark Vandermaas. The OPPA had no reason to believe that Gary McHale or Mark Vandermaas were promoting hatred, flaunting the judicial system or inciting violence by organizing a demonstration in Caledonia.*[50]

Karl Walsh showed his true colour (it was red, the colour of the Liberal party) when he decided to run in the Ontario election in the hopes of becoming a member of McGuinty's Liberal caucus. It was funny, in a very sad way, that Walsh's moral outrage over dozens of officers being injured was no impediment to supporting the very person responsible for the dreadful policy. Walsh was quoted as saying that he had "developed a strong sense for politics and how to be the Liberal voice..."[51] He and I agree on that point – he *does* know how to be a Liberal voice, so much so that the Liberal party was willing to have him as a candidate. Although one could legitimately say he did a very good thing by helping Christie Blatchford confirm that everything we were saying about Caledonia was true, Walsh has shown himself to be someone who is willing to remain silent in the face of ongoing injustice and to shift blame away from those truly responsible for public discord by claiming those standing up for equality and justice are responsible for all the problems. In all these ways, Karl Walsh has proven that he is a very good Liberal indeed.

Too bad for him he never got the chance to sit in McGuinty's caucus. When the provincial election rolled around, Walsh was defeated.

1   OPP policy, Sept. 2002, *"The Promise of the O.P.P." (Values and Ethics).* *
2   Ontario Polices Service Act, 2011. http://www.e-laws.gov.on.ca/html/statutes/english/elaws_statutes_90p15_e.htm.
3   Office of the Commissioner for Federal Judicial Affairs Canada, March 12, 2004, *Stenhouse v. Canada* (Attorney General) (F.C.), 2004 FC 375, [2004] 4 F.C.R. 437. http://reports.fja.gc.ca/eng/2004/2004fc375.html. *
4   *CBC News*, March 19, 2004, Dismissed RCMP officer ordered reinstated. *
5   Ontario Court of Justice transcripts, OPP Constable Jeffrey Bird, testimony April 27, 2009, pp. 44-46. *
6   Ontario Ministry of Finance, public Sector Salary Disclosure. http://www.fin.gov.on.ca/en/publications/salarydisclosure/pssd/.
7   *National Post*/Canada.com, July 29, 2006: Embattled OPP boss accepts Irish Offer. *
8   The *Hamilton Spectator*, June 8, 2006, OPP brass sacrificing safety: Officers. *
9   *Tekawennake News*, Aug. 15, 2007: Band Council and citizens clash. Former Chief David General says "he does not consider Kanonhstaton [Douglas Creek Estates] sacred land, citing two reported rapes and several other unseemly acts which have been reported from the reclamation site." *
10 OPP radio transmissions, Dec. 1, 2007, Part of disclosure given to Gary McHale.
11 Ontario Provincial Police, Professional Standards Bureau report, *Police Service Complaint for False Arrest* (re: Gary McHale arrest, Dec. 16, 2006), Oct. 18, 2007, Witness #3 – Sgt. Ben Gutenberg, pp.20-21. *
12 See online photos and video from Dec. 3, 2011. *
13 Court transcripts, Feb. 20, 2013, *R. v. Toulouse*, OPP Sgt. Brad Moore testified the roads on Douglas Creek Estates were owned by the County and McHale and his group are allowed to use it.
14 Court transcripts, Nov. 25, 2008, *R. v. McHale* – preliminary hearing, OPP Officer Paul MacDonald testified. *
15 Caledonia Victims Project, Feb. 23, 2011: Queen's Park 'Truth & Reconciliation' news conference. *
16 Prime Minister of Canada Stephen Harper, June 11, 2008: Prime Minister Harper offers full apology on behalf of Canadians for the Indian Residential Schools system. http://www.pm.gc.ca/eng/media.asp?id=2149.
17 Photo, circa May 2006: Palestinian flag flying on occupied Douglas Creek Estates w/ Mohawk Warrior and Six Nations flags. *
18 Canadian Union of Public Employees (CUPE) 3903 (York University) First Nations Solidarity Working Group, Nov 15/09: Report of the CUPE 3903 First Nations Solidarity Working Group to the 2009 AGM. *
19 *Regional News*, Gary McHale column, Nov. 4, 2009: Have you heard of Tom Keefer? *
20 Concordia University, Thursday Report Online, April 25/02: Keefer and Marouf ban lifted. *
21 VoiceofCanada.ca, June 07, 2011: *BULLETIN: Crown drops Assault charge vs. Gary McHale.* *
22 Online photos and videos are available. *
23 *R. v. Asante-Mensah*, 2003 SCC 38, [2003] 2 SCR 3. http://www.canlii.org/en/ca/scc/

doc/2003/2003scc38/2003scc38.pdf.

24 *R. v. Beaudry*, 2007 SCC 5, [2007] 1 SCR 190. http://www.canlii.org/en/ca/scc/doc/2007/2007scc5/2007scc5.pdf.

25 OPP Press Release, July 24, 2012, Three Charged As A Result Of Altercation. *

26 *Regional News*, Gary McHale, Feb. 01, 2012: 'No Blacks, Whites or Jews Allowed by Order of McGuinty.' *

27 VoiceofCanada.ca, Feb. 13, 2012, Queen's Park news conference – NGO's stand with Caledonia activists for release of Caledonia Act recommendations to end racial policing. *

28 Video of event is available on-line. *

29 Video of event is available on-line. *

30 JeffParkinson.ca, April 24/12: Video – Two arrested for race in Caledonia. *

31 Sun News Network, March 5, 2012, Michael Coren interview of Gary McHale on *The Arena*.

32 VoiceofCanada.ca, April 27, 2012: Vandermaas email to OPP officer re April 21 DCE rally before two 'breach of peace' arrests. *

33 *Hamilton Spectator*, Sept 19/08: Caledonia tense after native arrested. *

34 Canadian Advocates for Charter Equality, July 13, 2008: OPP tell CanACE: Land Title deeds do NOT prove ownership. *

35 Ontario Court of Justice, July 08/08: *McHale v. Ruby Montour & Floyd Montour*. *

36 Caledonia Lawsuits & Court Actions: *1536412 Ontario Ltd. v. HCCC, HDI, Ruby & Floyd Montour, Hazel Hill (Cayuga occupation, May-June 2008)*; see para 29(2). *

37 Cayuga, Hagersville, Brantford Superior Court rulings. *

38 *Henco Industries Limited v. Haudenosaunee Six Nations Confederacy Council*, 2006 CanLII 41649 (ON CA). http://canlii.ca/t/1q58j.

39 Email on Feb. 10, 2011 from the OPP Lawyer stated, "Inspector Periversoff was the interim Detachment Commander of the OPP's Haldimand Detachment from May 17, 2006 – June 23, 2006, from Nov. 10, 2008 – January 6, 2009 and from June 12, 2009 to December 27, 2009. Inspector Periversoff has been the permanent Detachment Commander since Dec. 28, 2009."

40 OPP Insp. Periversoff's message to the residents of Haldimand County as posted on the County website, March 12, 2010. *

41 'Truth & Reconciliation Rally in Caledonia' news conference, Queen's Park Media Studio, Feb. 23, 2011. See Mark Vandermaas presentation. *

42 Ibid. See Gary McHale presentation. *

43 On-line video is available. *

44 *R. v. Parkinson*, 2009 CanLII 729 (ON SC). http://canlii.ca/t/224jp.

45 Ibid,. See paras 23, 26 and 28.

46 *McHale v. Attorney General*, ruling July 2, 2009 by Superior Court Judge D. Marshall. See para 43. *

47 Takefman c. Court of Québec (Criminal and Penal Division), 2012 QCCS 6295 (CanLII). http://canlii.ca/t/fw2qt

48 Christie Blatchford, *Helpless: Caledonia's Nightmare of Fear And Anarchy, And How The Law Failed All Of Us*, Doubleday Canada, 2010, pg. 143, 222. *

49 The *Hamilton Spectator*, June 8, 2006, OPP brass sacrificing safety: Officers. *

50 Ontario Superior Court of Justice, Memorandum of Settlement of the Plaintiffs and Defendants (*Gary McHale & Mark Vandermaas vs. Karl Walsh and Ontario Provincial Police Association*), June 11, 2011 (terms to be confidential).

51 OPPA news release, July 8, 2011, OPPA, Gary McHale and Mark Vandermaas Resolution of Litigation. *

* See http://www.GaryMcHale.ca/book for additional information, links to documents, videos and photos

153

Chapter 9

McGuinty's Ipperwash Cover-Up: The Caledonia Legacy

Many people have said that much of what happened in Caledonia is a direct result of how the OPP handled a similar crisis in Ipperwash, Ontario – and they would be correct, but for the wrong reasons.

We wanted to understand the role that Ipperwash and the subsequent inquiry[1] played in policing Caledonia so, after Ipperwash activist (later named an honorary CanACE founder) Mary-Lou LaPratte spoke at my first March for Freedom on October 15, 2006, Mark Vandermaas visited the area for a guided tour and to obtain access to the extensive collection of evidence LaPratte had amassed at her lawyer's office. What we found was astonishing. The common assumption is that the OPP's racist, Native-biased policing in Caledonia is the result of policy changes made after Dudley George's death in 1995. In reality, the reverse is true: the evidence clearly shows that George died because the OPP and the Department of National Defence refused to enforce the law against Native radicals in the years prior to his death. This led to the escalating violence against non-Natives (and other natives as well) that eventually claimed his life. Here, for example, is a news report from just over one month before George's death on September 7:

> **Native rowdies run amok** (Toronto Sun – Aug 5, 1995). [...] The base was bought outright for $50,000 in 1962 by taxpayers from a native group. Complaints by some natives led to the forking out of another $2.1 million in 1980... but a handful of natives started making trouble. In 1993 an Armed Forces helicopter was hit by gunfire and training was suspended. Since then, the problems multiplied. Gunfire was commonplace. Fences were torn down. Trespassing occurred. Stolen cars were

stored on the property. This year, a building was firebombed, military police and civilians were assaulted, weapons fired and vehicles damaged. The last straw was on July 29 when two kids drove a school bus right into the camp's drill hall and got into a fight with military personnel. [Military] evacuation followed to avoid confrontation [...][2]

On March 14, 2007 we released our Ipperwash Papers project (www.IpperwashPapers.ca) at a news conference in the Queen's Park Media Studio. It consists of over 400 pages of documents that never made it into the inquiry, documents that show how non-Natives were first victimized by police and Native radicals, and then later by an Inquiry that deliberately excluded them and their testimony.

On November 13, 2010, the *Toronto Sun* published an article by its legendary founder Peter Worthington – "Caledonia Crisis of Facts" – detailing many facts about the Ipperwash report which the media had overlooked. He wrote:

The Linden [Ipperwash] Report is more concerned about pacifying Indians than recognizing abuses to non-aboriginals. It's as if aboriginal status gives immunity from laws that apply to everyone else... Mark Vandermaas, Mary-Lou LaPratte and Gary McHale challenge the Ipperwash Report and its recommendations. The three held a press conference at Queen's Park that was largely ignored. They had a two-part article published by the Caledonia-based Regional News — virtually the only media to give them a hearing... Their 400-page report on lawlessness and racial policing has largely been ignored — but deserves scrutiny.

In fact, the Ipperwash Inquiry avoids the issue of preventing lawlessness, and is cited in Caledonia to justify racial policing, which others view as 'illogical, disingenuous and illegal.' Commissioner Lewis' arguments notwithstanding, certainly non-Natives at Caledonia saw themselves as living in a de facto war zone, with no rights to be protected by the OPP, who were ostensibly the 'peacekeepers.'[3]

What follows is the two-part article written by Mark Vandermaas, Mary-Lou LaPratte and me that was published in the Regional News This Week between February 18-25, 2009 and which Worthington credits in his Toronto Sun story. A PDF copy, complete with citations, can be downloaded from the CanACE website.[4]

* * *

MCGUINTY'S IPPERWASH COVER-UP: THE CALEDONIA LEGACY

PART 1: Race-based Policing in Ipperwash

On the sandy roads and beautiful Lake Huron beaches of Ipperwash, 35 kilometres north of Sarnia, Ontario there are few signs of the turmoil that once ripped apart an entire community and set others on a collision course with land claim anarchy thanks to a public inquiry that wasn't.

Imagine if a future government invested $20 Million and three years on an inquiry into the Caledonia crisis, but refused to allow a single resident to testify, and deliberately excluded every shred of evidence of crimes against them by native protesters. What if this inquiry was then used to hold natives blameless and justify a 'hands off' policy against land claim lawlessness in other Ontario towns? This is the legacy of Premier McGuinty's Ipperwash Inquiry.

On March 14, 2007, two and a half months prior to release of the Inquiry's report, with the assistance of MPP Toby Barrett, the authors held a news conference in the Queen's Park Media Studio to release their Ipperwash Papers project – 400 pages of documents showing how residents of Ipperwash were victimized by land claim lawlessness, government inaction and racial policing. Afterwards, they provided McGuinty and leaders of the Opposition with a press kit summarizing the Inquiry's failures.[5]

The Ipperwash Papers show that the OPP, Provincial and Federal governments allowed race-based policing to exist long before the shooting of Dudley George, and that it was the root cause of both his death and the community's suffering since 1992. The authors correctly predicted that the yet-to-be-released Inquiry report could never make a single credible recommendation for preventing violence against residents because *the Inquiry never allowed the issue to be explored.*

The Ipperwash saga began in 1942 when land was expropriated from natives for a military base. $50,000 was paid, and families were relocated to a nearby reserve. An additional $2.5 million was paid in 1981 with a promise the land would be returned when no longer needed.[6] Tired of waiting, natives occupied part of Camp Ipperwash in May 1993, but were not evicted even after a helicopter was shot.[7] In February 1994, the federal government agreed to return the base. On July 29, 1995 native children were used to crash a bus through the main gate as decoys during a violent takeover of the entire base.[8] Military personnel were cited for protecting "life and property" during the evacuation.[9] The adjacent provincial park was occupied September 4th. During a confrontation with natives two days later OPP officers, believing they had taken fire, shot and killed Dudley George.

Victimization of residents began in earnest with a land claim filed against their homes in 1992. Former Ipperwash community leader Mary-Lou LaPratte recounts:

> *As soon as the occupations and land claim on the West Beach started we noticed a disturbing OPP policy evolving. Natives coming off the occupied lands into surrounding areas to harass, threaten, intimidate, steal from, or assault innocent homeowners and tourists, were exempt from criminal charges upon reaching the safe haven of the disputed land. In the West Beach land claim, which was going through a court process, a native anywhere on the properties, for any reason, would not be charged. Our lives became a daily nightmare of threats, intimidation, and harassment tactics which, over the years, became home invasions and physical assaults.*[10]

LaPratte herself was a victim of a 2 a.m. home invasion. When her husband called the OPP he was asked if the intruder was native, whereupon he was instructed not to touch the man or face arrest.[11]

In May 1994, the *Sarnia Observer* published an editorial, '*Police must enforce laws*' stating, "Regardless of any land claim, natives must obey the law. They simply cannot be allowed to do as they please..."[12] Within sixteen months, natives had launched their violent takeover of Camp Ipperwash, Dudley George was dead and terrified residents were abandoned for weeks by the OPP who pulled out to a distance of 6-10 km for fear of native retaliation, leaving residents and the unsecured shooting scene under control of native occupiers.[13]

The OPP eventually returned, but residents complained bitterly to provincial and federal governments about the lack of OPP protection against rampant native crime. Elected officials wrote back saying it was the responsibility of the OPP to enforce the law. The correspondence offers startling insight into how utterly paralyzed the Canadian democratic system can become when police refuse to do so.[14]

In 1996, hundreds of residents wrote victim impact statements to Federal Liaison Robert Reid who held a position similar to that of David Crombie in Caledonia.[15] The Ipperwash Papers includes thirty-four letters, one of which was written by the town's Chief Administrative Officer blaming the Department of National Defence for George's death:

> *DND, through it [sic] failure to remove illegal occupiers, failure to permit the law to be upheld, failure to protect its boundaries, failure to ensure safety at one of its military facilities and ultimate retreat from and desertion of Camp Ipperwash in the middle of the night has created a situation that led to the death of at least one individual, the takeover*

and destruction of public property, terrorizing of a municipality, destruction of property values, and the tearing apart of a community and its way of life.

Repeatedly, over the two years preceding the fatal shooting of Dudley George, town officials advised provincial and federal government cabinet ministers, politicians and bureaucrats of the real potential for injury and death in the area. Unfortunately, unless real progress towards a solution commences immediately, we feel that more injuries and deaths will occur.[16]

In 1998 eight natives beat a man to unconsciousness leaving him with permanent damage to his hand. A witness had to call 911 seven times before OPP responded.[17] In 2002 and again in 2005, pieces of two human bodies were found in areas controlled by native occupiers.[18]

The Ipperwash Inquiry, called by McGuinty following his win over Mike Harris' Conservatives in October 2003, was given a mandate to "inquire and report on events surrounding the death of Dudley George" and "to make recommendations that would avoid violence in similar circumstances in the future." Ipperwash residents were hopeful it would examine the lawlessness they had endured so the people of Ontario – especially those living in Caledonia – could understand the terrible dangers of race-based policing.

Their hope was badly misplaced.

PART 2: How the Ipperwash Inquiry suppressed evidence and put Ontario communities on a collision course with anarchy

On October 15, 2008 MPP Toby Barrett announced that his petition for hearings into the Caledonia crisis had been rejected by Aboriginal Affairs Minister Brad Duguid with the excuse that, "Justice Linden's comprehensive report arising out of the Ipperwash Inquiry includes a road map for progress in our relations with First Nations and Metis people and the government is following those guidelines."[19]

The Inquiry's report contains 100 recommendations, but not one specifically addresses the issue of preventing violence against residents.[20] How could this even be possible given the extreme lawlessness in Caledonia during the year prior to its release?

The Ipperwash Inquiry began with seven days of testimony by two experts on aboriginal culture and history going back to the 17th century.[21] While the Inquiry was keen to understand, in excruciating detail, aboriginal history predating Confederation, they did not want to hear how today's aboriginals had terrorized innocent residents in the 1990's. They refused to allow LaPratte to testify despite her position as president of the 600 member Ontario Federation for Individual Rights and Equality (ONFIRE) – a group formed one month after the death of Dudley George to give beleaguered residents a voice – and, arguably, the most knowledgeable person alive regarding the impact of land claims and associated crime on innocent third parties.[22]

Derry Millar, lead counsel for the Inquiry, was well acquainted with both LaPratte and the suffering of Ipperwash residents. He and his law firm successfully defended the West Ipperwash Property Owners Association – of which LaPratte was the Public Relations officer – against the native land claim filed against their homes in 1992.[23] The case went to the Supreme Court of Canada, and on May 19, 1998, the native claim was dismissed.[24] It cost residents $500,000 for the legal defence of their homes.

Despite Millar's knowledge of the residents' agony, none were permitted to testify about the native crime and violence they had experienced. Out of 139 witnesses, not one was a non-native resident.[25] Mary-Lou LaPratte's 29-page chronological history of Ipperwash from the residents' point of view, submitted on behalf of ONFIRE in July 2004, is not listed on the Inquiry website.[26] Not one symposium was held on the subject of preventing violence against innocent residents during land claim protests.

During the three-year inquiry, the non-native victims of Ipperwash were allotted a total of just 90 minutes to address Commissioner Linden during a town hall meeting that took place on June 21, 2006 at the height of the violence in Caledonia. The now-mayor of Lambton Shores, Gord Minielly, a councillor at the time, echoed residents' concerns and expressed his sympathy for Caledonians:

> *I have listened to all of the seminars, and am most aggrieved that all the work in the last ten years among the governments, OPP and the Natives was of no help in the Caledonia dispute. Violence must not be tolerated. It only serves to leave the area in question paralyzed by fear and a sense of hopelessness.*[27]

The Inquiry's minutes of this 'Community Consultation' however, give the false impression there were no significant problems between residents and natives expressed.[28]

Since the Inquiry never examined the issue of preventing lawlessness against innocent residents, and does not have the force of law, the use of it to justify racial policing in Caledonia is illogical, disingenuous, and illegal.

The best evidence for this can be found in the testimony of OPP Commissioner Julian Fantino himself on August 29, 2007 when he told Shawn Brant's lawyer:

Mr. Rosenthal, there's nothing in the spirit, the intent, or the written word in this document [Ipperwash Inquiry report] that justifies criminal conduct or that exonerates people from accountability from criminal conduct, or that it absents me as a law enforcement officer from exercising discretion or using the authority bestowed upon me to effect a lawful purpose.[29]

McGuinty and Fantino have stated that police are 'peacekeepers' – as though citizens victimized by land claim lawlessness are living in a de facto war zone with no right to full police protection mandated under the Police Services Act.[30] Both men know they are allowed – and required – to enforce the law before innocent people become victims. They simply choose not to do so in Haldimand County.

The authors briefed Mayor Trainer prior to releasing the Ipperwash Papers who was shocked by the eerie similarities between Ipperwash and Caledonia. "If you just change the names," she said, "this could be Caledonia." Her observation highlights the most disturbing and far-reaching consequence of the suppression of evidence from residents: dangerous policy-making resulting from the Inquiry's inability or unwillingness to identify the root cause of Dudley George's death as race-based policing.

If the law had been properly enforced in Ipperwash in the years prior to 1995 without regard to race it is quite likely that Dudley George would not have been part of the escalating violence that claimed his life just as Caledonia builder Sam Gualtieri would not have been nearly beaten to death by native thugs if OPP had removed the initial occupiers of the Douglas Creek Estates.

Not one MPP has ever risen in the Legislature to denounce the suppression of evidence by the Ipperwash Inquiry, or the inappropriate use of its flawed recommendations. The Opposition has silently allowed the Inquiry to become a legalized myth justifying racist policing practices that have already been permitted by Conservative and Liberal governments at both the provincial and federal levels.

The authors believe the key reason Ipperwash residents were never permitted to testify was because the Inquiry was not about justice or reconciliation, but about attacking the Mike Harris Conservatives. It should not have surprised anyone that its report was made public a few months before the last provincial election – an obvious attempt to silence the Conservatives regarding law and order in Caledonia.

Since June 2006 ordinary Canadians have been leading the fight to ensure any new inquiry was about justice and law & order, and not about scoring political points. On June 5, 2007 however, PC leader John Tory called for an inquiry into Caledonia stating the purpose of such an inquiry was to review the 'absence of communication and lack of leadership by Premier McGuinty and his Liberal government,' and not to examine OPP race-based policing.[31]

MPP Toby Barrett's February 05, 2009 call to examine the validity of land claims, and allegations of political interference in policing[32] follows in Tory's footsteps by ignoring the clear wishes of the 7,000 people who have signed the current petition demanding an inquiry into the actions of the OPP.[33]

Ontario's political parties believe Caledonia is a mere 'drop' of water in the political landscape. Real change within the OPP and the Ontario government is possible, however, thanks to a growing grassroots movement to hold all politicians accountable for allowing racial policing to exist. When you sign the petition, you become one of the thousands of 'drops' in a river that will one day wash away the illegal actions of the OPP.

* * *

An illegal peacekeeping mission on Canadian soil

Mark Vandermaas, a former UN peacekeeper himself, gave a presentation at our 2011 *Caledonia: No More Nightmares* event in Ottawa[34] which discussed the most troubling recommendations of all from the Ipperwash Inquiry:

> *The Ipperwash Inquiry includes four recommendations which suggest the OPP, other police forces and the Minister of Community Safety & Correctional Services enact so-called 'peacekeeping' policing policies during aboriginal disputes.[35] Both the Premier of Ontario and the former Commissioner of the OPP have referred to the OPP role in Caledonia as being that of 'peacekeepers.' On May 02, 2007 the Premier actually joked on TV about having to issue blue helmets to the OPP.'*

> *The obscenity of this joke is underscored when one reviews a list of countries where UN peacekeepers are currently deployed: Liberia; Ivory Coast; Haiti; Sudan; Lebanon; East Timor; Darfur; Kosovo; Chad; and the Congo.[36] The UN says this about the role of peacekeeping in restoring the Rule of Law in failed states:*

>> *Rule of Law is the legal and political framework under which all persons and institutions, including the State itself, are accountable. Establishing respect for the rule of law is fundamental to achieving a durable peace in the aftermath of conflict. Laws need to be publicly promulgated, equally enforced and independently adjudicated and be consistent with international human rights norms and standards. Peacekeeping works to strengthen police, justice and corrections institutions, as well as the institutions that can hold them accountable.*

> *Since 1999, all major peacekeeping operations, and many special po-
> litical missions, have had provisions to work with the host country to
> strengthen the rule of law.* [37]

> *Obviously, then, peacekeeping missions are not deployed to undermine
> the rule of law in stable democracies by withholding law enforcement
> protection from innocent civilians to appease armed aggressors of a fa-
> voured race. Strangely, not one politician or journalist has ever thought
> to ask some seemingly-obvious questions:*

> 1. *Who has the authority to authorize a peacekeeping mission on Ca-
>   nadian soil?*

> 2. *What legal authority exists for substituting a peacekeeping policy in
>   place of the legal protections of the Charter of Rights and Ontario's
>   Police Services Act during any land claim, let alone an imaginary
>   one?*

> 3. *If Canadian citizens in Caledonia have so much in common with
>   those in failed states such as Haiti, Darfur, Kosovo and Liberia that
>   they require a peacekeeping mission, why have our federal and pro-
>   vincial governments turned blind eyes to their plight?* [38]

* * *

The very use of the word 'peacekeeping' by police and government should act
as a red flag, warning that they have done – under cover of a racist inquiry –
what they could never have done through legislation: authorized police officers
and government ministries to refuse to protect us from violent interest groups.

As you have read, not a single non-Native resident was allowed to testify at
Premier Dalton McGuinty's Ipperwash Inquiry. The inquiry did not look into
the violence unleashed by Natives during the land claim protests; its scope of
inquiry was limited to violence committed against Native protesters. Although
you wouldn't know it by mainstream media coverage of Ipperwash, Dudley
George wasn't the only fatality in Ipperwash. You will find hundreds of stories
about George's death, but you will search in vain for references to William
MacMillan or Jason Lane whose dismembered bodies were found on the occupied Ipperwash Army Base in 2002 and 2005 respectively.[39] The deaths of
MacMillan and Lane, however, didn't fit the Native-only victimhood propaganda. That meant that the untold number of violent acts residents suffered at
the hands of Natives and the two dead bodies (other than George, of course)
found at the occupation site, were of no interest to the Inquiry or the media.

When the Ipperwash Inquiry released its final report in April 2007, it did not
include the voice of even a single Ipperwash resident. Ironically, it does quote
something I said on my website in 2006:

163

Is it a question that the OPP are completely inept? Is it a question that the OPP are completely clueless? Or is it just that they don't care about the safety of people? Whichever it is, it is time to talk about disbanding the whole OPP force.[40]

The report then offers this statement by Premier McGuinty:

"I understand that there are, in some quarters, some impatience and some frustration, but we are dealing with this in a peaceful manner... We are determined to resolve this, but we will do this in a way that results in no incident and in no compromise to public safety."[41]

Nice words, Mr. McGuinty. What a shame they did nothing to help Sam Gaultieri, who was nearly killed in Caledonia and left with permanent brain damage after the OPP allowed Native thugs to aggressively and illegally occupy the Stirling development site.[42] (Uncharacteristically, and within a few days of the September 2007 attack on Gaultieri, the OPP moved in with hundreds of officers and removed the radical Native thugs who had taken over the subdivision and attacked Gaultieri. Five years later there has not been one case of violence at Stirling. Doesn't that tell us that using force works as a deterrent? Doesn't it underscore the fact that once the police say "No more," law and order will be restored?) Meanwhile, McGuinty and the OPP continue to tell the public that "at least no one was hurt in Caledonia". I suppose Sam Gaultieri is "no one." I guess the two dead men found in pieces in Ipperwash are "no ones," too.

The Ontario government knows full well the Ipperwash Inquiry did not allow the vital issue of native violence against residents to be studied, yet it continues to use its skewed recommendations to justify the wholesale subversion of the protection non-natives are entitled to under the Police Services Act and the Charter of Rights. It is frightening that the lessons of Ipperwash have gone un-learned. The only politician to ever publicly point out the failures of the inquiry is Senator Bob Runciman, who was Ontario's Solicitor General at the height of the Ipperwash crisis.[43] Even as of today, however – six years after we released our Ipperwash Papers project at Queen's Park – not one MPP has ever stood up in the Ontario Legislature to condemn this dangerously-flawed inquiry that has truly put our province on a collision course with anarchy.

---

1   Ipperwash Inquiry Report. www.attorneygeneral.jus.gov.on.ca/inquiries/ipperwash.
2   *Toronto Sun*, Diane Francis, Aug 5/95: Native rowdies run amok. *
3   *Toronto Sun*, Peter Worthington, Nov. 13, 2010: Caledonia crisis of facts. *
4   *Regional News This Week* series, Mark Vandermaas, Gary McHale, Mary-Lou LaPratte, Feb. 18-25, 2009: *McGuinty's Ipperwash Cover-Up: The Caledonia Legacy.* *
5   Ipperwash Papers project. www.IpperwashPapers.ca.
6   Camp Ipperwash payments & negotiations: Dept. of Indian & Northern Affairs: *Fact*

Sheet – Camp Ipperwash Negotiations. *

7   Helicopter shooting: *Toronto Sun*, Diane Francis, Aug. 5, 1995: Native rowdies run amok. (IpperwashPapers.ca, K-5) *

8   Children used to crash bus through gate of Camp Ipperwash: Ipperwash Inquiry, Volume 1, Chapter 7, pp. 130-132). *

9   Canadian Forces Base Toronto, *Recommendation for Commendation, LFCA Commander's Commendation*, July 17, 1996 (IpperwashPapers.ca, I-1). *

10 Mary Lou LaPratte re Native crime against residents: LaPratte speaker's notes, March for Freedom, Caledonia, Oct. 15, 2006. (IpperwashPapers.ca, D-14). *

11 LaPratte home invasion: Mary Lou LaPratte affidavit w/chronology as submitted to Ipperwash Inquiry, July 2004. (IpperwashPapers.ca: A-1, para 7). *

12 *Sarnia Observer* editorial, May 25/94: Police must enforce laws (IpperwashPapers.ca, K-4). *

13 Victim impact statements re OPP abandonment: Mary Lou LaPratte affidavit w/chronology as submitted to Ipperwash Inquiry, July 2004. (IpperwashPapers.ca: A-1, paras 31-43). *

14 Correspondence with elected officials: (IpperwashPapers.ca, H-1 to H-27). *

15 Victim impact statements by residents, 1996: (IpperwashPapers.ca, F-1 to F-34, G-3). *

16 Town of Bosanquet, CAO victim impact statement, March 13, 1996. (IpperwashPapers. ca, F-34). *

17 Mary Lou LaPratte affidavit w/chronology as submitted to Ipperwash Inquiry, July 2004. (IpperwashPapers.ca, A-1, para 77) *

18 Body parts found on occupied former Camp Ipperwash: OPP Special Circular, April 7, 2004 re William (Bill) Gordon McMillan. (IpperwashPapers.ca, L-22) *

19 MPP Toby Barrett email, Oct. 15, 2008: McGuinty axes land dispute hearings – uses Ipperwash as excuse. *

20 No specific recommendations for preventing native violence against residents. *

21 Expert testimony re Aboriginal culture: Ipperwash Inquiry, Witnesses Who Have Testified (Darlene Johnston, Joan Holmes); Also, w/numbering of witnesses added (IpperwashPapers.ca, O-2). *

22 Mary Lou LaPratte & Ontario Federation for Individual Rights and Equality (ONFIRE); refusal to allow LaPratte to testify. *

23 Inquiry lead counsel Derry Miller represented Ipperwash residents during land claim against their homes: West Ipperwash Property Owners Association (WIPOA) newsletter, July 16, 1993; Derry Millar of Weir & Foulds new lawyer. *(IpperwashPapers.ca, C-1). *

24 Supreme Court of Canada, *Chippewas of Kettle and Stony Point v. Canada*, [1998] (IpperwashPapers.ca, C-4). *

25 Ipperwash residents not allowed to testify: *Report of The Ipperwash Inquiry, Witnesses Who Have Testified.* *

26 Mary Lou LaPratte chronology of Ipperwash not listed on Inquiry website: Mary Lou LaPratte affidavit w/chronology as submitted to Ipperwash Inquiry, July 2004. (IpperwashPapers.ca: A-1, para 8 of affidavit). *

27 Lakeshore Advance, June 28, 2006: June 28, 2006: Asking for compensation. (IpperwashPapers.ca, O-4). *

28 Ipperwash Inquiry, Community Consultation, Thedford Arena, June 21, 2006: Notes. (IpperwashPapers.ca, O-3). *

29 OPP Commissioner Fantino on limitations of Ipperwash Inquiry report: Shawn Brant trial transcript: Fantino testimony, Aug. 29, 2007 (pp. 28-29). *

30 Premier McGuinty & OPP Commissioner Fantino re OPP as 'peacekeepers.' *City TV News*, May 2, 2007: Caledonia Convoy. *

31 MPP Toby Barrett email, Feb. 10, 2009: Time for an inquiry into area land disputes. *

32 MPP Toby Barrett news release, Feb. 5, 2009: Time to determine the truth about Caledonia. *

33 Residents' petition for inquiry into OPP: *Dunnville Chronicle*, Jan. 17, 2009: Petition asks for inquiry into Fantino and OPP. *

34 *Caledonia: No More Nightmares*, Ottawa, ON, March 22, 2011; sponsored by Free Thinking Film Society and International Free Press Society. *

35 Ipperwash Inquiry, 'peacekeeping' recommendations, Recommendations: Volume 2, Policy Analysis, See #38, 45, 47 and 49. *

36 United Nations Department of Peacekeeping Operations: Current Peacekeeping Operations. http://www.un.org/en/peacekeeping/operations/current.shtml.

37 United Nations Department of Peacekeeping Operations: Rule of Law. http://www.un.org/en/peacekeeping/issues/ruleoflaw.shtml.

38 Mark Vandermaas presentation notes, Caledonia: No More Nightmares, Ottawa, March 22, 2011. See Part 2: Caledonia Myths & Policy Issues (Illegal Peacekeeping Mission on Canadian Soil), pp. 12-13. *

39 Body parts found on occupied former Camp Ipperwash: OPP Special Circular, April 7, 2004 re William (Bill) Gordon McMillan. (IpperwashPapers.ca, L-22). *

40 Ipperwash Inquiry, Volume 2, Chapter 2: Primer on Aboriginal Occupations, p. 29. *

41 Ibid, p. 30. *

42 Attack on Caledonia builder Sam Gaultieri: *National Post*, Sept. 3, 2011: 'He shouldn't be free because I'll never be free,' says victim after Caledonia conviction. *

43 Senator Bob Runciman condemnation of Ipperwash Inquiry & 'peacekeeping' recommendations: Senator Bob Runciman, Inquiry needed into Caledonia occupation, *Toronto Sun*, July 12, 2011. *

* See http://www.GaryMcHale.ca/book for additional information, links to documents, videos and photos

Chapter 10

Standing Up Against Institutionalized Racism

In Canada we often speak of Aboriginals as if they are all the same, have the same experiences, suffer from the same problems, and experience the same kind of victimization. Using that reasoning, it follows that they must all be treated in the same way. However, that logic is faulty. Ironically, it employs the same type of stereotyping that Canada's human rights codes specifically and explicitly reject. And it is ironic, too, that when we make such generalized statements about one group, we start down the road of institutionalized racism against another group.

It is hard to imagine that Natives who live on Six Nations, close to jobs in Hamilton and other big cities, experience the same economic hardship as Natives who live on remote reserves in Northern Ontario. While, certainly, there are similarities, it would be inaccurate to characterize their way of life – or the way other Natives live in other parts of Canada – as being exactly the same.

We should also realize that Native people aren't the only ones who have and who continue to suffer: Canada opens its doors to immigrants arriving from places where people are oppressed and victimized. And yet, we ask that they leave the laws of their homelands behind and accept that, here in Canada, there is one justice system for all. That means, even if you happen to come from a place where, for example, women are treated as second class citizens, and men can literally get away with murder for committing so-called "honour" crimes, you cannot expect our justice system to consider and incorporate legalisms that are at variance with our laws.

In effect, however, that is exactly what Canada is doing when it comes to Natives. Our political masters, government lawyers, judges and the Supreme Court of Canada have all decided that, because of their background and history, Native people who commit the same crimes as non-Natives *must* receive a lesser sentence *because they are Natives*. The intention behind this sort of inequity may be good, and may be seen as a way of trying to correct the wrongs of history. However, the policy of meting out different punishments based exclusively on the group a perpetrator happens to belong to is, at its core, a racist one.

It doesn't matter how many judges sign off on it: racism is still racism. As Dr. Martin Luther King Jr. pointed out, government lawyers and judges in Nazi Germany "legalized" all the government's illegal actions. King was born and raised in an extremely racist society where authorities took an active role in discriminating against black people. People may claim that, had they lived at that time and in in that place, they would have known that such racism was wrong, and would have done everything in their power to change it. But then, it is easy to make such a claim in our time and in our place – a country that is sensitive (perhaps even hyper-sensitive) to societal inequities and that is dedicated (via a nationwide human rights apparatus) to rooting out every last bit of discrimination against certain designated victim groups (one of which is Aboriginals). As always, though, hindsight is 20-20, and history provides one example after another of those living in dark times who could have challenged the immorality and injustice going on around them but who, for reasons of ignorance, cowardice, powerlessness or expediency – or some combination of two or more – failed to do so.

Canada has certainly come a long way from the ugliness of its past that saw Chinese people being forced to pay a head tax and Japanese-Canadians being interred in camps during World War II. A past in which Native children were separated from their parents and forced to attend schools where they were often abused, and in which Native people were barred from our courts and hiring their own lawyers. (That situation prevailed until the 1950s. As wards of the state – their status since the 1800s – Natives, it was then held, had no need to use the courts or hire lawyers because the state would look out for them. Technically, Natives who remain on reserves today are still wards of the state, with few rights.)

And yet, in taking those many steps forward, we have also taken a tremendous step backwards. For, instead of embracing the principle of equal rights for all, we have set up a system whereby certain groups receive special rights, ones that are granted, shockingly, *because* of a person's skin colour, religion and/or creed. To paraphrase a famous line in George Orwell's novel *Animal Farm*: All Canadians are equal, but some Canadians are more equal than others.

In and of itself, such a system is wrong – and, yes, evil. It is as wrong in Canada today (a Canada, we are told repeatedly, where all are afforded equality by our Charter of Rights and Freedoms) as it was in the American south of Martin Luther King Jr.'s time, and as it was in Adolf Hitler's Germany. If today in Canada Natives have been privileged and non-Natives are now the ones facing state-sanctioned inequity, that does not redress the wrongs of history. Rather, it merely institutionalizes a whole new set of wrongs.

The fallout from this sort of set up is immense – and immensely damaging. It corrupts police, who are forced to make (or not make) arrests using inherently racist criteria. It corrupts politicians, who jump on the "more rights for some" bandwagon because they have been persuaded that it is a way to keep a lid on a potentially explosive situation, and is thus being done for the greater good of all. It corrupts the judicial system, as special consideration is granted to members of certain designated victim groups, while others, who can point to no such membership, are hit with the full force of the law.

How did we arrive at such a situation? How could we have allowed such an unfair system to set down roots in Canada, a long-established democracy that looks back to freedoms asserted centuries ago in the Magna Charta, and that claims to hold its Charter of Rights and Freedoms in such high esteem? I suggest that you can blame it in on good intentions motivated by guilt and fear.

How is this guilt/fear manifested? It starts with policing. As we know, the OPP has codified a policy (the *"Framework"*) that instructs officers to enter into negotiations with Native people rather than make arrests. In Caledonia and other places in Ontario, such a policy results in police turning a blind eye to the blatant criminal activity of native protesters. In that way, police and those controlling them hope to placate angry Native protesters who might be inclined to act out in a violent way and potentially spark another Oka or Ipperwash crisis that made both police and the government look very bad indeed. At the same time, this policy is obviously unfair to non-Natives who, because they don't belong to the select group, cannot expect to be the beneficiaries of the "negotiate, don't arrest" directive.

The guilt/fear – and unfairness – continues during the prosecution/sentencing phase. For example, directives on the Ontario Attorney General's website instruct Crown prosecutors to treat Natives in a different way. Section 718.2 (e) of Canada's Criminal Code states that, during sentencing, the court should consider "all available sanctions other than imprisonment that are reasonable in the circumstances should be considered for all offenders, with particular attention to the circumstances of aboriginal offenders." Native offenders, because they are Natives, deserve to have "particular attention" paid to their circumstances; attention, it is clear, that is not owed to non-Natives. And the

Supreme Court of Canada has confirmed its support for this special treatment policy for Natives when they are sentenced for their crimes.

The most common argument for special treatment to keep native criminals out of jail is that aboriginals are "over-represented" in prison. The silliness of this position becomes obvious if I were to suggest to you that since men far outnumber women in prison we should, therefore, have special provisions in the law to keep men out of prison. Those who support the racist, native-biased laws also never seem to consider that native communities are the ones who suffer when violent native offenders are released because of politically-correct racism in the form of low expectations. Surely, law abiding native people deserve protection from the courts, too.

The danger of preferential treatment based on race or religion was foretold by the Manitoba Court of Appeal back in 1977 when it warned:

In a civilized country priding itself on equality of all people before the law, a special dispensation in favour of a particular group would hardly be a matter suitable for public discussion... So what we have here is a clear case of the exercise of a purported dispensing power by executive action in favour of a particular group. Such a power does not exist...

Not every infraction of the law, as everybody knows, results in the institution of criminal proceedings. A wise discretion may be exercised against the setting in motion of the criminal process. A policeman confronting a motorist who had been driving slightly in excess of the speed limit may elect to give him a warning rather than a ticket. An Attorney General faced with circumstances indicating only technical guilt of a serious offence but actual guilt of a less serious offence may decide to prosecute on the latter and not on the former. And the Attorney General may in his discretion stay proceedings on any pending charge, a right that is given statutory recognition.

But in all these instances the prosecutorial discretion is exercised in relation to a specific case. It is the particular facts of a given case that call that discretion into play. But that is a far different thing from the granting of a blanket dispensation in favour of a particular group or race. Today the dispensing power may be exercised in favour of Indians. Tomorrow it may be exercised in favour of Protestants, and the next day in favour of Jews. Our laws cannot be so treated. The Crown may not by executive action dispense with laws. The matter is as simple as that, and nearly three centuries of legal and constitutional history stand as the foundation for that principle. [1]

How shocking that, in just over 30 years, the very situation the Manitoba

Court of Appeal warned us about has now come to pass. We must reject – out of hand – the notion that people should be treated differently by our criminal justice system based on their race or religion, and we must not shy away from calling such treatment what it is: racism, pure and simple.

* * *

If I accept that my rights come from the state, I must also accept that the state can, if it so desires, take them away. But the fact is that I don't need the state to tell me that everyone is equal, and to treat people equally, because my rights as an individual are inalienable and innate in me as a human being; they are not derived from the creation of England's Bill of Rights (1689) or Canada's Bill of Rights (1960) or even from our Charter of Rights and Freedom's (1982). As I have come to see, even in a professed free society such as we have here in Canada, when it comes to our rights, it's a case of "use them, or lose them." As the saying goes, **"The only thing necessary for the triumph of evil is for good men to do nothing."**

I, and the people who stand with me, have heeded this warning. I believe that, as Canadians, we have a far greater obligation to unite to battle injustice, even if the hurdles to overcoming it seem great, because we live in a system that allows for protest. That truth struck Mark Vandermaas, for one, when the Canadian Society for Yad Vashem (Israel's official memorial agency for victims of the Holocaust) sponsored him to bring a bus load of people to Ottawa to take part in the National Holocaust Remembrance Day on April 23, 2012. Mark was profoundly moved when he was asked to help light the final candle in the ceremony.[2] As I watched him perform this act of honour and remembrance, I thought to myself that it was only two days ago that he had been arrested in Caledonia for standing up for the rights of Canadians.[3] In another honour, a tree was planted in Israel for Merlyn Kinrade by the Jewish Defence League of Canada.

Neither Mark nor Merlyn stood up for freedom and equality because the state told them they had a duty to do so. They did it because they, the freeborn citizens of a democracy, felt a duty that came from within.

Of course, it's easy to rationalize sitting back and doing nothing. You can tell yourself that, while you don't like what's happening, you don't want to do anything that might compromise you and your family's safety, and/or your ability to provide for them. It's easy to think that, since you're a taxpayer, the government can and should "fix" all the problems. After all, isn't that why they were elected? Unfortunately, it doesn't work that way, and every generation must address the reality that the state rarely corrects an injustice unless pressured to do so. Further, as the example of Caledonia and other examples demonstrate, when the state tries to correct one injustice (the historical injustice done to

Canada's Native peoples), it can end up instituting a new injustice such as the unequal treatment meted out by police and courts to Natives and non-Natives.

My response to the injustice in Caledonia was inspired by the courageous, non-violent actions of Dr. Martin Luther King Jr. in the American South. And, as his example shows, the sort of change he was working for – to change the heart of a nation – can take a long time to accomplish. That's why I tell those who join us in Caledonia that they should be prepared for the long haul. They should steel themselves to withstand abuse, not only from the militants and their anti-capitalist allies, but especially from the police and court system. One speech, one rally, one more event, won't bring the resolution we seek. It will take many speeches, many rallies, and likely many, many years. But if you are single-minded, and you know you have right on your side – as Dr. King knew – eventually, you will prevail. You just need to stand the test of time.

* * *

Canadians should be aware that they have an additional legal option for redress, one that is rarely used and is uniquely Canadian. It has never been allowed in the United States and has been done away with in most democratic countries. I am speaking of the right of Canadians to lay criminal charges via the private prosecution provisions of the Criminal Code – even against government officials and police. While such a law has the potential for abuse, Parliament has accepted it as a legitimate measure. In 1986, a legal report issued to Parliament said as much:

> As will become evident it is our belief that a criminal justice system that makes full provision for private prosecution of criminal and quasi-criminal offences has advantages over one that does not. In any system of law, particularly one dealing with crimes, it is of fundamental importance to involve the citizen positively. The opportunity for a citizen to take his case before a court, especially where a public official has declined to take up the matter, is one way of ensuring such participation....

> For reasons which follow we have concluded that as nearly as possible, the private prosecutor ought to enjoy the same rights as the public prosecutor in carrying his case forward to trial and ultimately to final disposition on appeal. This is a modest proposal but an important one, since it underscores our belief in the value of citizen/victim participation in the criminal justice system and serves to reinforce and demonstrate the integrity of basic democratic values" ... we believe that private prosecutions are not only desirable but also necessary for the proper functioning of the Canadian prosecution process... [4]

Canadian citizens have always had the right to perform citizens' arrests and pursue private prosecution, but the way the law was constructed provided loopholes whereby the police and Crown could ignore these rights. Over the past 50 years the Supreme Court of Canada ruled in ways that were consistent with Parliament's expressed interest in gradually increasing the rights of citizens and gradually lessening the control of Crown prosecutors. In 2002 the federal government started adjusting the Criminal Code to ensure that every citizen had the unimpeded right to lay criminal charges. The thinking behind it was that if you give people access to the courts they can resolve their issues without resorting to criminal behavior. Virtually every area of the Criminal Code has been adjusted since then. Even the title "Crown prosecutor" has been changed to "the prosecutor" to better reflect the fact that average citizens can act as prosecutors. In theory it is now easier for the average person to prosecute cases, set bail conditions and handle appeals.

I must stress that this development has not been entirely to the liking of the police or the Crown. My own view is that, quite simply, they are arrogant, and don't like this power being put in the hands of the people. Many may recall the case of Toronto shop owner David Chen who, exasperated at being ignored by police, performed a citizen's arrest of an individual who had repeatedly robbed him. The Toronto police's absurd response was to arrest the shop owner along with the thief. The local Crown attorney added insult to that injury by dropping charges against the thief so that he could testify in court against the man he had robbed (Chen was later acquitted).[5] Even the federal New Democratic Party joined others in insisting that the government change the law to end such foolishness. As a result of those changes, individuals have a stronger right to make citizens' arrests, and it is harder for police to victimize them, as they did Mr. Chen.[6]

Police and the Crown have been very slow to acknowledge the revised laws, however. A week after the citizen's arrest law came into effect, I placed two Native protesters – one who had assaulted me with a lacrosse stick and one who was a thief – under citizen's arrest. The OPP, apparently not caring about these laws, simply released the Natives and arrested me "to prevent a breach of the peace" (in other words, to stop Native protesters from continuing to assault me). But since my citizen's arrests were completely legal, both cases were set for trial, and, as of this writing, the Native who assaulted me has been convicted.

Jeff Parkinson, a founding CanACE member, was a real trail-blazer. He was the first of our group to act as his own prosecutor. The circumstances: Jeff and Merlyn Kinrade were talking to Buck Sloat, an elected Haldimand County councilor. Sloat became outraged when Merlyn kept asking him pointed questions as Jeff taped the discussion. All of a sudden, Sloat grabbed Jeff by the shoulder, took his tape recorder, and threw it on the sidewalk. He then walked away. The OPP refused to do anything (it was, after all, an elected official assaulting a member of CanACE, a group the OPP despised), so Jeff filed a private prosecution against Sloat, and a Justice of the Peace ordered Sloat to face a criminal charge. Later on, Jeff laid charges against two OPP officers he caught helping Native protesters build a barricade to prevent the rightful (non-Native) property owner from using his own Hagersville property, and became (after an extended court battle with the Crown) the first citizen in Canadian history to compel a Justice of the Peace to issue criminal charges against government officials.

Historically, we've always had the right to lay charges, but the Justice of the Peace could disallow them with no appeals process available; changes in 2002 to the Criminal Code included the right to seek an 'Order of Mandamus,' an appeal process to a higher court. (I say that Jeff "compelled" the Justice of the Peace because during the hearing – called a 'pre-enquete' – for Jeff's charge, the Justice initially followed the Crown and agreed that no charge should be issued, in part because of Jeff's "bias" against OPP officers. I had Jeff file a Mandamus application to compel the Justice to issue the charge. This led to an unintended bit of comedy; I vividly remember the day Crown attorneys stood before Superior Court of Ontario Judge Marshall and, in their ignorance, actually declare that he had no authority to issue Jeff's Mandamus. After a two-day hearing, Judge Marshall issued our Mandamus, which ordered the original Justice of the Peace to sign the paperwork that would allow Jeff's charge against the two OPP officers to be issued.[7])

Since then we have submitted several Mandamus applications and won all but one (against the best government lawyers your tax dollars can buy). I even won a Mandamus that prevented the Crown from withdrawing charges prior to a ruling by the Justice of the Peace. The Crown didn't want an independent JP reviewing evidence about whether government officials had committed a crime, and wanted to interfere so that it could cover for these officials. Judge Marshall of Superior Court disagreed, emphasizing the importance of the case we were bringing forward in his *McHale v. R.* ruling by quoting Alexander Hamilton, one of the fathers of the U.S. constitution:

> [45] *This case raises the important issue of a citizen's right to lay criminal informations against public officials and for those informations to be heard before an independent judge. This is a long held and hard fought right.*

> [46] Indeed, Alexander Hamilton wrote in The Federalist Papers at page 78: *"Considerate men...ought to prize whatever will tend to...fortify that temper in the courts (independence); as no one can be sure that he may not be tomorrow the victim of a spirit of injustice, by which he may be a gainer today."*[8]

The Crown appealed, but the Court of Appeal for Ontario ruled in our favour.[9] This ruling was most recently cited at length by the Quebec Superior Court.[10] In short, private prosecution allows citizens to take their evidence before the court and have criminal charges issued against government officials. Such an option is not available anywhere else in the world. However, this uniquely Canadian process should be used only in the clearest instances of officials who have violated the law. While such officials may not be terribly concerned when civil lawsuits are launched against them, since government will cover their costs, they care very much about criminal charges, because a conviction is against them personally. Even when the Crown drops a charge, it is still on the record that the Court found that there was enough evidence to issue the charge.

So far, we have successfully laid criminal charges against one politician; five OPP officers (including one commissioner, one deputy-commissioner – who is now the present commissioner – a superintendent, a sergeant and one constable); and two of the most proactive native occupation leaders in the region.[11] While there are still legal loopholes which enable the local Crown to interfere with private prosecutions, the battle to ensure that average citizens have the legal means to stand up against injustice goes on – and will continue so long as injustice persists.

1   Manitoba Court of Appeal, Nov 14/77: *R. v. Catagas.* *
2   IsraelTruthWeek.org, April 26, 2012: Israel Truth Week friends travel to National Holocaust Remembrance ceremony in Ottawa. *
3   VoiceofCanada.ca, April 27, 2012: Vandermaas email to OPP officer re April 21 DCE rally before two 'breach of peace' arrests. *
4   Law Reform Commission of Canada, 1986, Working Paper 52 – *Private Prosecutions.* *
5   *National Post*/Canada.com, Oct. 29, 2010: Toronto shopkeeper cleared in citizen's arrest case. *
6   *TorontoStar*.com, July 16, 2013: New citizen's arrest powers come into effect in Canada. *
7   Ontario Superior Court of Justice, Endorsement – Application for Judicial Review, Jan 12/09: *Jeffrey Parkinson v. Her Majesty the Queen.* *
8   Ontario Superior Court of Justice, Reasons for Judgement, July 2, 2009: *Gary William McHale v. Her Majesty the Queen.* *
9   Court of Appeal for Ontario, May 17, 2009: *McHale v. R.,* 2009. *
10 Takefman c. Court of Québec (Criminal and Penal Division), 2012, QCCS 6295 (CanLII). http://canlii.ca/t/fw2qt
11 CanACE private prosecutions: see online list of cases. *

* See http://www.GaryMcHale.ca/book for additional information, links to documents, videos and photos

Chapter 11

Five Myths of the Caledonia Occupation that Threaten Our Rule of Law

In order to understand the impact of Caledonia on Ontario and Canada, we must look beyond the fact that one group of people was allowed to use violence against another group. The real danger is a direct attack on the Rule of Law.

The vast majority of our work consists of court action arising out of our protests, arrests, and education of the public, police, politicians and members of the media. This is done through our various websites, private communications/meetings, town hall meetings, news conferences at Queen's Park, conferences sponsored by others, and in-depth reports that have been downloaded a combined total of over 300,000 times. Our 101 page *Human Costs of Illegal Occupations report* [1] filled the need for a comprehensive reference about Caledonia's misery until the 2010 release of Christie Blatchford's *Helpless,* [2] for which we provided significant evidence and sources.

In 2008, we released *Legalized MYTHS of Illegal Occupations* [3] to help business people and landowners, especially, understand that the reasoning behind police refusal to protect them from illegal occupations was based on complete legal fiction. What the OPP, the McGuinty government and Crown lawyers could not accomplish in court (because racist policing is illegal in Canada), they accomplished by propagating myths. Through endless repetition, these myths have, in effect, become the truth. Though both false and illegal, the myths now drive, and are used to justify, the actions of police, the provincial government and the Crown.

177

Myth #1: A Native occupation is justified by "Colour of Right"

There is no greater issue facing property owners in Ontario than whether or not Native Protesters are exempt from the Criminal Code of Canada. The issue obviously affects developers: an article entitled HELD HOSTAGE in the Spring, 2007 edition of the *Ontario Homebuilders Association* magazine expresses builders' frustration at how the government was allowing Native protesters to occupy and shut down construction sites.[4]

The OPP claims Native protesters have the legal right to enter private property and to block and stop construction because of "Colour of Right." That's a legal concept that means a person is exempt from prosecution if he believes that what he is doing is legal. What is crucial here is intent: if Natives honestly believe the land they are occupying belongs to them, then there is no intent to do something wrong, and their actions can thus be legally justified. Here's how the Ontario Ministry of the Attorney General explained "Colour of Right" in its June 28, 2006 submission to the Ipperwash Inquiry:

> As a defence to a criminal charge, colour of right involves a lack of mens rea. In that sense, colour of right is "an honest belief in a state of facts or law which, if it existed, would be a legal justification or excuse." If upon all the evidence it may fairly be inferred that the accused acted under a genuine misconception of fact or law, there would be no offence committed because there is colour of right.[5]

Another reference to "Colour of Right" can be found in our Criminal Code: Colour of Right – section 429(2) "No person shall be convicted of an offence under sections 430 to 446 where he proves that he acted with legal justification or excuse and with colour of right."[6]

Is the Attorney General's definition of "Colour of Right" correct? Yes. Does the Criminal Code mention "Colour of Right" and thus, exempt people from being charged criminally? Yes. However, does that mean that Native protesters are automatically exempt from being prosecuted just because they claim land rights or treaty rights? No, it most certainly does not.

As well, "Colour of Right" applies to *all* citizens, not just to Natives. Say, for instance, you come home one night, find you have locked yourself out, and break a window to get in. You cannot be charged and convicted of break and enter because it is your property, your intent wasn't wrongful, and "Colour of Right" thus applies. Here's another example: suppose you park your car in a lot and discover you have left your keys inside after locking the car. Again, you decide to break a window. Seconds later you realize your car is actually in the next lane, and that you have smashed the window of a car that looks exactly like yours. Should that happen, you would likely not be charged with a crime (though, of course, you would still be legally responsible for repairing the damage).

In other words, every property owner in Canada has "Colour of Right" over his property. But does that mean Native protesters have "Colour of Right" over these same properties, as the OPP has repeatedly told property owners? Under Canadian laws, occupations (trespassing, mischief, intimidation, extortion, etc.) are illegal, plain and simple. There is no law or legal ruling that legalizes criminal behaviour. And the fact that police refuse to lay a charge, citing "Colour of Right," doesn't alter the reality that a crime has been committed and that the occupation is illegal.

I may speed down a highway, but even if police do not pull me over and charge me, I have still broken the law. If an officer does pull me over and, using his discretion, decides to let me off with a warning, that does not establish my legal right to speed down the highway. Unfortunately, far too many police officers have come to believe a crime is committed only if they decide to lay a charge. (Using the same logic, it was legal for whites to beat blacks in the pre-Civil Rights era American south because police did not lay charges). Remember that a crime is committed whether or not police lay a charge.

Furthermore, all courts in Canada have rejected Native claims of "Colour of Right" during these illegal occupations. Courts have recognized that, just because a protester who happens to be Native honestly believes that what he is doing is right, that doesn't turn criminal actions into non-criminal ones. Imagine the violence and chaos – the anarchy – that would ensue if everyone used "Colour of Right" as an excuse to commit crimes.

For the record, both the Attorney General of Ontario and the OPP brass know full well "Colour of Right" does not justify Native occupations because the Attorney General's own report to the Ipperwash Inquiry in 2006 contained dozens of court rulings establishing that Native protesters are *not* exempt from the law by virtue of "Colour of Right." The report concluded with this blunt assessment:

> *There is no jurisprudence, even as it has evolved to date, that supports the view that the concept of "colour of right" entitled the Aazhoodena to act as they did in occupying Ipperwash Provincial Park in September, 1995.[7]*

Here is one of the rulings, cited in paragraph 50:

> *As noble and honourable his motives might be they are really irrelevant in our considerations pertaining to "colour of right". Unless it can be demonstrated to this Court, that his honest belief in the existence of a state of facts, in this case title to the subject lands, is based on a mistake*

179

of fact or law, his defence cannot succeed on moral conviction alone. Moral convictions though deeply and honestly felt, cannot transform illegal actions into legal ones; only the "rule of law" must prevail. [8]

It is immediately followed by this one:

The test for the presence of an honest belief is subjective, but there must be an air of reality to the claim before the defence is put to the jury. [9]

In another ruling in the Attorney General's report, *R. v. Roche*, the Court considered the "air of reality" test requirement [that any proposed defence must have an evidentiary foundation] in relation to an aboriginal protest concerning land at the Goose Bay Airport. The court found that denial of the fact of Canadian sovereignty over the land and jurisdiction of the Canadian courts was "not a reasonable or practical assertion in the 1990's," and therefore the "air of reality" requirement had not been met. The Attorney General quoted *R. v. Roche* to point out that Aboriginals can be charged with a crime even if they deny the fact of Canadian sovereignty and reject the jurisdiction of Canadian courts. [10]

Later, the report cites *R. v. Billy*:

56. An aboriginal right does not exist merely because it has been asserted to exist. In the context of "Colour of Right," there must be some basis for a belief in the existence of aboriginal title beyond a bare assertion. R. v. Billy *[2005] B.C.D. Crim. 250.30.55.00-02 (B.C.S.C.) at pars.11, 15*

57. The case of R. v. Billy *involved the blockade of the road to B.C.'s Sun Peaks resort area, a road that had existed as a public highway for more than 20 years. The accused were convicted of intimidation and their appeal was dismissed. The appellate judge had this to say about the protesters' bare assertion of ownership:*

Asserting aboriginal title on a roadway that has existed for some time, as the appellants in this case do, is not sufficient to raise a prima facie case as to their entitlement. The trial judge commented that the appellants' claim was based on a "presumed entitlement" and that they "posit an entitlement to....lands which, rather than having title, they claim title.

.....The trial judge rightly concluded that a bare claim of ownership of the land was insufficient [to establish colour of right]. [11]

The Attorney General's legal team goes on in paragraph 58 to show that Native protesters cannot simply ignore indications of ownership by others and break the law:

58. The case of R. v. Penashue *also involved a protest, by Innu [Aboriginals] at the Goose Bay, Labrador airport. Protestors gained entry to the airbase that had been in use for over 40 years by rushing the gate and going under barriers, despite warnings by a security guard and a request by the R.C.M.P. that they leave the premises. The trial judge reviewed the law with respect to "Colour of Right" and rejected the defence. In his decision, the judge observed that only legal means could be used to protest wrongs or assert rights:*

> *It is clear from the evidence that the accused was involved in a protest. Furthermore, **even using a subjective test, while he felt he and his people owned the land it is clear he also knew that by fences, signs, a barricade, etc., that he was not authorized or permitted to go inside the fence and to do so would likely mean he was committing a breach of the law.** I do not feel the accused honestly believed he was not doing something unlawful when he went onto the base...*

> *If the acts of the accused amounted to a defence in this case this would basically mean that if one believes in a cause, no matter what surrounding circumstances exist, illegal means can be used to promote that cause. There are obviously lawful methods to reacquire property that has been improperly possessed including civil proceedings...*

> *Certainly no one can breach the criminal law even to protest a civil wrong committed against them. Only legal means can be used to protest such acts.* [12]

Please reread the emphasised section (my emphasis) which, all by itself, destroys the protesting Natives' "Colour of Right" argument. The mere fact that a construction company has put up signs and fences on a construction site is enough to establish to any reasonable person that someone has a claim on that land, and that, should you enter that property, you are likely violating the law. But in Caledonia, the OPP and Native protesters tell property owners exactly the opposite – that it is reasonable for Natives to enter and occupy a construction site, and that it is not a violation of the law to do so. Property owners – and all Canadians – should know that this is a myth; when there are signs a property owner is using his property, especially when he erects a fence and posts "No Trespassing" signs, "Colour of Right" does not give Natives the right to enter that property.

In recognition of this truth, every single injunction application sought by property owners in the Haldimand Tract resulted in court orders calling for police to remove Native trespassers.

Even though the report rejecting the 'Colour of Right' defence to illegal occupations was prepared during his service as Attorney General (Oct. 2003-Oct. 2007), former Aboriginal Affairs Minister Michael Bryant once tried to convince Hal-dimand County councillors at a public meeting that took place on April 22, 2008 that it was a legitimate legal reality. We provided Mayor Marie Trainer with a copy beforehand and, when Bryant finished speaking, she read out the conclusion cited earlier and asked him to respond. Jeff Parkinson captured the stunned Bryant's nonsensical, caught-with-his-hand-in-the-cookie-jar reply on camera.[13]

Myth #2: Police in Caledonia can and do exercise discretion

In a widely publicized January 15, 2013 YouTube video responding to criti-cism of police response to the Idle No More protests, OPP Commissioner Chris Lewis stressed the fact that individual police officers have the discretion to decide whether or not to lay a charge.[14] He is correct that police discretion is part of a proper justice system but wrong to assert that the OPP practices such discretion in a proper legal manner.

Police discretion refers to the ability of individual police officers to use their own experience and judgment to decide whether or not to lay a charge at a par-ticular moment. It is thus completely different from officers being told what to do by superiors, a situation which, by its very nature, strips officers of the abil-ity to use their own discretion. So when Commissioner Lewis says, on the one hand, that individual officers can exercise discretion, and on the other hand that he is proud he helped create and institutionalize the OPP *"Framework,"* a document which essentially deprives officers of their discretion by telling them to avoid arresting Natives as a matter of police policy, he is speaking out of both sides of his mouth.

The OPP may believe that its *"Framework"* takes precedence over an individu-al officer exercising discretion, but the Supreme Court of Canada begs to differ. It has made clear that, while policies such as the *"Framework"* can influence how individual officers make their decision, they cannot control the officer's actions. For example, the court heard the case of a police officer who had been convicted of obstructing justice because he failed to take breath samples of a fellow officer and, as a result, that officer could not be charged with impaired driving. At trial, the accused claimed that he had exercised police discretion in a proper way. However, the Crown argued otherwise, saying he used his discretion to give a fellow officer preferential treatment, an improper use of that power.

As proof of preferred treatment the Crown argued that police policy was to al-ways take a breath sample and thus, because the officer failed to do so, he used his authority improperly. The Supreme Court disagreed, stating that police policies couldn't interfere with police discretion: "... It should be pointed out that these [administrative] directives do not have the force of law. They therefore cannot alter the scope of a discretion that is founded in the common law or a statute... An officer's duties and hence his or her responsibilities cannot be equated with instructions as to how those duties and responsibilities should be carried out. Police policies speak to the manner in which police should carry out their responsibilities, but do not define or limit those responsibilities." [15]

When Commissioner Lewis says the "*Framework*" allows for the proper exercise of police discretion, he is not being truthful. To repeat, the "*Framework*" does just the opposite. Despite that, police officers serving in Caledonia are forced to apply it, and to forget about exercising their own discretion. Commissioner Lewis admitted as much in his YouTube video when he said that police had followed the "*Framework*" in over 60 Idle No More protests – how is it possible that at every single one of these events officers independently decided to follow the "*Framework*" unless they are automatically bound by a top-down directive to follow it?

The Supreme Court also made it clear that when an officer does use his discretion NOT to make an arrest that race should not play a role in it. The court stated: "a police officer who has reasonable grounds to believe that an offence has been committed, or that a more thorough investigation might produce evidence that could form the basis of a criminal charge, may exercise his or her discretion to decide not to engage the judicial process. But this discretion is not absolute. Far from having *carte blanche,* police officers must justify their decisions rationally... a decision based on favouritism, or on cultural, social or racial stereotypes, cannot constitute a proper exercise of police discretion. However, the officer's sincere belief that he properly exercised his discretion is not sufficient to justify his decision."

In chapter 10 I quoted from the 1977 Manitoba Court of Appeal which held that the government cannot exempt people from laws based on that person's race, culture, religion or ethnicity.[16]

What we see from these court rulings is that discretionary authority isn't in the hands of OPP brass at all. Legally, it is in the hands of average, front-line officers who, based on their own experience, decide on the best approach to take. Despite that, officers have testified in court that they believed they would be punished if they did not treat Native and non-Native protesters differently.

We should recall, as well, what the court ruled regarding the OPP's use of authority during the 2008 illegal occupation in Cayuga: "The police have the right to use their discretion in the enforcement of the law and private property rights. A blanket refusal to assist a property owner or a class of property owners, however, would be an abuse of that right."[17] When faced with criticism of the force's refusal to protect property owners being victimized by Native protesters in Caledonia, both former OPP Commissioner Julian Fantino and current Commissioner Chris Lewis have cited the number of charges laid as 'evidence' they are not engaged in racial or political policing. In response to a highly critical National Post editorial published June 27, 2013 Lewis wrote:

> *Since April 2006, the OPP has laid 191 criminal charges against 96 persons relating to the Douglas Creek Estates...The OPP has exercised the proper use of discretion in the interests of public and officer safety. Rather than inflame a volatile situation, police will sometimes gather evidence and wait for a safer time to make an arrest. The proper use of police discretion should not be confused with lack of enforcement.*[18]

By way of comparison, the London Police Service laid 175 charges against 68 suspects in connection to a riot that lasted just one day in March 2012.[19] The Vancouver Police have so far laid 763 charges against 246 suspects in connection with the hockey riots of 2011, again, just one day of lawlessness.[20] Contrast these numbers with the OPP's statistics for *seven years* of chaos in Caledonia, and it becomes obvious that OPP officers are not using their discretion, but are acting under orders from above in the form of '*The Framework*' to conduct racist policing practices to the benefit of Native protesters at the expense of non-Natives.

Furthermore, OPP Association President Karl Walsh was outraged by the low number of arrests that OPP officers were allowed to make. In an October 2010 article published in the Hamilton Spectator, Walsh's view, as reported in Christie Blatchford's book Helpless, stated, "But the grumbling among the rank-and-file had already started to percolate. Most of the complaints were directed to Ontario Provincial Police Association boss Karl Walsh, who later coined the phrase 'two-tiered justice system.' Walsh was alarmed by the scant number of charges that had been laid against the protesters, who had blocked public highways, knocked out a hydro substation, torched a rail bridge, hijacked a police vehicle and thrown a van over a bridge. They had also looted houses in full view of the police and media."[21]

It should be noted that not one charge was issued for any of the offences Walsh lists above. So much for Commissioner Lewis' proud statement about the number of charges issued.

Myth #3: Businesses and landowners must consult with and accommodate Natives

Native protesters say that, because of treaty rights, the Crown has a duty to consult with and accommodate them, and that's correct. However, when they declare that businesses are similarly obligated, that is simply not so. The Supreme Court has ruled that the Crown – i.e. Federal and Provincial governments – has a duty to consult and accommodate Natives where possible, but that obligation does not apply to individual citizens, businesses and corporations. (Local municipalities are corporations and thus are not considered to be the Crown.) Therefore, a business does not have to consult with Natives, and Native protesters do not have the right to occupy a business and force it to negotiate with them. Despite that, however, the OPP, instead of informing Caledonia business owners of their rights, has chosen to remain silent all the while acting, in effect, as security guards for Native protesters to keep lawful owners from using or developing their property.

In fact, it is common practice for the OPP to disregard the rights of non-Native property owners as a way to force them to consult with Native protesters as it did, for example in the Cayuga occupation.[22] The Ontario Superior Court objected to this practice, stating: "The remaining defendants' [Native protesters'] resort to self-help, taken with the authorities' refusal to defend the plaintiff's property rights, has put the plaintiff in a most unfair position. The same government that advises the plaintiff not to pay extra-governmental development fees refuses to enforce its property rights and threatens to arrest its agents if they try to enforce these rights on their own."[23]

In another case, *Haida Nation v. British Columbia (Minister of Forests)*, the Supreme Court of Canada held that, Weyerhaeuser Company Limited, a forestry company did not have to consult with Natives before cutting down trees on provincially-owned land. The court ruled: "The duty to consult and, if appropriate, accommodate cannot be discharged by delegation to Weyerhaeuser. Nor does Weyerhaeuser owe any independent duty to consult with or accommodate the Haida people's concerns... Third parties cannot be held liable for failing to discharge the Crown's duty to consult and accommodate. The honour of the Crown cannot be delegated, and the legal responsibility for consultation and accommodation rests with the Crown."

Furthermore, it is a myth that the duty to consult means that Native protesters have veto rights over government policies and decisions. The duty to consult does not mean the government is bound to reach a deal, only that it must make a 'good faith' attempt to accommodate. In the Supreme Court ruling of *Taku River Tlingit First Nation v. British Columbia* the court stated, "On the principles discussed in Haida, these facts mean that the honour of the Crown placed the Province under a duty to consult with the TRTFN in making the decision to reopen the Tulsequah Chief Mine... It did so, and proceeded to make accommodations. The Province was not under a duty to reach agreement with the TRTFN, and its failure to do so did not breach the obligations of good faith that it owed the TRTFN."[24]

The Cayuga builders whom we assisted by laying charges of Extortion, Intimidation and Mischief against the ringleaders of an occupation[25] reported that they had cited our *Legalized MYTHS* report information about 'Duty to Consult' during a meeting with the natives who were trying to extort money from them.[26] The occupiers were shocked to discover that the builders knew the truth.

Myth #4: Canada stole land from Six Nations and violated their treaty rights

The narrative constantly propagated by Native militants and their anti-capitalist supporters is that an evil, colonialist England stole land from the indigenous Six Nations people and has violated its treaties with them which they now want honoured. The OPP have bought into this revision of history; it is quite the sight to see OPP Officers telling non-Natives that treaty rights, and their inability to resolve 'First Nations' underlying land claims' are the reasons police cannot enforce the law. But when you tell these same officers that Six Nations doesn't have any treaties with Canada they look at you as if you have three heads. They've been lied to by their brass for so long that they are clueless about the facts.

The truth is that the people of Six Nations are not First Nations citizens in Canada, nor does Canada have any signed treaties with them, nor were they 'indigenous' to Canada. They originally came from the United States where they were dispossessed of their land after the Revolutionary War. The Crown rewarded them for their service as loyal allies after the war by purchasing the Haldimand Tract from the Mississauga Indians as a refuge for them as per the Haldimand Proclamation of 1784. The Six Nations people were treated honourably by a grateful Crown: Canada did not steal land from them, it bought it for them so they could settle here in safety. Six Nations later surrendered large portions of the tract to be sold by the Crown for their benefit.[27]

There is an amazing CHCH TV interview with a First Nation chief from Mississaugas of the New Credit (i.e. a real First Nation) which shows him screaming at Six Nations' protesters illegally occupying a subdivision in Hagersville, "We legally sold the land to the developer." And yet, Six Nations from the United States think they have veto power over Canadian First Nation Natives.

What the public doesn't know (because the OPP, government and media refuse to tell them) is that the issues in Caledonia have nothing to do with land claims. First of all, the federal Justice Department does not recognize the Douglas Creek Estates as a valid land claim,[28] and legal counsel for the Six Nations band council (not the protesters) have repeatedly told the courts and landowners in Haldimand County that Six Nations is *not* making any claim for possession or return of land. According to three different Superior Court judges who have ruled against three other illegal occupations in Cayuga, Hagersville and Brantford, the recognized representatives of Six Nations have not made any claim for possession or return of surrendered portions of the Haldimand Tract, and such a claim would not succeed even if they did.

The only claims Six Nations have made is for monetary compensation that may be owing. In 2010, for example, a Superior Court judge granted Brantford an injunction against violent occupations that were destroying the city's economy. After reviewing a report on the Haldimand Tract land transfers prepared by an expert from the Ipperwash Inquiry and the related documents he ruled as follows:

> *For more than 150 years the Six Nations did nothing to indicate to innocent third-party purchasers that there was any problem with title to their lands. Property has been bought and sold over that time period. The Six Nations did commence a claim in 1995 against the federal and provincial governments seeking compensation but never for return of the land. Still there was no notice to private landowners, when that action was commenced or after, of any problem with their title. [...] It was not until this case commenced that the Six Nations claimed to have the right to control the activities of private landowners on the basis that the private land within the City of Brantford belonged to the Six Nations. I conclude such an argument must fail.*[29]

So despite the impression conveyed by the OPP, government, and media, Six Nations are *not* First Nations, they have no signed treaties with the Canadian government , and no basis under which to make a property claim. Maybe that explains why some on Six Nations (which includes the Mohawk Warriors) resort to violence – because it's the only way to get the government to submit to their will, and because every court has ruled against them.

(Interestingly, while hundreds of Native groups in Ontario live in peace with non-Native communities, the violent occupations at Oka, Ipperwash, Caledonia and Deseronto have all involved Six Nations Mohawks whose settler ancestors were taken in by the Crown as refugees out of respect for their contributions to the British cause.)

But let's say for a moment that Six Nations did have treaty rights in Canada. What treaty would allow them to burn down bridges or attack power stations? What treaty right permits them to assault police officers and residents? What section of which treaty grants Native protesters the right to wear masks and carry baseball bats to threaten and intimidate others?

The answer: no treaty ever written would accord them such rights. And the fact that OPP officers behave as though Native protesters have such rights by virtue of imaginary land claims and a non-existent treaty between Canada and Six Nations goes to show how badly individual officers have been brainwashed.

Myth #5: The government cannot direct police

The government is required by law to direct the police. Otherwise, we would be living in a police state. In fact, in all democracies, Canada included, politicians have authority over police forces and the military. That means that police and the military are accountable to politicians, and politicians are accountable to us, the people who elect them. Both the government and police are responsible for police policies, but the government cannot direct police in individual cases.

Our law requires governments to direct the police via the minister in charge of policing; in Ontario, it's the Minister for Community Safety and Correctional Services – referred to as the Solicitor General in the Ontario Police Services Act. The minister's legal duties under Section 3(2) (*Duties and powers of Solicitor General*) include the following:

(a) monitor police forces to ensure that adequate and effective police services are provided at the municipal and provincial levels

(b) monitor boards and police forces to ensure that they comply with prescribed standards of service

(e) conduct a system of inspection and review of police forces across Ontario

(f) assist in the co-ordination of police services

(g) consult with and advise boards, community policing advisory committees, municipal chiefs of police, employers of special constables and associations on matters relating to police and police services

(j) issue directives and guidelines respecting policy matters[30]

Furthermore, Section 4(2) (*Core police services*) states:

Adequate and effective police services must include, at a minimum, all of the following police services:

1. Crime prevention.

2. Law enforcement.

3. Assistance to victims of crime.

4. Public order maintenance.

5. Emergency response.[31]

Therefore, the law clearly requires Ontario police services – within reasonable limits of discretion – to take action when they see crimes being committed. It does not permit them to stand by and do nothing. As per the Act, police are expected to aid victims, enforce the law, prevent crime and maintain public order. That's the "minimum" of what they're expected to do. Should police fail or refuse to provide the "minimum" service, the minister in charge is required by law to step in and direct the police force to do its job or to make changes that will ensure it will do so. Of course, politicians love to say that they cannot direct the police – a way for elected officials to avoid being held accountable – but recent events demonstrate just how false this is.

In December 2012 and January 2013, a so-called grassroots political movement called Idle No More organized protests around Ontario, illegally blocking highways, border crossings and railway lines. In response to the blockades, CN Rail went to court and got injunctions ordering police to remove the protesters, an order the city of Sarnia's police force refused to heed. One of the force's sergeants went even further than non-compliance; he was caught on videotape joining protesters in a drumming ceremony, a clip shown repeatedly on SUN News TV. (SUN News often covers what it calls the "Caledonia Disease," which refers to the police practice of doing nothing while Native protesters commit crimes, a precedent set in Caledonia and in Ipperwash before that.) Reacting to this negative coverage, OPP Commissioner Chris Lewis created the YouTube video I mentioned earlier in Myth #2, the one in which he supports the Sarnia police decision to ignore a court injunction. Of course, in so doing he only created more media attention.

By mid-January, 2013 the media were reporting that Ontario Association of Chiefs of Police (OACP) president Steve Tanner had asked Ontario Community Safety Minister Madeleine Meilleur for guidance on how to enforce court orders involving Idle No More protests.[32] In other words, Tanner who, along with being OACP president, is also chief of the Halton Regional Police, was asking the government to tell him how police should proceed. He would not – he would never – have done such a thing if the government could not direct police action. And yet, the myth that the government lacks that power remains the official line.

The truth is that government not only sets the laws, it is supposed to ensure that those laws are enforced. Police are subject to the government, which is accountable to the people. Police cannot make something legal when the government has enacted a law or laws that have made it illegal. And when an entire police force blatantly refuses to uphold the law or respond to court orders, the government is duty bound to correct that wrong.

Mark Vandermaas and I were invited by Dr. Frances Widdowson (co-author of the *Disrobing The Aboriginal Industry*)[33] to speak at the 2010 New Directions in Aboriginal Policy conference at Mount Royal University in Calgary, Alberta where, for first time ever, the voices of the victims – Aboriginal and non-Aboriginal – from Ipperwash and Caledonia were heard at a public policy forum. Mark's presentation was entitled, *Listening to Victims: A Fresh Approach to Healing and Reconciliation* while mine focused on rule of law issues, including the dangers to Native communities: "The Rule of Law exists not just to protect non-Natives but also Native people. God forbid the day ever comes when a group of non-Natives believes they have the right to systematically attack Native People. If it does happen then what will Native People cry out? That people are not subject to the Law, or will they demand that the Rule of Law be enforced to protect them and their children?"[34]

In fact, as cited in Chapter 8, *Cashedonia*, Native people are being victimized by the failure of government to order the OPP to enforce the law in Caledonia: Rapes. Gun violence. Assaults. Arson. When does it stop? When will Ontario's Solicitor General order an end to the racial policing that threatens our rule of law?

1   Canadian Advocates for Charter Equality (CanACE), December 2007: The Human Costs of Illegal Occupations. *

2   Christie Blatchford, Doubleday Canada, 2010: *Helpless: Caledonia's Nightmare Of Fear And Anarchy, And How The Law Failed All Of Us*. See also: www.helplessbyblatchford.ca.

3   Canadian Advocates for Charter Equality (CanACE), May 2008: Legalized MYTHS of Illegal Occupations. *

4   *Ontario Homebuilders Association* magazine, Spring 2007, HELD HOSTAGE. *

5   Attorney General For Ontario, June 28, 2006: Submissions of the Province of Ontario [to Ipperwash Inquiry], Part 1 – Submissions on the Evidence, Colour of Right, pp. 17-25, para 47. *

6   *Criminal Code of Canada*, Colour of Right, section 429(2). *

7   Attorney General For Ontario, June 28, 2006: Submissions of the Province of Ontario [to Ipperwash Inquiry], Part 1 – Submissions on the Evidence, Colour of Right, pp. 17-25, para 74. *

8   Ibid., para 50. *R. v. Drainville* (1991), 5 C.R. (4th) 38 (Ont.Ct.(Prov.Div.)) at pp. 12-13.

9   Ibid., para 51. *R. v. DeMarco* (1973), 13 C.C.C. (2d) 369 (Ont. C.A.). – *R. v. Robertson* (1987), 58 C.R. (3d) 28 (S.C.C.).

10 Ibid. para 52.

11 Ibid. paras 56-57. *R. v. Billy* [2005] B.C.D. Crim. 250.30.55.00-02 (B.C.S.C.) at pars.14, 15

12 Ibid. para 58. *R v. Penashue* (1991), *90 Nfld. & P.E.I.R. 207 (Nfld.Prov.Ct.)* at paras. 27, 28, 38

13 CaledoniaWakeUpCall.com feature: Michael Bryant & the Colour of Right. *

14 OPP Commissioner YouTube Video, Jan. 15, 2013, Idle No More – OPP Commissioner Chris Lewis' internal message. *

15 *R. v. Beaudry*, 2007 SCC 5, [2007] 1 SCR 190. http://canlii.ca/t/1qbk6.

16 Manitoba Court of Appeal, Nov 14/77: *R. v. Catagas*. *

17 Ontario Superior Court of Justice, Injunction Endorsement, June 10, 2008: 1536412 *Ontario Ltd. v. Haudenosaunee Confederacy Chiefs Council*, Haudenosaunee Development Institute, Hazel Hill, Ruby Montour, Floyd Montour (para 29(2)). *

18 *National Post*, Full Comment, Today's letters, June 19, 2013: OPP Commissioner Chris Lewis letter, Ontario police are not politicized. *

19 *London Free Press*, July 6, 2012: *1 riot, 68 suspects, 175 charges & a $500K tab. Was it worth it?* *

20 Vancouver Police Department, Vancouver Riot 2011: Stats (accessed July 17, 2013). https://riot2011.vpd.ca/.

21 The *Hamilton Spectator*, Oct. 15, 2010, A nightmare of fear and anarchy. *

22 Ontario Superior Court of Justice, Injunction Endorsement, June 10/08: *1536412 Ontario Ltd. v. Haudenosaunee Confederacy Chiefs Council...* para 6. *

23 Ibid, para 28.

24 *Taku River Tlingit First Nation v. British Columbia* (Project Assessment Director), 2004 SCC 74, [2004] 3 SCR 550. para. 22. http://canlii.ca/t/1j4tr

25 Ontario Court of Justice, July 08, 2008: *McHale v. Ruby Montour and Floyd Montour.* * http://voiceofcanada.files.wordpress.com/2008/02/080708-decision-ontcourtjustice-montour-prosecution.pdf

26 Ontario Superior Court of Justice, Injunction Endorsement, June 10, 2008: *1536412 Ontario Ltd. v. Haudenosaunee Confederacy Chiefs Council, Haudenosaunee Development Institute, Hazel Hill, Ruby Montour, Floyd Montour* (paras 6, 7, 8). *

27 Ontario Court of Appeals, Oct. 04, 1974: *Isaac et al. v. Davey et al.* (paras 8-15). *

28 *Hamilton Spectator*, Jan. 26, 2007: Land claim would fail in court: report. *

29 (Brantford) Superior Court of Ontario, Reasons For Judgement, Nov 18, 2010: *City of Brantford v. Ruby Montour, Floyd Montour, Charlie Green, David Martin, Hazel Hill, Aaron Detlor and the Haudenosaunee Development Institute* (para 55). *

30 *Ontario Police Services Act*, R.S.O. 1990, CHAPTER P.15., last amended 2009. *

31 Ibid.

32 SUN News, Jan. 15, 2013, Police chiefs ask government for advice about Idle No More blockades. *

33 Frances Widdowson, Albert Howard, McGill-Queen's University Press, 2008: *Disrobing the Aboriginal Industry: The Deception Behind Indigenous Cultural Preservation.* *

34 Caledonia Victims Project, May 4, 2010: 2010 '*New Directions in Aboriginal Policy*' forum hears Caledonia's pain...and hope. *

* See http://www.GaryMcHale.ca/book for additional information, links to documents, videos and photos

Chapter 12

How We Won Caledonia in the 2008 Federal Election

In 2008 I decided it was time to put an end to all the propaganda being spewed by the OPP and government which claimed that the people of Caledonia were against us and wanted us to go away. I decided that the best and quickest way to do so was to run as an independent in the federal election in the hopes of representing Haldimand-Norfolk in Parliament. That way the public could cast their vote either for or against me.

To say the least, the odds were not in my favour. Elections are expensive, and I had no financial resources to help pay for a campaign. Nor, because I was an independent, did I have the financial and organizational backing that goes along with being a candidate from a major political party. I had never run for office and I had no campaign organization. Even more problematically, because I was running as an independent, I lacked the crucial recognition factor that comes with being the candidate of one of the main political parties (the average independent candidate gets just over 300 votes). Another problem: the Crown was still prosecuting me for the now-infamous Counselling Mischief Not Committed charge, and I was forced to heed travel restrictions that barred me from both Caledonia and nearby Hagersville. That meant that, for the first time in Canadian history, someone facing a possibility of a five-year jail term was running for federal office. How would the public respond?

I was up against some serious competition. The Haldimand-Norfolk electoral district had become a Conservative stronghold and was represented by Diane Finley, one of Prime Minister Stephen Harper's cabinet ministers. Finley's husband, the late Doug Finley, ran Harper's election campaign and who later, courtesy the P.M., was named a senator. The Liberals, who had held the riding for many years before Finley's win, were desperate to get it back. To that end, they brought in a star candidate, Dr. Eric Hoskins, an internationally renowned humanitarian with an Order of Canada to his credit. (Hoskins is now a cabinet minister in Ontario's Liberal government.) The stage was set for me to be publicly humiliated.

The first hurdle to overcome: who was going to work in my campaign – experienced insiders or average people? Right away the key members of CanACE jumped aboard, and my campaign was up and running. The second hurdle: how was I going to get around the OPP's ridiculous travel restrictions? A bail review of my travel restrictions could take months, so Superior Court Judge David Marshall conducted a "negotiation" meeting with the Crown. While he lacked the authority to order changes, he did enable both sides to speak to each restriction. In the end the Crown agreed to change the restrictions somewhat, but I was still limited in my ability to campaign. I was now allowed to go to Caledonia and Hagersville (but only for the duration of the election). However, I was not allowed to travel on certain roads, to visit certain homes, to remain at a Tim Horton's if more than 10 people were there to hear me, or to be part of any gathering consisting of more than 50 people without first notifying the police.[1] The Crown told the court that these conditions were necessary because without them I could cause a riot.

I can remember when the Crown insisted to Judge Marshall that I could not be allowed to speak to more than 10 people at a Tim Horton's. I asked the Crown, "So what do I do if I am speaking and the eleventh person comes over to listen to me?" To which the Crown replied, "Tell them you are on court restrictions and leave." "Well, that is going to really help my election," I said. "You will get more votes because of it," said Judge Marshall.

I think Judge Marshall knew how the public felt about the way the OPP and Crown were prosecuting me; many lawyers and judges were also upset by what they saw as the OPP's and Crown's outrageous abuse of the judicial system. After Judge Marshall passed away in 2009, his son, Albert Marshall, wrote one of my letters of reference when I applied to law school as a mature student. In his letter he mentioned his father's high regard for me. When my wife and I met with the dean of the university, he said, "You come highly recommended by judges and lawyers." (One of their letters included these flattering remarks: "Mr. McHale has, through his court work and social activities, developed and defined Canadian law. I daresay he has made more law to date than most lawyers do in a lifetime.")

What shocked the mainstream political parties was that my campaign was so well-run. I had volunteers running my website,[2] fundraising, and putting up election signs and, I was running full-page ads in several newspapers outlining exactly what I would do if I was elected. The core message of my campaign was to ask voters to 'DARE TO BELIEVE' that things could be better:

> **Dare to Believe** *that one vote, one voice and one riding can make a difference when average people can take back control of their future from the hands of governments that have run amok due to party politics. Dare to Believe that this election enables you, the voter, to say 'Enough is enough!' Dare to Believe that average people, determined to demand more from government, can change the system. You deserve better and do not have to settle for the status quo.* [3]

It was a bold message to proclaim in a country where the central powers in political parties exert control over what their MPs and MPPs – and those running to attain those offices – say and do. But since, unlike Hoskins and Finley, I was an independent, I could, and did, speak freely, with only my conscience as a guide. I even published my religious beliefs in some of my Dare To Believe ads so that voters would know exactly who I was as a person:

> *When I was in my early twenties, I had to decide whether a life of anger, hate and crime was a path I was going to take. Through that process I became a Christian and came to believe that love is greater than hate, peace overcomes anger and lawlessness never solves anything.*

> *Christianity to me is something you live and something you must pay a price for. Throughout history those who have stood up for Justice, for Equality and for the Truth were always the ones who paid the price so others could live Free and have Justice. Those who came before me fought in wars and against injustice in our society so that I could have the freedom to speak up today.*

> *Why did I get involved and why will I not back down? Simply because, as a Christian, there are more important things in life than the next new car or having a big screen TV. Truth, Justice and Equality are not just words but the very heart of a community and of a country.*

My celebrated opponent Dr. Hoskins (who was born in the area and whose parents still lived there) didn't take my candidacy seriously. He predicted that I would get a total of only 348 votes. However, he began to see that I was shaping up to be more of a real threat to him during a televised debate sponsored by the *Hamilton Spectator*. According to the paper's report:

> *The well-spoken Rhodes Scholar and war zone humanitarian was upstaged by Gary McHale, the well-known Caledonia activist (or, if you prefer, rabble rouser) who is running as an Independent. Hoskins un-*

dermined his own position by first identifying the native land claims as the most urgent issue facing the riding, but offered no solution other than a deadline for negotiations which would be tepidly followed by mediation in case of an impasse. Gee, that would be different. By contrast, McHale promised to rattle cages and maintain a media spotlight on the issue until it was solved, threatening to be the worst nightmare for the OPP and provincial and federal powers that be. While Hoskins responsibly offered more of the same, McHale dared frustrated voters to take a risky walk with him along the edge.[4]

In most areas in Canada, election debates are typically not well attended so, when I contacted the organizers of the Caledonia debate and kept suggesting they book the largest hall they could find, they laughed at me and said people don't come out to debates. I was proven right when the hall in Caledonia was packed and people overflowed into the street. Even the washroom door was open for extra space as people filled every square foot of the hall. Political parties put a lot of effort into making it look like they have strong support at these debates by bringing in people with signs and banners to give them the photo op, but it was clear that the public was believing in my campaign. When Ian Nichols, the NDP candidate, saw people responding to me, he leaned over and whispered in my ear, "Looks like this is your town."

Mayor Marie Trainer gave me an unofficial endorsement when she was interviewed by Monte Sonnenberg of the *Simcoe Reformer* who wrote:

Despite the OPP's and the McGuinty government's attempts to cast McHale as a troublemaker, Haldimand Mayor Marie Trainer thinks his candidacy is positive. With McHale in the race, Trainer says Haldimand's quest for peace, law and order, stability and justice will feature prominently in the coming campaign. She says McHale will force the other candidates to state their position on the issue of two-tiered justice. "I definitely think he'll get some votes," Trainer said. "No doubt in my mind. We'll have to wait and see what happens on election night. People will change their minds right up to when they step in the polling booth. He will keep the land claims issue in the forefront." [5]

When the votes were counted, it sent shockwaves through provincial halls of power. I didn't win the riding, but I had won the majority of votes in Caledonia itself. The final tally there: 1,822 for me; 1,668 for the Conservative incumbent; 1,189 for the Liberals; and 567 for the NDP. In the riding as a whole, I received 10% of total votes cast, over 4,800 votes, unheard of for an independent candidate. Best of all, in Caledonia I had come first in nearly every poll and second in the others. That was a kick in the pants, so to speak, to those who had done their utmost to try stop me, and sweet, sweet vindication in the form of a huge vote of confidence from the people of Caledonia for me. Sixty-two percent of my votes came from outside Caledonia, signifying that there was a broad base of support for our efforts.[6] It amounted to a stunning rejection of the deliberate, obsessive official campaign to discredit me, and of all the propaganda targeting CanACE, not just from the OPP, but also from Ontario's then-Minister for Aboriginal Affairs, Michael Bryant (a former Attorney General of Ontario). Bryant had condemned Mark Vandermaas and me for daring to use peaceful and legal means (in this case, our complaints to the Ontario Human Rights Commission regarding our December 16, 2006 arrests) – rather than violence – to resolve Charter violations against us. He claimed:

> *Most people don't have much sympathy for Vandermaas or McHale after their tense rallies in the divided town... their activity, generally-speaking, is extremely harmful and, as far as I can tell unwelcome by everybody. I know a lot of people in Caledonia feel that they're individuals who are just trying to get attention for themselves and are, in fact, stirring it up.*[7]

Obviously, the election results proved otherwise – that Caledonians appreciated our efforts and were glad we were there.

It had never mattered to me if only 30-50 people showed up for our rallies. I knew that many families lived in fear – fear of being targeted by Native protesters, but also and equally – fear that the OPP and the Ontario government would retaliate against them should they have the temerity to stand with CanACE. Caledonians knew that to do so put them at risk of, say, a sudden and unexpected visit from Children's Aid, or the OPP stopping your vehicle for the pettiest of reasons. And who, if they could avoid it, would want to be on the receiving end of that extra – and obviously, politically-motivated – scrutiny?

The fact that so many people voted for me to be their elected representative in Ottawa sent a powerful message to the OPP and the Ontario government. Conservative Diane Finley, the incumbent and eventual winner, must have heard it loud and clear because, not long after the election, she became one of the 5,000 Haldimand residents who signed the petition demanding that Julian Fantino be removed as OPP chief and a public inquiry be called into two-tier justice in Haldimand.[8]

For many years the OPP and the provincial government – with a lot of support from mainstream media with a pronounced leftist bias – have claimed again and again that people didn't support our efforts to restore the rule of law in Caledonia. It turned out that those living there were my strongest supporters, because they knew exactly how the OPP had failed them.

1   Copy of conditions are available on-line. *
2   Gary McHale website for 2008 federal election (http://garymchale.wordpress.com).
3   298 *Regional News This Week*, Oct. 6, 2008, Gary McHale campaign advertisement, Dare to Believe; see also *Simcoe Reformer*, Oct. 7, 2008, Gary McHale campaign advertisement, Dare to Believe. *
4   *Hamilton Spectator*, Oct. 6, 2008, Simple or smooth – you choose. *
5   Monte Sonnenberg, *Simcoe Reformer/Brantford Expositor*, Sept. 8, 2008: McHale seeks H-N seat in federal election. *
6   Gary McHale election website, Oct. 15, 2008: Gary captures 10% of H-N votes. *
7   *Toronto Star*, April 7, 2008, Fantino asked to attend rights mediation. *
8   Residents' petition for inquiry into OPP. *Dunnville Chronicle*, Jan. 17, 2009: Petition asks for inquiry into Fantino and OPP. *

   * See http://www.GaryMcHale.ca/book for additional information, links to documents, videos and photos

Chapter 13

Hope For The Future

Christie Blatchford's book, *Helpless: Caledonia's Nightmare of Fear and Anarchy, and How the Law Failed All Of Us*, captured the reality of how thousands of families felt – helpless and betrayed. Most of us live out our lives believing the system will work and that those who have sworn an oath to serve and protect the public will carry out that duty. We naturally respect police officers because they have the life-threatening job of going after those who commit crimes.

However, now we have police officers who believe that, for the "greater good," they are required to stand by and watch even while their fellow officers and average citizens are harmed, and even when, say, a Native protester places a knife to the throat of an American federal agent. All the police officers I have spoken about in this book would tell you they are upholding the rule of law, maintaining the peace, following the standard protocols and ensuring public safety. The new logic of law enforcement seems reasonable to those in power, but of course it isn't, and ordinary Ontarians are paying the price.

This book isn't about being helpless. It is about how average citizens are the last line of defence in a democracy. It is the people who can and must stand up to the corruption within the justice system when we are failed by elected officials, big business and the PhDs. This is a book about hope and how those few who stand for what is right can and, ultimately, will change the course of history.

'Ten things that have changed in Caledonia since 2006'

After numerous flag raising rallies (including one at Julian Fantino's home)[1]and arrests of law abiding Canadians we were finally able, on July 12, 2009, to raise

199

a Canadian flag across from the entrance to the Douglas Creek Estates.[2] It took nearly another three years and more arrests of 'freedom volunteers' to reach the point, on February 18, 2012, when we finally established the right for all citizens to walk down the county roads on DCE.

Merlyn Kinrade was assaulted that day as were police officers. Although the OPP did not arrest the man who assaulted Merlyn and their officers, they did something that they had never done before – they arrested a native person during the commission of a crime at one of our protests. Teresa Jamieson was carried out by four officers for attempting to strike me with a pipe (it was actually a Native man who stopped her from hitting me, not the OPP).[3] Afterwards I, the victim of the intimidation and assault, was arrested to…you guessed it… prevent more breaches of the peace.[4]

Five days later the *Hamilton Spectator* published a letter by a Six Nations occupation supporter named Tracy Bomberry who was, no doubt, annoyed by the concept that non-Natives should be able to peacefully walk down a road. She accused me of inflaming "a situation that has been on simmer for the past six years," and closed by saying, "Feb. 28 will be the sixth anniversary of this land dispute…and sadly nothing has changed."[5] On that anniversary, marking the start of Caledonia's nightmare in 2006, the *Spectator* published my reply:

Ten things that have changed
Letter to Editor, Hamilton Spectator (Feb. 28, 2012) by Gary McHale

While to some it appears inherently wrong ever to disagree with a native person, I have to say that Ms. Bomberry's view that nothing has changed since 2006 is not supported by the evidence. Here are 10 things that have changed since 2006.

1. *Contrary to the Native occupiers' view, Six Nations Band Council has repeatedly told the court there is no claim on title to people's property. Judges have agreed.*

2. *Courts have repeatedly disagreed with the OPP's refusal to enforce the law and have even rebuked the OPP for targeting legal property owners instead of Native protesters.*

3. *The OPP has been forced to accept that property owners do have the right to have Native trespassers arrested.*

4. *Both Native protesters and the OPP have been forced to acknowledge that non-Native people do have rights in this country.*

5. *Most on Six Nations have rejected the use of violence and terrorism to force land claims upon others.*

6. *The media has been forced to acknowledge that Natives are not always the victim of the evil white man and that some Natives are indeed radicals who commit serious crimes against innocent people.*

7. *The myth that Six Nations people are not subject to Canadian laws has been shattered.*

8. *The rights of private citizens to lay criminal charges against Native protesters, police and government officials is now well established in law.*

9. *The general public has accepted the view that the policies of the OPP are based on the race of the person involved and are unacceptable in a society that believes in equality.*

10. *The greatest accomplishment of all is that we have shown peaceful protests can defeat those who prefer violence.6*

* * *

Since my letter was published, some great things have been accomplished.

In September 2012 we conducted a series of weekly protests that resulted in more arrests of non-Natives for non-crimes. On September 2, the 'Caledonia 8' expanded to become the 'Caledonia 11' as more people volunteered to be arrested for trying to walk down the road through DCE.[7] On September 30, the final protest of 'Freedom Month' – just one week before our great friend and ally, Merlyn Kinrade, passed away – we sat in lawn chairs at the entrance to DCE with our backs to the OPP and the few remaining occupiers behind them – and had pizza delivered to us. Unthinkable just a few months before.

Developments in the past few weeks of the summer of 2013, as I finish the final chapters of this book, have shown that our no-nonsense reputation for defending the rule of law may be acting as 'incentive' for police to do their jobs. When the Hamilton Police refused to remove occupiers (which included Six Nations occupation ringleaders Floyd and Ruby Montour) from Enbridge's #9 Pipeline pumping station in Westover, the company was unnecessarily forced to obtain a court injunction, but the police still didn't remove them.

In the early morning of June 26 I sent Chief Glenn De Caire a letter notifying him that if the occupiers weren't gone by the following week, I would bring my people in to document the crimes and file private prosecution charges. I also told him that I might also arrest and prosecute any officer who obstructed justice by preventing us from gathering evidence. I concluded by saying, "At the bare minimum it is our goal to expose any police force that allows a two tier justice system to be institutionalized. Your department has forced a company to get an injunction solely because you decided not to enforce the law."[8]

The Hamilton Police moved on the occupiers later that day. It could have been just a coincidence, but the media didn't see it that way; the *Toronto Star* and the *Hamilton Spectator* mentioned my letter, but Brian Lilley of SUN News expressed his absolute delight on his *Byline* show (note that Lilley's own comments about the Hamilton Police response as quoted in the Spectator are included in square brackets below):

> *I applaud McHale for taking a stand and taking action...Essentially, McHale was telling the cops 'do your damn jobs before we do it for you.' But, it worked, because this morning they arrested the folks squatting on Enbridge property...This is the type of thing I'm calling for when I say we've got to stand up, we've got to take action, we've got to refuse to let our leaders ignore the rule of law. Now, if you doubt that McHale's actions had any impact on the decision of the police chief to order the removal, then I want you to pay attention to what was being said by the police last night; Hamilton Police, their response to a court order to remove the protesters and barricades...was to send in their labour negotiator. Here's another quote from the* Hamilton Spectator: *'We are doing that with our dialogue with them [enforcing the court order]. They are co-operating with us. When we ask them to do something, they are doing it [other than leaving]. Our role is to keep the peace and to facilitate co-operative action between the folks that are there and ourselves and Enbridge.' That was Superintendent Ken Weatherill.*
>
> *Oh great...cops as facilitators, negotiators. Are they there to enforce the law or are they there to make sure that everyone gets the same number of sprinkles on their organic, fair trade, gluten-free cupcakes before we all start a consensus session? Give me a break!...Gary McHale's actions forced the cops to act and we need to learn from this.*[9]

OPP Commissioner Chris Lewis publicly disagrees with the Crown

Commissioner Lewis may have had a revelation during this summer for he began to see things in an entirely new light. On July 24, 2013 Sun media broke the story that Lewis was publicly disagreeing with the Crown's decision not to prosecute Native protesters who blocked rail lines near Deseronto, Ontario. It is unheard of for police to publicly make negative statements against Crown prosecutors – after all, the police and Crown work hand-in-hand to ensure those who commit crimes are held accountable. Lewis is reported as saying, "the case was discussed with the local Crown attorney, and it was the decision of the Crown that it was not in the public interest to proceed with charges against those responsible... I fully respect the judicial process and the role of the Crown attorney therein, but I fundamentally disagree with the decision in this particular case."

One could ask Lewis why it is okay for the OPP to overlook the crimes committed at over 100 illegal occupations this year, but the Crown cannot overlook the token charges the OPP brought forward at just one occupation? Superior Court judges throughout Ontario have repeatedly rebuked the OPP for their failure to enforce the law and now somehow Lewis is upset that the Crown follows in the OPP's footsteps of race based enforcement of the law.

I will give Lewis some credit – he has created the opportunity for the public to review not just OPP racial policing, but how the Crown prosecutors in Ontario use their own racist policies to give Native protesters special treatment. We have seen this policy play out in Caledonia many times where Crown prosecutors make a half-hearted attempt to present a case in court against Native protesters or simply drop charges.

If however, Lewis has suddenly seen the light and realized that government officials – i.e. police and Crown prosecutors – cannot give exemptions to people based on their race then I would suggest Lewis could start by removing the OPP's *Framework* policies that have created so much harm to the citizens of Ontario. At least he could apologize to the people of Caledonia for forcing upon them race based policing.

I will not hold my breath because I believe Lewis' real motive isn't that he suddenly is against racist enforcement of the law, but an attempt to blame the Crown for why the OPP has such a negative public image. Maybe Lewis sees the writing on the wall that the Liberal government is now doomed to be defeated and he is preparing a way to explain why the OPP failed to lay the thousands of charges for crimes that OPP officers stood by and watched occur. It is clear there will be a public inquiry into the OPP regarding Caledonia and officers are starting to abandon the sinking ship.

The mere fact that Lewis feels the need to say something publicly demonstrates just how far we have come in exposing to all citizens in Ontario the harm caused by OPP racist policies. Even Lewis knows the OPP can no longer ignore public disillusionment with the force.

Canadian Taxpayers Federation

Over the years countless people have thanked CanACE and me for our efforts. That includes government officials, elected politicians, police officers, business owners and average Canadians. While I never doubted that one day the general public would be so outraged by the injustices that even the police and politicians would have to take note, we are grateful when individuals and organizations have stepped forward and taken a stand.

One of the first organizations to publicly denounce what was happening in Caledonia was the Canadian Taxpayers Federation. It had issued various press releases relating to Caledonia, and it provided us with a written statement that was read out during our October 2007 'Remember Us' Rally (which was held two days before the provincial election, just a month after Sam Gaultieri was nearly killed).[10] Here is that statement, which is still posted on the CTF website:

Caledonia March Statement (*October 7, 2007*) *by Kevin Gaudet, Canadian Taxpayers Federation*

Today is a day when we should all be at home with family celebrating Thanksgiving. Instead, sadly enough, you are here making an important point about freedom: freedom of expression, freedom of speech, freedom of association, and freedom not to live in fear in your own homes and your own city. We have been blessed to live in Canada, a country that usually celebrates these freedoms even when they challenge us on sensitive issues such as this.

Everyone wants to see a peaceful resolution to the troubles in Caledonia. Everyone wants a quick resolution to the troubles and disagreements in Caledonia. Governments need to step up to facilitate an end to the standoff so freedom can be returned to Caledonia.

The Canadian Taxpayers Federation is a national, not-for-profit organization with 68,000 supporters. Our mandate is to fight for lower taxes, less waste and greater accountability in government. The standoff has cost taxpayers over $50 million dollars and government has not been accountable for the tremendous hardships all have faced. People like the Gaultieri's and the Brown's, injured OPP officers and so many others can attest to that.

It has been more than 19 long months since this standoff began and it appears no closer to resolution today. Thanks to the unfortunate acts of a few, the failure of governments and the failure of police to act, all are suffering.

This growing rift is not the result of the Six Nations reserve and residents of Caledonia wanting to continue the standoff. It stems from complacency shown by politicians in Queen's Park and Ottawa.

There is no clear-cut evidence that the people of the Six Nation's reserve have a legal claim to disputed land. That is what the legal system will help determine. A swift decision on the land issue would be desirable. However, governments should not negotiate with occupiers or those who support them or fail to condemn them. When governments offer cash settlements to occupiers and their supporters they damage the principle of the rule of law. They also give the appearance that there are different laws for native lawbreakers than for non-native lawbreakers. The government should enforce the rule of law.

In Toronto on June 3rd a group of women anti-poverty activists held their own protest and occupied an abandoned building. Toronto police had them removed and four were arrested in a matter of a few hours. This double standard should not be allowed.

Lawbreakers should be charged and the amount of the settlement offer from the government should be reduced by the amount it has cost taxpayers during this standoff.

It is time for governments to act. We are at the end of the provincial election, a time when promises are flying left and right. Instead of promises we need to see action to end this standoff and quickly and fairly settle the land claims. Thank you for your time.[11]

* * *

On November 13, 2007 the CTF announced a petition calling upon all levels of government:

- To enforce the rule of law equally in Ontario;
- Not to undertake negotiations when there are illegal occupations and blockades;
- To make every effort to recover from occupiers, blockaders and bands all unusual costs incurred due to standoffs; and,
- To work diligently and quickly to resolve outstanding land claims.[12]

The CTF also had the courage to demand that then-Commissioner Julian Fantino be fired for threatening Haldimand Council. In a statement issued April 12, 2007 it stated:

The Canadian Taxpayers Federation (CTF) today called on OPP Commissioner Julian Fantino to apologize to the citizens of Caledonia and Ontario for threatening to quit policing the area and also requests Premier McGuinty confirm for the residents that there will be a police presence for as long as is required. "If the Commissioner won't apologize then the premier should replace him immediately with someone who will keep the peace," said CTF Ontario Director Kevin Gaudet. "Mr. Fantino needs to apologize for threatening to abandon the people of Caledonia. Does he think 'peace, order and good government' means he will keep the peace only if government follows his orders? Instead of threatening Caledonians Mr. Fantino should be urging politicians and Native leaders to end the standoff."[13]

CanACE, and all those who have supported our work were honoured when the Canadian Taxpayers Federation awarded me the Queen's Diamond Jubilee Medal on February 1, 2013.[14] The usual radical leftist characters harassed the CTF, and the Governor General himself received emails trying to stop the award (one writer was forced to apologize in writing after I notified her of my intent to sue for defamation). It is events such as this, where an organization like the CTF takes a stand against the failed and inequitable policies in Caledonia, that give me hope for the future.

And it's not just the CTF I would like to thank. Tribute must also be paid to SUN TV, which has changed the entire course of Caledonia-related media coverage. It had been impossible to get CBC, CTV or Global TV to pay continued attention to the Caledonia issue, and to report on how non-Native residents there have been victimized. None of these networks appear to care about how non-Native residents are being treated, and how they have been subjected to harassment by Natives and illegal arrests by the OPP. (What if the OPP were treating Natives this way – arresting them when they were being assaulted by non-Natives. Can you imagine the outcry from the media? How quickly do you think these outlets would race to the scene to cover every last outrage?) Only SUN TV had the courage to show how the OPP is illegally arresting non-Natives, and give us access when we had important news and background to share. It alone has been willing to publicly name individual officers who have violated the rights articulated in our Charter of Rights and Freedoms.

I could write a whole book on the failure of the media to report the truth about the Caledonia situation, and how SUN TV has filled the gaping hole of media coverage. Again and again, SUN TV hosts such as Ezra Levant; Michael Coren; Brian Lilley; Charles Adler; David Menzies; and Jerry Agar have demonstrated their willingness to report on government abuses and how those in positions of power are harming average Canadians. These members of the media stand for freedom, and are willing to pay the price to do so.

In Caledonia there were two newspapers – The *Regional News* and *The Sachem*. The *Regional News*, owned by Chris and Kevan Pickup was, according to Christie Blatchford (whose *Helpless* book signing event was hosted at their office), a "brave, feisty voice" that confronted local politicians and exposed the failure of the OPP to help local residents.[15] For over two years The *Regional News* allowed me to have a weekly column to report on what was happening in the courts and throughout the county.[16] They were also the only media outlet to publish our '*McGuinty's Ipperwash Cover-up*' series (reprinted in chapter nine). After Mayor Hewitt was elected, however, Haldimand Council punished the paper by transferring all their advertising to The Sachem and, in return, Mayor Hewitt received a weekly column which enabled him to promote himself. [17] As a result The *Regional News* went under as did the *Dunnville Chronicle*. Now the *Sachem* simply refuses to hold accountable either Haldimand Council or the OPP and so many news stories go unreported.

Chris and Kevan Pickup paid a price for standing against injustice when, after forty years in business, they were forced to close their doors.[18] Their final edition of February 8, 2012 included this editorial – defiant to the end, standing for what was right to the end:

> *This present council will likely dance on our grave today, but someone needs to hold them accountable. The Sachem's viewpoint has been bought and paid for by council... the proof is in their editorial pages and the mayor's fatuous weekly columns, so it obviously won't be them. Besides, they've never been critical of anything; cowardice seems to be in the news genes over there.*

> *Then there's our favourite subject – believe me I wish it didn't have to be! – the OPP. That's another organization that will join council in the dance... it will have to be a bloody big grave. But there again, they need to be held accountable. They can't just be allowed to shove their oaths under the bed because it's convenient for the provincial government to avoid the truth, as they have avoided many and many a truth over the last few years and left this province as thoroughly have-not as it is. It seems to us so many police organizations have lost their way, from the RCMP out in B.C. to Hamilton and Toronto officers who have botched so many drug raids by targeting innocent families.*

> *But the OPP is ours, and it's allowing politicians to designate which laws they should and should not enforce. I have nothing but respect for Gary McHale and Merlyn Kinrade and the rest of CanACE who have personally given so much over the last six years and got so much disrespect from those who should know better.*[19]

* * *

Our allies in the Never Again Group from Hamilton have been a great blessing. Not only have they worked to make Israel Truth Week a success, they were the first pro-Israel group to come and stand with us at various protests in Caledonia. Their unofficial spokesperson, Stuart Laughton, a musician of world renown,[20] has proudly shared a jail cell with us; defended our raising of a 'No Jews Allowed by Order of McGuinty' sign at our Queen's Park 'Caledonia Act' news conference[21] (more on that later); served as emcee for two Israel Truth Week conferences; and volunteered hundreds of hours to help edit this book. Others, such as Al Gretzky and Mary Lou Ambrogio of the International Free Press Society came to support us as well. Mary Lou also spoke at our 'Caledonia Act' news conference.

There are many others who helped us along the way with donations of time, money, information, and encouragement and/or by their presence at rallies and court hearings; too many to try to acknowledge here, but they know who they are

Missing in action

Then there are those who, frankly, should have done more, but didn't:

The struggle would have been much easier if the Conservative Party of Ontario had stepped forward and demanded change. I'm speaking here of Ontario Conservative leader Tim Hudak. His riding is right next to Haldimand County, so you might have expected him to take a special interest in what was going on there. Unfortunately, and disappointingly, Mr. Hudak has preferred to ignore the problems; he couldn't manage to find time to visit Caledonia during the 2011 election; he made his first and only trip there because he was under pressure to do so from SUN TV after we invited him to march with the 'Caledonia 8' against racism.[22]

It would have been easier if local businesses had united against injustice, but they didn't. They remain silent and many even opposed the Caledonia Class Action lawsuit; but were quick to line up and get a cheque once the lawsuit was settled for $20 million.

It would have been easier if church leaders – those claiming to be Christian – did more than just hide within the four walls of the church, but they didn't. They reminded us of Dr. King's frustration with the "white ministers, priests and rabbis" who opposed his work outright; and with the others whom he felt were "more cautious than courageous and have remained silent behind the anesthetizing security of stained-glass windows."[23] (We should never forget that although Dr. King eventually became a civil rights icon, he was harshly judged by many of his contemporaries.)

It would have been easier if the Haldimand municipal council had the courage to take a stand. However, as history shows, those in positions of power and leadership are rarely willing to pay the price that taking such a stand is likely to cost them. With very few exceptions they behaved as cowardly appeasers when their community needed them most, and they worked against those of us standing up for justice. The only exception was Mayor Marie Trainer who did speak out in 2006 and was censured for it.

Other than MPP Toby Barrett who spoke at my first rally on October 15, 2006 not one politician ever agreed to speak in defence of Caledonia's victims at any of our protests. Even after Sam Gaultieri was nearly murdered in 2007 by Native protesters, none would share the stage with Sam's brother and 15 year-old Pam 'Dancer' Dudych from the Sixth Line[24] at our pre-election 'Remember

Us' Rally – including Toby Barrett, Marie Trainer and John Tory. It was pitiful that those who were paid to defend our rights and our safety were not willing to stand with the victims when they had the chance to do so.

More illegal peacekeeping missions as the 'Caledonia Disease' spreads

While there is hope for the future, we must be aware that the very OPP policy that has caused so much harm in Haldimand County is now moving across the province and infecting other police forces, and according to *"The Framework,"* there will always be a group sacrificed on the altar of political correctness to ensure that a favoured group is allowed to commit crimes without police interference.

It should come as no surprise that Premier McGuinty extended Julian Fantino's contract as OPP Commissioner so that he could influence policing during 2010's G8/G20 Summit, which he did – that summit is now infamous for its awful policing which saw police turning a blind eye to property destruction and other crimes, and then the victimization of innocent protesters and bystanders. Not a shock there: McGuinty had publicly supported Fantino when he'd done exactly the same in Caledonia. Which begs the obvious question: So, Torontonians: how do you like that Caledonia-style policing?

Thanks to Dalton McGuinty (a failed premier who has since folded up his tent and skulked away, leaving politics, and a great big mess behind him), and thanks to the OPP, the justice system has been twisted into an unrecognizable shape. The legacy of the McGuinty government will affect policing throughout the province for many years to come. The Charter of Rights and Freedoms of individuals will be violated in the name of some greater good. Look, for example, at the riot in London, Ontario in the summer of 2012. Once again the police stood by and watched as rioters destroyed both public and private property. It was only after it was over that police started to make arrests, a lot of them, yes, but not in time to stop a news truck from being torched. In so doing, police have sent a message that comes through loud and clear to every radical group in Ontario and Canada: go ahead and be as violent as you like because the police won't touch you.

On the other hand OPP Sgt. Dan Michaud has admitted to me that Native protesters elsewhere in Ontario have gone to jail for committing the exact same crimes being perpetrated with impunity by Natives in Caledonia. Our conversation concerned protesters near Thunder Bay known as the KI 5 (5 Natives from Kitchenuhmaykoosib Inninuwug First Nation), and in Frontenac, 60 miles north of Kingston. In the latter case, the conviction of the jailed Native protesters was upheld by the Ontario Court of Appeals, which shows that *some* Native protesters are subject to the law once you start pushing back.

In Caledonia, by contrast, police have in effect created a state of martial law whereby the OPP and McGuinty government summarily rescinded the Charter Rights and Freedoms of the entire community so Natives there won't face criminal charges. While the police have made some arrests (which have resulted in some Natives being convicted), the vast majority of the crimes have been ignored. Officers have been trained to turn a blind eye to them, and to not assist victimized non-Natives.

Having established this precedent in Caledonia, police and governments now feel they can follow it in other areas as well. Remember how McGuinty secretly approved special "no-go" zones in downtown Toronto during the G20 summit?[25] It didn't matter what the law said because the police quickly became puppets of the politicians, believing they could do anything as long as their political masters backed them up. We should think about the fact that every single officer who served in Caledonia faced a clear moral question regarding his or her oath of office and duty to individual citizens. Each officer had to choose between aiding victims of crimes, or standing by and watching crimes being committed, and each had to decide whether to accept the standing order that allowed one people to victimize another people. Each officer had to decide whether his or her own paycheque was more important than the victims in Caledonia.

Our police are 'pre-wired' to appease Islamic supremacists

Police and governments throughout the West are facing an ominous new challenge. Just take a look at what's been happening in France, England and even the U.S. (for example, in Dearborn, Michigan) and you can see that police and politicians are responding to Muslim radicals there in much the same way that the OPP have appeased the Native extremists in Caledonia.

Speaking of radicals, we should be clear that there is only a small minority within Six Nations who support the use of violence against their neighbours, but those few who have employed violence are the ones whose actions guide the policies of the OPP and government. (Six Nations councillor Helen Miller has – courageously – made it clear that the radicals don't speak for the people of Six Nations).[26] And if our provincial police can't withstand violent radicals in Caledonia, how can we expect them to handle that small group who hide behind their Muslim faith to justify violence?

The day is coming when there will be a million peaceful Muslims living throughout Ontario, and a few hundred or a few thousand who will choose to use violence. How will the police deal with them – like Native protesters in Caledonia, another group which is so quick to play the victim card and complain about persecution? Will the police uphold the laws equally or will the policies in Caledonia suddenly kick in whereby those who have chosen violence are appeased and innocent, peaceful people will have to pay the price in order to keep the violent ones from being "offended," and from acting out because of it? How will the police and governments stand up to those who want to see the oppressive Sharia law become part of our body politic, and who cleverly use the smokescreen of victimhood and "human rights" to do it?

Dearborn, Michigan provides a cautionary tale. Christians in that Detroit suburb have been arrested for handing out free Bibles or reading from the Bible while on a public sidewalk. We spent three days in Toronto training with a former Sharia courts judge (who is a consultant to politicians in Europe, Great Britain and the U.S.) and a Dearborn activist who explained the ways in which Dearborn police and local politicians are appeasing a few radical Muslims, and where they have, for example, refused to take 'honour' violence seriously. The same thing has been happening in Canada. In Kingston, Ontario, four female members of the Shafia family (three young daughters and the first wife), originally from Afghanistan, were murdered. This 'honour' crime was committed by the father, his second wife and the son. While we can take pride in the fact that they were arrested, prosecuted and convicted (as would anyone else who had committed the crime), we should not be proud of the fact that, for three years before the crime, these women cried out to authorities, who did nothing to help them before they were murdered. And there is little doubt that authorities failed to intervene because these women were Muslim, and because they were worried that doing so might offend the women's abusers, and perhaps even other Muslims outside the family.

Personally, I am all for the religious freedom of any group. At the same time, though, equality before the law *must* be upheld. There was a time when Protestants and Catholics in England killed each other, and whoever was in power had the upper hand. Our laws cannot operate this way. We cannot allow any group to be favoured, whether it arises from good motives or because of fear of violence. Feeling guilty because of past wrongs – and because of fear that certain groups will turn to violence – should never be the basis of public policies. Unfortunately, in our modern society we refuse to learn from the past, and all too often we react out of guilt and fear.

Preserving Our Freedom: What Should Be Done?

On February 10, 2012 we released a comprehensive list of legislative and policy recommendations for preventing future breakdowns in the rule of law at our 'Ending Race–Based Policing: *The Caledonia Act*' news conference in the Queen's Park Media Studio. [27] We made recommendations for changes at both federal and provincial levels of government. Here are some of them:

1. (Federal) Change the Criminal Code to make civil rights violations a federal offence as America did during the civil rights era

I see no option other than to enact new laws to ensure that police must enforce the law equally. When the USA was faced with the reality that certain states would not prosecute white criminals who victimized blacks, the Federal government made it a Federal crime to violate anyone's civil rights. This is needed in Canada, too; currently, the only legal remedy for Charter violations is a civil lawsuit. When the Ontario government is willing to sacrifice a whole community because of their race in order to appease a favoured group then it is time to enact laws that would see people like McGuinty, Fantino, Lewis and numerous other OPP officers face jail time for wilfully violating the Charter of Rights and Freedoms. These new laws must be prosecuted in Federal court, not at the provincial level, since Crown attorneys are not about to prosecute the very people with whom they work.

Furthermore, we need to change the law to ensure that Crown prosecutors cannot automatically drop private prosecutions against police and government officials.

2. (Provincial) Better civilian oversight

We need to change the way complaints against police are investigated. By now it shouldn't surprise anyone that 100% of the complaints filed regarding policing in Caledonia have resulted in every officer being cleared of wrongdoing. When you have OPP officers investigating OPP officers you virtually ensure that that will be the outcome.

We need to set up a completely separate group of investigators to deal with all complaints, Canada-wide, against police officers, and the Ontario Ombudsman must also be given the authority it currently lacks to review the conduct of police services, especially in regards to complaints of systemic refusal to uphold the law as in Caledonia.

3. (Federal) Seize transfer payments to Native reserves that support lawlessness

Many of the Native occupation protests are simply a way of forcing the government to turn over more money, whether or not there is any real land claim. The larger Native community that doesn't support lawlessness has nevertheless seen a financial benefit in having a small group of Native protesters break the law. The illegal occupation in Caledonia has provided Six Nations and various Native individuals with millions of dollars. We tell our children that crime doesn't pay, but the truth is that some crime does pay – the crime that occurs behind a smokescreen of 'Native land claims.' Whether or not a land claim has validity should be determined by the courts. It should not be resolved by the rule of lawless thugs.

Companies and communities lose millions and even billions of dollars to violence during these illegal occupations. The quickest way to stem this loss is to allow people to sue the Native bands. If the suit is successful, application can be made to the court to seize assets. Thanks to Canada's Indian Act, Natives on reserves don't have assets, so these would have to be transfer payments from the Federal and Provincial governments. I can guarantee you if companies can apply to seize transfer payments to a Native band, no chief will go on TV and tell his people to block roads and railways. (To state the obvious, no non-Native mayor or council in Ontario would encourage his or her community to block roads and interfere with rail lines, something Native chiefs do on a regular basis.)

One simple change in the law allowing people to seize transfer payments, and all illegal occupations would quickly end. Talk about an easy and peaceful way of ending the violence!

4. (Provincial) A public inquiry and an apology

Finally, there must be a public inquiry into the OPP's conduct in Caledonia; we must scrap the OPP '*Framework*' or direct that it is to be amended to make it clear that it applies to all citizens; and the OPP and Ontario government must issue an apology to the people of Caledonia.

Freedom isn't a given; you must do your part

Even though the OPP and Ontario government have tried everything they could to stop us - arrested us, sued us, defamed us, violated our rights, harassed and intimidated us - they have failed to break our spirit nor will we ever surrender our rights and freedoms. The purpose of this book is to expose what the OPP and government have been up to, so that Canadians can have a clear picture of what has been happening and learn from our experiences. I hope that the successes CanACE and our supporters have had in confronting the evils of racial policing in Caledonia will serve to inspire other 'ordinary' citizens to act boldly when police refuse to protect them.

As Thomas Jefferson reminds us - and it is a message that is not American, or Canadian, but is universal - "Eternal vigilance is the price of freedom." Freedom isn't a given, and unless each and every one of us is prepared to do what it takes to preserve it, we should not expect to remain free.

The self-evident truth is this: Canada's future is in your hands!

1   CanACE video, Jeff Parkinson, March 02, 2008: Julian Fantino's Home – the flag raising. *
2   VoiceofCanada.ca, July 12, 20, 2009: THE END OF THE BEGINNING! *
3   Ontario Provincial Police news release, Feb. 19, 2012: Assault With A Weapon (Teresa Jamieson). *
4   VoiceofCanada.ca, Feb. 19, 2012: McHale arrested in Caledonia because Native man assaults 77 yr old former Navy vet/UN peacekeeper & OPP officers. *
5   *Hamilton Spectator*, Opinions, Letters – Tracy Bomberry: Gary McHale pulling a scab off a wound. *
6   *Hamilton Spectator*, Opinions, Letters – Gary McHale, Feb. 28, 2012: Ten things that have changed: McHale. *
7   CanACE video, Sept. 2, 2012: 11 Arrested for having wrong skin colour in Caledonia ('Caledonia 11': Larry Stephens; Bonnie Stephens; Mark Vandermaas; Christine McHale; Gary McHale; Randy Fleming; Doug Fleming; Peter Kammerman; Ted Harlson; Jack Vanhalteren; Hettie Vanhalteren). *
8   Gary McHale/CanACE letter to Hamilton Police Chief Glenn De Caire, June 26, 2013: Illegal Occupation of Enbridge Line #9 Pipeline. *
9   312 SUN News Network, Byline w/Brian Lilley, June 26, 2013: Accommodating activist thugs. *
10 CaledoniaWakeUpCall.com, Sept. 28, 2007: New Photos of Sam Gaultieri. *
11 Canadian Taxpayers Federation, statement for 'Remember Us' rally, Kevin Gaudet, Oct. 7, 2007, Caledonia March Statement. *
12 Canadian Taxpayers Federation news release, Kevin Gaudet, Nov. 13, 2007: CTF releases S.O.S. (Stop Ontario's Standoff) Caledonia Petition. *
13 Canadian Taxpayers Federation news release, Kevin Gaudet, Oct. 7, 2007, Fantino Should Apologize or McGuinty Should Fire Him. *
14 *Simcoe Reformer*, Feb. 11, 2013: McHale reaches out to Six Nations chief. *
15 Christie Blatchford, *National Post*, February 10, 2012: Caledonia loses brave, feisty voice as Regional shuts its doors. *
16 Gary McHale, *Regional News* weekly column archive. *
17 *The Sachem* is part of the *Toronto Star* newspaper chain. Prior to becoming Mayor of Haldimand County, in 2006 Ken Hewitt was strongly against the Caledonia Class Action lawsuit. During Hewitt's attempts to discourage residents from suing the Liberal government he made statements resulting in John Findlay, lawyer for the Caledonia Class Action lawsuit, filing a defamation claim against Hewitt and the *Toronto Star*. Not surprisingly Hewitt and *The Sachem* fit well together. *
18 VoiceofCanada.ca, February 8, 2012: Caledonia, Canada lose heroic watchdog of democracy as Haldimand *Regional News* closes. *
19 VoiceofCanada.ca, Feb 9, 2012: Stories & letters from final edition of *Haldimand Regional News*. See editorial by Chris Pickup. *
20 Wikipedia.org: Stuart Laughton. http://en.wikipedia.org/wiki/Stuart_Laughton.
21 VoiceofCanada.ca, Feb. 13, 2012: Stuart Laughton, Never Again Group speech at Caledonia Act news conference: Individuals are the ultimate minorities. *
22 CanACE/Caledonia Victims Project joint media release, Feb. 22, 2012: Caledonia 8 invite PC Leader Tim Hudak to march in Caledonia against racism. *
23 Dr. Martin Luther King, Jr., April 16, 1963: *Letter From Birmingham Jail*. *
24 Caledonia Victims Project, April 13, 2010: Caledonia's youngest hero: 14 year old Pam 'Dancer' Dudych. *
25 *Toronto Star*, July 7, 2010, McGuinty invokes Trudeau and Nixon to defend G20 actions. *
26 Helen Miller letter to *Brantford Expositor*, July 14, 2009: Only elected council can speak

for Six Nations ("As for who represents Six Nations let me put it this way: The Mohawk Workers, Women of the Mohawk Nation, the Men's Fire or individuals like Steven "Boots" Powless or Ruby and Floyd Montour were not elected, appointed or authorized by the people of Six Nations to be their representatives or to speak on their behalf. Nor is the Haudenosaunee Development Institute (HDI) supported by the elected council or the community at large. Truth is today the majority of Six Nations people who I've spoken with are fed up with the protests, fed up with these groups of people and individuals claiming to speak for them and fed up with the smoke shops on Highway 6. So people who fear another Caledonia can put their fears to rest."). *

27 VoiceofCanada.ca, Feb. 13, 2012: Queen's Park News Conference – NGO's stand with Caledonia activists for release of Caledonia Act recommendations to end racial policing. *

   * See http://www.GaryMcHale.ca/book for additional information, links to documents, videos and photos

CPSIA information can be obtained at www.ICGtesting.com
Printed in the USA
LVOW13s1634261113

362899LV00006B/698/P